£16.50

THU?
TECHNICAL
LIBRA

D1581640

00320863

Children Act 1989—
A Practical Guide

Children Act 1989— A Practical Guide

Linda Feldman LLB
Solicitor
&
Barbara Mitchels LLB
Solicitor

LONGMAN

©Longman Group UK Ltd 1990

ISBN 0851 21553 X

Published by
Longman Law, Tax and Finance
Longman Group UK Ltd
21/27 Lamb's Conduit Street
London WC1N 3NJ

Associated offices:
Australia, Hong Kong, Malaysia, Singapore, USA

Typeset by Kerrypress Ltd, Luton, Beds.
Printed in Great Britain by
Biddles of Guildford Ltd

Contents

Contents

Contents

Table of Cases

Table of Statutes

Table of Statutes

Table of Statutes

xv

Table of Statutes

Table of Statutes

Table of Statutes

Table of Statutes

Table of Statutes

Table of Statutory Instruments

Glossary

Section 105 of the Act gives the interpretation of many specified terms used within the Act, and these are reproduced below. Other sections of the Act also define terms used, and these are also included here. In the text we have used some terms of our own, and these, too, are included in the glossary. We have indicated with an asterisk those terms which are not defined within the Act, to avoid confusion. The wording of the Act itself where it is included in the definitions below is indicated by quotation marks.

adoption agency 'a body which may be referred to as an adoption agency by virtue of s 1 of the Adoption Act 1976'.

authorised person in relation to care and supervision proceedings, means a person (other than a local authority) authorised by order of the Secretary of State to bring proceedings under s 31 of the Act (for a care or supervision order) and includes any officer of a body so authorised. In the Act there are other persons authorised to carry out specified functions, ie to inspect premises used for private fostering. There is insufficient space to set them all out here, but these are each discussed in the appropriate chapters below.

bank holiday 'a day which is a bank holiday under the Banking and Financial Dealings Act 1971' (includes all the usual bank holidays in the UK).

care order an order made under s $31(1)(a)$, (placement of a child in the care of a local authority) including an order made under s 38 (an interim order placing a child in the care of a local authority except where an express provision to the contrary is made); and 'includes any order which by or under any enactment has the effect of, or is deemed to be, a care order for the purposes of this Act; and any reference to a child who is in the care of an authority is a reference to a child who is in their care by virtue of a care order'.

child 'a person under the age of eighteen'.

child assessment order means an order under s 43 of the Act to produce the child and to comply with the court's directions relating to the assessment

xxv

of the child. There are restrictions on keeping the child away from home under this section.

child in care   a child in the care of a local authority pursuant to an order made under s 31(1)(*a*) or an interim order under s 38 of the Act.

child in need   a child is taken to be in need if:
(a) he is unlikely to achieve or maintain, or to have the opportunity of achieving or maintaining, a reasonable standard of health or development without the provision for him of services by a local authority;
(b) his health or development is likely to be significantly impaired or further impaired, without the provision for him of such services; or
(c) he is disabled.

child minder   is defined in s 71 as a person who looks after one or more children under the age of eight for reward for total period(s) exceeding two hours in any one day. A person is not deemed to provide day care for children unless the total period(s) during which the children are looked after exceeds two hours in any day.

child of the family   in relation to the parties to a marriage, means:
(a) a child of both of those parties
(b) any other child, not being a child who is placed with those parties by a local authority or voluntary organisation, who has been treated by both of those parties as a child of their family.

child looked after by a local authority   is a child who is in the care of a local authority by virtue of a care order, or provided with accommodation by a local authority.

child provided with accommodation by a local authority   is a child who is provided with accommodation by a local authority in the exercise of its functions, particularly those under the Act, which stand referred to their social services committee under the Local Authorities Social Services Act 1970 (includes children in what was previously called voluntary care).

children's home   defined in s 63 as a home which provides (or usually provides or is intended to provide) care and accommodation wholly or mainly for more than three children at any one time. Obviously many homes contain three or more children and the section lists several exceptions, including the homes of parents, relatives, or those with parental responsibility for the children in question.

community home   is defined in s 53 and may be:
(a) a home provided, equipped and maintained by a local authority, or
(b) provided by a voluntary organisation but in respect of which the local authority and the organisation—
   (i) propose that, in accordance with an instrument of management,

the management, equipment and maintenance of the home shall be the responsibility of the local authority; or
(ii) so propose that the management, equipment and maintenance of the home shall be the responsibility of the voluntary organisation.

contact order is defined in s 8(1) 'an order requiring the person with whom a child lives, or is to live, to allow the child to visit or stay with the person named in the order, or for that person and the child otherwise to have contact with each other'.

development means physical, intellectual, emotional, social or behavioural development.

disabled is defined in s 17(11) and 'in relation to a child, means a child who is blind, deaf, or dumb or who suffers from mental disorder of any kind or who is substantially and permanently handicapped by illness, injury or congenital deformity or such other disability as may be prescribed.

district health authority is defined in the National Health Service Act 1977 as the authority for a district, whether or not the name incorporates the word 'district'.

domestic premises any premises (including any vehicle) which are used wholly or mainly as a private dwelling.

education supervision order means an order under s 36(1) of the Act, putting the child with respect to whom the order is made under the supervision of a designated local education authority.

emergency protection order an order made under s 44 of the Act:
(a) operates as a direction to any person . . . in a position to do so to comply with any request to produce the child . . .;
(b) authorises
(i) the removal of a child to accommodation provided by or on behalf of the applicant and his being kept there; or
(ii) the prevention of the child's removal from any hospital or other place in which he was being accommodated immediately before the making of the order; and
(c) gives the applicant parental responsibility for the child.

family assistance order an order made under s 16 of the Act appointing a probation officer or an officer of the local authority to advise assist and befriend a named person for a period of six months or less. Named persons may include parents, guardians, those with whom the child lives, or the child himself.

family proceedings defined in s 8(3) as any proceedings:
(a) under the inherent jurisdiction of the High Court in relation to children; and
(b) under Parts I, II and IV of the Act; the Matrimonial Causes Act 1973; the Domestic Violence and Matrimonial Proceedings Act 1976; the Adoption Act 1976; the Domestic Proceedings and Magistrates'

Courts Act 1978; Sections 1 and 9 of the Matrimonial Homes Act 1983; and Part III of the Matrimonial and Family Proceedings Act 1984.

functions includes powers and duties.

guardian means a guardian appointed under s 5 of the Act for the child but not for the child's estate.

harm is defined in s 31(9) and means ill-treatment or the impairment of health or development, and where the question of whether the harm is significant or not turns on the child's health and development, that child's health and development should be compared with that which could be reasonably expected of a similar child.

health means physical or mental health.

health authority means any district health authority and any special health authority established under the National Health Service Act 1977.

health service hospital a hospital vested in the Secretary of State under the National Health Service Act 1977.

hospital any health service hospital, and accommodation provided by the local authority and used as a hospital. It does not include special hospitals, which are those for people detained under the Mental Health Act 1983, providing secure hospital accommodation.

ill-treatment is defined in s 31(9) and includes sexual abuse and forms of ill-treatment which are not physical.

independent school is the same meaning as in the Education Act 1944 and means any school offering full time education for 5 or more pupils of compulsory school age not being a school maintained by a local education authority.

local authority means a council of a county, a metropolitan district, a London borough, or the Common Council of the City of London. In Scotland, it means a local authority under Social Work (Scotland) Act 1968 s 12.

local authority foster parent means any person with whom a child has been placed by a local authority under s 23(2)(*a*) of the Act. Local authority foster parents may include a family; a relative of the child; or any other suitable person.

local education authority means in relation to any area for which a joint education board is constituted as a local education authority under Part 1 Sched 1 of the Education Act 1944, the board; or the council of the county; or the council of the county borough.

local housing authority as defined in the Housing Act 1944, meaning the district council; London borough council; Common Council of the City of London; or council of the Isles of Scilly.

mental nursing home as defined in the Registered Homes Act 1984 any premises used . . . for the reception of and provision of nursing or other medical treatment . . . for one or more mentally disordered patients, whether exclusively or in common with other persons.

non-parent with parental responsibility a person who is not a natural parent of a child, but who has parental responsibility for the child.

nursing home as defined in the Registered Homes Act 1984 any premises used or intended to be used for reception or nursing for sickness, injury or infirmity; and for pregnant women or childbirth; or certain specified medical procedures, including termination of pregnancies.

parent the natural mother or father of a child, whether or not they are married to each other at the time of the birth or of conception, and adoptive parents.

parental responsibility defined in s 3, including all the rights, duties, powers, responsibilities and authority which by law a parent of a child has in relation to the child and his property.

parental responsibility agreement defined in s 4(1) an agreement between the father and mother of a child providing for the father to have parental responsibility for the child (a father married to the mother of their child at the time of the birth will automatically have parental responsibility for that child, but a father not so married will not).

parent with parental responsibility this term will exclude the natural father of a non-marital child who has not acquired parental responsibility under the Act, unless child legitimated by subsequent marriage of parents.

person with parental responsibility includes a parent with parental responsibility or any other person who has parental responsibility under the Act.

prescribed means prescribed by regulations under the Act.

privately fostered child defined in s 66. 'To foster a child privately' means looking after a child under the age of 16 (or if disabled, 18), caring and providing accommodation for him or her; by someone who is not the child's parent, relative, or person with parental responsibility for the child.

prohibited steps order defined in s 8(1). Means an order that no step which could be taken by a parent in meeting his parental responsibility for a child, and which is of a kind specified in the order, shall be taken by any person without the consent of the court.

protected child is a child protected under the Adoption Act 1976, ie a child who is living with the applicant to adopt that child, who has given notice to the local authority of his or her intention to apply to adopt. The child is subject to the supervision of the local authority during the period of protection, which continues until one of a number of specified circumstances occur.

recovery order   order under s 50 for the recovery of a missing child who is subject to a care order.

refuge   a voluntary home, registered childrens' home or foster home certified by the Secretary of State under s 51 as a refuge for children at risk of harm.

residential care home   defined in s 1 Registered Homes Act 1984. Basically, an establishment where 4 or more people in need of personal care because of old age, disablement, past or present dependence on alcohol or drugs, or mental disorder, must be registered as a residential care home, with the result that conditions may be imposed as to its use.

registered children's home   defined in s 63 a home, registered under the Act, which provides (or usually provides or is intended to provide) care and accommodation wholly or mainly for more than three children, who are not siblings with respect to each other, at any one time. The Act provides a number of exceptions to the category of children's homes in s 63.

registered pupil   in relation to a school, a pupil registered at that school.

relative   in relation to a child means a grandparent, brother, sister, uncle or aunt (whether of the full blood or of the half blood or by affinity) or step-parent.

residence order   an order under s 8(1) settling the arrangements to be made as to the person with whom a child is to live.

responsible authority   a local authority to be notified under s 85 when child accommodated for more than 3 consecutive months by a health authority or a local education authority.

responsible person   defined in Sched 3, para 1 in relation to a supervised child means:
(a)   any person who has parental responsibility for the child; and
(b)   any other person with whom the child is living.
and in relation to s 49 means person responsible for child whilst in police protection or subject to a care order or an emergency protection order.

service   in relation to any provision made under Part III of the Act (local authority support for children and families) means any facility.

*signed   in relation to any person includes the making of his mark. In some circumstances, (such as the appointment of a guardian) an appointment may be signed at the direction of the appointer, but the signature must be attested by two witnesses.

special educational needs   these arise when there is a learning difficulty which calls for special educational provisions to be made; the Education Act 1981, s 1(1), sets out the meaning of 'learning difficulty'.

special health authority   defined in the National Health Service Act 1977 a special body established to perform functions on behalf of an area or district health authority, or Family Practitioner Committee.

specific issue order means an order under s 8(1) giving directions for the purpose of determining a specific issue which has arisen, or which may arise, in connection with any aspect of parental responsibility for a child.

supervision order means an order under s 31(1)(*b*) and (except where express provison to the contrary is made), includes an interim supervision order made under s 38.

supervised child and **supervisor** in relation to a supervision order or an education supervision order, mean respectively the child who is (or is to be) under supervision and the person under whose supervision he is (or is to be) by virtue of the order.

upbringing in relation to any child includes the care of the child but not his maintenance.

voluntary home means any home or other institution providing care and accommodation for children which is carried on by a voluntary organisation, with certain exceptions set out in s 60 of the Act.

voluntary organisation means a body (other than a public or local authority) whose activities are not carried on for profit.

Chapter 1

Introduction

1.1 Historical background

The Children Act 1989, referred to in this book as the Act, provides for the first time a unified and consistent code for the care and upbringing of children applicable to public and private law. The Act reforms the existing law on child care and family services and the emergency protection of children. It also reforms and consolidates the various statutory provisions relating to children under the private law. Nine Acts of Parliament are wholly repealed (see Appendix 6) and many others are amended in what has been described by the Lord Chancellor as 'the most comprehensive and far reaching reform of child care law . . . in living memory'.

The historical roots of the Act may be traced to a report of the House of Commons Social Services Committee published in 1984 which recommended a thorough review of child care law. As a result an interdepartmental working party was set up in July 1984 and its report, the Review of Child Care Law, was published in September 1985. The report reviewed in detail the existing law and considered proposals for reform. Its recommendations formed the basis for the White Paper, The Law on Child Care and Family Services, published in January 1987 (Cmnd 62) on which Parts III, IV and V of the Act are based.

At much the same time the Law Commission was giving thought to the need to reform the law on guardianship and custody. Its Report on Guardianship and Custody (Law Commission No 172) published in 1988 contained innovative proposals for reform upon which Parts I and II of the Act are largely based.

Other events influenced the movement towards reform. Just as the death of Maria Colwell in 1969 led to much needed reform

1

of the legislation then in force, so the reports into the deaths of Jasmine Beckford, Kimberley Carlile and Tyra Henry highlighted the areas where the existing law had failed or was unable to protect children at risk. The law's failure to strike an acceptable balance between the need to protect children from harm and the rights of parents was illustrated most tragically in the events in Cleveland in 1987 when the government set up a statutory inquiry to investigate an unprecedented rise in the diagnosis of child sexual abuse. The result was Lord Justice Butler-Sloss's Report of the Inquiry into Child Abuse in Cleveland 1987 published in July 1988 (Cmnd 412). The Report broadly endorsed the proposals in the White Paper with certain reservations. Some, but not all, of these have been taken into account in the Act.

No historical account of initiatives for reform of child care law can end without mentioning the Family Court. This was first seriously mooted in the report of the Finer Commission in 1969. Since then pressure for its introduction has never subsided. The Act does not introduce a family court. Nevertheless, its provisions for concurrent jurisdiction and the transfer of cases between courts constitute in the words of the Lord Chancellor 'an important first step towards a more general examination of the arrangements for family business'. They derive from a consultation paper, Improvements in the Arrangements for Care Proceedings, published by the Lord Chancellor in July 1988 in swift response to certain recommendations made in the Cleveland Report. The Lord Chancellor has made it clear that the Act 'is not intended to be a substitute for family courts or to lay a foundation for them'. He has, however, publicly stated that he will consider the whole question of family courts once the reform of substantive law contained in the Act is in place.

1.2 Outline of main provisions

The Act contains 12 parts and 15 schedules. These are discussed in this book as follows:

Chapter 2: General principles This covers Part I of the Act which lays down the general principles and matters which are to govern decisions relating to a child's upbringing, introduces the new concept of parental responsibility, amends the law of guardianship and provides for welfare reports to be available in proceedings under the Act.

Chapter 3: Family proceedings This covers Part II of the Act which introduces a new range of orders which may be made in respect of children in family proceedings.

Chapter 4: Local authority support for children and families This covers Part III of the Act which sets out the responsibilities of local authorities to children and their families.

Chapter 5: Care and supervision This covers Part IV of the Act which makes new provision for the making of care, supervision and other related orders and for the representation of children in certain proceedings.

Chapter 6: Protection of children This covers Part V of the Act which makes new provision for the protection of children at significant risk of harm and sets out the investigation responsibilities of local authorities.

Chapter 7: Community homes This covers Part VI of the Act which deals with the provision, management and conduct of community homes.

Chapter 8: Voluntary homes and organisations This covers Part VII of the Act which provides for the registration and regulation of children's homes provided by voluntary organisations and for the welfare of children accommodated in them.

Chapter 9: Registered children's homes This covers Part VIII of the Act and provides for the registration and regulation of private children's homes and the welfare of children accommodated in them.

Chapter 10: Private arrangements for fostering children This covers Part IX of the Act which provides for the notification and regulation of private fostering arrangements and the welfare of privately fostered children.

Chapter 11: Child minding and day care This covers Part X of the Act which provides for the registration and regulation of child minding and day care services for children under the age of eight.

Chapter 12: Supervisory functions of the Secretary of State This covers Part XI of the Act which contains powers for the Secretary of State to supervise and assist other bodies with functions, duties and responsibilities under the Act.

Chapter 13: Welfare of children living away from home This discusses ss 85 to 87 of the Act which require local authorities to be notified and exercise a welfare duty when children are accommodated away from home in certain circumstances.

Chapter 14: Jurisdiction and procedure This covers ss 92 to 99 of the Act which specify which courts are to have jurisdiction under the Act, the procedural matters to be covered by rules of court, special provisions which may apply with regard to evidence and arrangements for legal aid.

Chapter 15: Restrictions on the use of wardship This discusses the controversial provision in s 69 of the Act restricting the use of wardship jurisdiction by local authorities.

Chapter 16: Care and supervision orders in criminal proceedings This discusses s 90 of the Act which abolishes the power of courts to make care and supervision orders in criminal proceedings.

Chapter 17: Adoption This covers s 88 of the Act which amends existing adoption legislation.

Chapter 18: Miscellaneous and general provisions This covers the general provisions in Part XI of the Act not otherwise dealt with including the transfer of orders between England and Wales and other jurisdictions, the issue of search warrants, the commission of offences by corporate bodies and the making of orders and regulations under the Act.

Chapter 19: Implementation and transitional provisions This lists the provisions of the Act already in force and discusses the transitional provisions contained in Sched 14.

The definitions contained in s 105 of the Act are reproduced in amplified form at the front of the book for easy reference. Appendix 1 reproduces the standard scale of fines currently applicable for offences under the Act. Appendix 2 contains a chart illustrating the effect and duration of orders under the Act. Appendix 3 lists secondary legislation which may be made under the Act. Schedules 12, 13 and 15 of the Act containing minor and consequential amendments and repeals are reproduced in Appendices 4, 5 and 6 respectively.

1.3 General principles

Part 1 sets out the basic principles upon which courts are to decide

4

issues relating to children. The welfare of the child is to be the paramount consideration whenever a court determines any question relating to a child's upbringing or property. Whilst the welfare principle, previously stated in s 1 of the Guardianship of Minors Act 1973, is not new it is now clear that it applies to all proceedings within the ambit of the Act. Courts are given a checklist of factors to be taken into account in care proceedings and certain other opposed applications. The ascertainable wishes and feelings of the child head the list. The primary responsibility for bringing up children is to rest with parents and courts are not, therefore, to make orders under the Act unless they consider that doing so would be better for the child concerned than to make no order at all.

The Act introduces a new concept of parental responsibility broader in scope than the concept of parental rights and duties previously defined in s 85 of the Children Act 1975. Married parents will automatically have parental responsibility. Unmarried fathers may acquire it by formal agreement or by court order thereby incorporating into the Act, with amendment, reforms originally introduced in the Family Law Reform Act 1987 which deals with the law of illegitimacy.

A coherent legislative structure is given to the law of guardianship, previously based upon a confusing patchwork of common law and statute. Appointment is simplified and the rights of surviving parents clarified and strengthened. The new provisions replace the statutory code previously laid down in the Guardianship of Minors Act 1971 and the Guardianship Act 1973.

Provision is made in Part 1 for courts to request welfare reports in any proceedings under the Act. Under the previous law such reports were not available in all types of cases. The Act remedies this and should ensure greater uniformity in the provision and content of reports and the manner in which they may be dealt with by courts.

Note that the concepts and principles set out in Part I are fundamental to the Act and to a proper understanding of its other provisions.

1.4 Family proceedings

Part II creates four new orders to be available in family and matrimonial proceedings and referred to collectively as 'section 8 orders'. These will replace custody and access orders. A residence order will settle who a child is to live with. A contact order will specify what contact he is to have with others. A specific issue order may deal with any specific issue relating to the child and a prohibited steps order may prohibit certain steps being taken without the court's consent.

Courts will be able to make the new orders in a wide variety of cases grouped together under the general heading of family proceedings. The term includes guardianship, adoption, matrimonial, domestic violence, wardship and care proceedings. It will be possible for a court to make an order of its own volition or on the application of any person entitled to apply or granted leave to do so. Those previously able to apply for custody under the Guardianship of Minors Act 1971 or custodianship under the Children Act 1975 will now be entitled to apply for the new orders instead. Others not previously able to seek orders, except perhaps in wardship proceedings, may now be able to do so with the leave of the court.

The new relationship between private and public law is interesting to note. Whilst courts will now have power to make residence orders in care proceedings brought under Part IV of the Act, the previous power to make a care or supervision order in family proceedings is abolished. The 'matrimonial' supervision order will to some extent be replaced by the new family assistance order which will provide for social work support for a maximum period of six months. In other cases where the court considers that a care or supervision order may be appropriate it will be able to refer the case to a local authority for investigation. It will then be up to the local authority to decide whether to apply in the same proceedings for a care or supervision order. In this way the Act seeks to create a comprehensive and flexible framework in which courts may make orders which are in the best interests of the children concerned.

1.5 Local authority support for children and families

Part III sets out the responsibilities of local authorities to children and their families. It covers children in need, disabled children and children being looked after by local authorities. It replaces, supplements and updates various provisions of the Child Care Act 1980 now repealed.

It sets out the services which local authorities must or may provide for children. It includes disabled children within the general code of child care law for the first time. It enables local authorities to provide accommodation for children in need, where necessary, and it specifies how they must treat all children they are looking after.

The existing machinery for voluntary reception into care will be replaced by the new concept of providing accommodation for children in need. This will be just one of the services which a local authority can offer to the child and his family. Wherever possible, voluntary arrangements will be made in partnership with parents who must be consulted as part of the decision-making process. To this end, parents will no longer have to give notice in order to remove a child and local authorities will no longer be able to assume parental rights by administrative resolution. Greater emphasis is placed throughout on the views of the child which local authorities will be obliged to ascertain and take into account in certain situations.

1.6 Care and supervision orders

Part IV contains new and important provisions governing compulsory admission into care to replace those in s 1 of the Children and Young Persons Act 1969, now repealed. It provides a single procedure and a single composite ground for local authorities to intervene in the care and upbringing of children. It broadens the range of interim orders available to courts. It introduces a system of timetabling to ensure the speedy disposal of proceedings. It imposes a duty on courts to consider parental contact before making an order and creates a new power for courts to give directions for medical or psychiatric examination. The role of the guardian ad litem is strengthened and the position of parents as a party to the proceedings is improved. The court has power to make a s 8 order in appropriate cases and a new education supervision order is introduced to deal with non-school attendance.

1.7 Protection of children

Part V deals with the most controversial area of law reformed by the Act. It introduces the emergency protection order,

7

supplemented by a more limited police power of protection, to replace the place of safety order and related provisions under the previous law. It creates the child assessment order to be used in less urgent situations. It imposes upon local authorities a more positive duty to investigate suspected child abuse and specifies, with great clarity and detail, the form that investigation should take.

The new emergency protection order is intended 'to strike a better balance between the need to protect children from harm and the need to enable parents to properly challenge any action taken' (David Mellor, Minister of State for Health). It will now be possible for local authorities (or the NSPCC) to apply for an emergency order if they are unreasonably refused access to a child at risk but the maximum duration of the order will be eight days, with provision for a further seven day extension in certain cases. The child or his parents will be able to apply for the order to be discharged after seventy-two hours. Guardians ad litem will now have a role to play in emergency proceedings and courts will have power to make orders relating to parental contact and medical examination. The applicant's responsibilities with regard to the child are clarified and there is a new and positive duty to return the child home once any risk has passed. The new provisions are supplemented by additional powers to order disclosure and issue search warrants in difficult cases.

1.8 Children's homes

Parts VI, VII and VIII govern the provision, conduct and management of the various categories of children's home. Part VI deals with community homes and re-enacts, with minor amendments, the provisions of Part IV of the Child Care Act 1980, now repealed. Part VII provides for the registration and regulation of voluntary homes and re-enacts, with minor amendments, Part VI of the 1980 Act. Part VIII governs the registration and regulation of private children's homes and largely re-enacts the provisions of the Children's Homes Act 1982, never fully implemented and now repealed. An important new provision in this section of the Act deals with a lacuna in the previous law relating to community homes and provides for the payment of compensation to local authorities when certain premises used as a home are disposed of or put to another use. The opportunity is taken to re-state the law with greater clarity and helpful definitions are provided. Certain basic principles, such as the need to safeguard and promote the child's welfare and to involve parent and child in the decision-making process, are to be observed whatever the category of home. The Act also seeks to ensure that the same matters are addressed in the regulations governing all types of home, wherever appropriate. This should ensure that high standards are maintained in local authority institutions and that children accommodated in homes provided by voluntary organisations or private bodies are not at a disadvantage.

1.9 Private fostering

Part IX replaces and amends in part the Foster Children Act 1980 which is now repealed.

Its purpose is to protect the welfare of privately fostered children. It requires the notification of private fostering arrangements and regulates arrangements so made.

There are exceptions (with safeguards) for schools which board children during the holidays, and certain other institutions.

Certain people may be prohibited from privately fostering children. Breach of a prohibition may result in prosecution. An offence is punishable with a fine or imprisonment. A prohibition may be appealed to the magistrates' court, county court or the High Court.

It is also an offence to advertise the undertaking of private fostering unless the advertiser's name and address are given in the advertisement.

1.10 Child minding and day care

Part X replaces the Nurseries and Child-Minders Regulation Act 1948 which is now repealed.

It enables local authorities to regulate the services offered by child-minders and others providing day care facilities for children under eight. It retains many features of the previous legislation, such as compulsory registration, but also introduces some new safeguards. Local authorities are given a right of entry to premises if it is believed that children are being cared for there in contravention of the Act. They will also have a duty to inspect registered premises at least once every year.

Certain people may be prohibited from providing day care services for young children. Breach of this prohibition may lead to prosecution. Failure to register under the Act will also be a criminal offence.

1.11 Supervisory functions of the Secretary of State

Part XI provides for the Secretary of State (or others authorised to act on his behalf) to inspect children's homes and certain other establishments; to conduct inquiries, where necessary; to fund research, training and the provision of secure accommodation and special facilities; to collect information from local authorities, courts and voluntary organisations and make this available to Parliament; and to keep under review the adequacy of child care training

Whilst many of these functions existed under the previous law, the Act is more explicit in spelling out exactly how the Secretary of State's functions are to be performed. Amendments are also introduced to take into account the increasing reliance on computerised record-keeping.

Most of the functions are expressed in the form of powers rather than duties. The exception is the new duty for the Secretary of State to keep under review the adequacy of the provision of child care training and to receive and consider information relating to this from the relevant agencies. The new function reflects the importance now attached to adequate and specialised child care training.

The Secretary of State's general supervisory role is reinforced by the power to make a default order where a local authority has failed to comply with any duty imposed under the Act.

1.12 Miscellaneous and general

Part XII contains provisions governing jurisdiction and procedure, appeals, evidence and legal aid. It introduces reforms which will affect wardship proceedings and the powers of the juvenile court in criminal proceedings. It also amends existing legislation relating to adoption and paternity tests and introduces a new duty to notify local authorities when children are accommodated away from home in certain situations.

Section 92 provides for the magistrates' court, the county court and the High Court to have concurrent jurisdiction in proceedings under the Act. The domestic branch of the magistrates' court, renamed the family proceedings court, will take over the jurisdiction previously exercised by the juvenile court in care proceedings. The Lord Chancellor is given power, by order, to specify which cases may be initiated in which courts and the circumstances in which they may be transferred from one court to another. The jurisdiction of certain courts will be limited to specified proceedings. The aim is to create a flexible system in which cases may be dealt with at an appropriate level within the court system with the minimum of administrative delay. It is not a family court but may, perhaps, be considered a move in this direction.

Section 93 specifies matters to be covered in proposed rules of court. In particular these will specify who may participate in proceedings as a party or otherwise, how proceedings are to be commenced, and what documents must be furnished and information given to the court and other parties.

Section 94 gives a general right of appeal to the High Court against any order made by a magistrates' court under the Act. This replaces the previous right of appeal to the Crown Court in care proceedings. There is also a right of appeal against the refusal to make an order. For the first time, therefore, local authorities (or the NSPCC) will be able to appeal against the refusal to make a care or supervision order. Under the previous law they could only appeal by way of case stated on a point of law.

Sections 96 and 98 relax the rules of evidence in civil proceedings relating children. The Lord Chancellor is given power, by order, to over-ride the hearsay rules and to provide for the admission of evidence in the form of audio or video recordings. Young children will be able to give evidence without taking the oath, as they may in criminal proceedings, provided that they understand the duty to tell the truth. Witnesses in proceedings under Parts IV and V of the Act will not be able to claim privilege against self-incrimination although any evidence they give as a consequence will not be admissible in criminal proceedings except for perjury.

Section 95 gives the court power to order the child to attend all or any stage of proceedings under Parts IV or V of the Act.

Section 97 provides for proceedings to be conducted in privacy and prohibits the publication of material intended or likely to identify the child. This prohibition applies to reports in the press and on television or radio.

Section 99 amends the Legal Aid Act 1988. Existing anomalies, such as the provision of legal aid under the criminal scheme in care proceedings, are eliminated. Civil legal aid will be available, subject to means, for all proceedings under the Act but not to local authorities or other bodies such as the NSPCC. Those who are automatically parties to applications for care or supervision orders will not have to satisfy the merits test before legal aid is granted and in urgent cases emergency certificates will be issued before an assessment of means has been carried out. Legal aid will be available, as of right, to any child who wishes to be legally represented in an application under s 25 of the Act to place him in secure accommodation.

Section 90 abolishes the power of the court to make a care order in criminal proceedings. Section 1(2)(*f*) of the Children and Young Persons Act 1969 (the offence ground for care proceedings) is specifically repealed, suggesting that this provision may be implemented before Part IV of the Act which totally reforms the law relating to care proceedings.

The 'criminal' care order is replaced by a new requirement which may be included in supervision orders requiring the child concerned to live in local authority accommodation for a period of up to six months. This separation of the care and criminal jurisdiction in respect of children marks a departure from the fundamental principles upon which the 1969 legislation was based.

Section 100 severely restricts the powers of the High Court in wardship proceedings so far as local authorities are concerned. The High Court may not make a care or supervision order in wardship proceedings, nor may it use it's inherent jurisdiction to place children in care or under supervision. The High Court is, instead, given the power to make care and supervision orders under Part IV of the Act. The new ground for care proceedings is intended to cover those cases in which wardship would have previously provided the only remedy. The message is clear. There is to be only one route into care.

The Act does, however, purport to leave a safety net for local authorities. They may still use the wardship jurisdiction, with leave,

12

for other purposes if they can show that the remedy sought is not available in any other proceedings and that, in its absence, the child will suffer significant harm. It is difficult, however, to envisage many situations which would satisfy these criteria since the Act expressly precludes wardship when a child is already the subject of a care order and prohibits the use of the jurisdiction to confer on a local authority the power to determine any issue relating to any aspect of parental responsibility.

For parents of children in care the position is unchanged. They may not invoke the jurisdiction to interfere in any way with those statutory powers and duties invested by Parliament in local authorities.

Section 85 introduces new provisions to safeguard the welfare of certain children accommodated by health or local education authorities. Section 86 makes similar provision for children living in residential care homes or private nursing homes. Those providing accommodation will have a duty to notify the local authority if a child is accommodated for a consecutive period of at least three months. Local authorities will then have a duty to safeguard and promote the welfare of the children concerned. Section 87 extends this welfare duty to pupils at independent boarding schools and reinforces this by giving local authorities a right of entry and inspection.

Section 88 amends existing adoption legislation in the light of the Act and also introduces some new provisions. Adoption proceedings are family proceedings under the Act and the court will therefore have power to make a s 8 order at any time. Section 14(3) of the Adoption Act 1976 is repealed. Courts will not therefore have to consider whether a custody (or equivalent) order would be more appropriate when a natural parent and a step parent apply to adopt.

The existing powers to free a child in care for adoption are clarified. It will only be possible to apply for an order without parental consent where a child is in the care of a local authority. It will not be possible to apply where a child is being looked after by a voluntary organisation even if that organisation is also an adoption agency.

Other reforms are introduced to enable adopted people to trace and contact their natural relatives more easily. The Registrar General is to set up an Adoption Contact Register. Relatives may

13

ask for their details to be included in the Register. These will then be passed on to any adopted person over the age of eighteen who has also registered. Adopted people wishing to obtain information about their birth records may now obtain the obligatory counselling interview anywhere in the world provided that it is carried out by a body approved by the Registrar General. Under the previous law counselling interviews could only be carried out in England, Wales or Scotland.

Various other miscellaneous matters are covered including provisions as to the effect and duration of orders under the Act; the recognition of similar orders made in courts in Northern Ireland, the Channel Islands and the Isle of Man; and the issue of search warrants to assist those exercising powers under the Act and certain other legislation.

The Act contains an extensive interpretation section which is reproduced (with additional definitions) in the glossary at the front of this book.

The final section of the Act provides for its implementation. Sections 89 and 96(3) to (7) and para 35 of Sched 12 came into force on 16 November 1989. Para 36 of Sched 12 will come into force in January 1990. The remainder of the Act will come into force by October 1991. For reference purposes Scheds 12, 13 and 15 are reproduced in appendices to this book. Schedule 14 is discussed in Chapter 19.

The Act applies to England and Wales. Certain provisions, notably those relating to day care services for children, also apply to Scotland. These are listed in s 108(11) and discussed in the text where relevant. The Act does not apply to Northern Ireland except for those provisions which relate to the recognition of orders made in other jurisdictions or the enforcement of orders abroad. The Secretary of State may extend provisions of the Act to the Isles of Scilly by order.

1.13 Financial effects of the Act

The government has estimated the resource implications of the Act. Parts I and II, being concerned with private law provisions, are expected to have no significant resource implications. Parts IV and V, being concerned with local authority care and supervision and emergency protection, are expected to result in increased court and legal aid costs. However, the government expects these to be partly offset by savings from limiting access to wardship and more effective management of cases. The net increase in court costs is estimated to be in the range of £0.6 million to £4.9 million, although this includes £1 million for judicial and staff training. The effect on legal aid expenditure is expected to range between a saving of £0.6 million and an increase of £1.7 million.

Local authority costs on court-related work are expected to increase in the region of £2.1 million per year. This takes into account an increased expenditure on guardians ad litem, but set against this are the savings which should be achieved by the transfer of most local authority wardship applications to care proceedings in the lower courts.

The additional welfare responsibilities imposed on local authorities by Part III of the Act are expected to cost approximately £1.7 million. Other local authority costs, including those relating to the registration and inspection of registered children's homes, are expected to increase by £0.2 million.

In all, the government estimates that the full annual cost resulting from the implementation of the Act is likely to be between £4 million and £11 million. Until the Act is fully implemented it is impossible to know whether the government has got its sums right. If the Act is to be implemented in a piecemeal manner, however, it will not be surprising if those provisions with the least resource implications come into effect first.

15

Chapter 2

General Principles

In 1988 the Law Commission published a *Report on Guardianship and Custody* (Law Commission No 172) referred to in the text below as 'the Report' which looked into the principles and guidelines upon which many of the proposed reforms discussed in Chapters 2 and 3 are based. Parts of the Report are quoted where relevant in order to better understand the provisions of the Act.

2.1 Welfare of the child

The Act sets out to state clearly the basic principles upon which the courts shall decide issues relating to a child.

It commences with a clear direction that the overriding concern in deciding matters affecting a child's upbringing or property shall be for the child's welfare:

1.—(1) When a court determines any question with respect to—
    (a) the upbringing of a child; or
    (b) the administration of a child's property or the application of any income arising from it,
the child's welfare shall be the court's paramount consideration.

This re-enacts the welfare principle previously set out in s 1 of the Guardianship of Minors Act 1971, now repealed. Under the previous law, the child's welfare was the court's 'first and paramount consideration'. The Lord Chancellor has made it clear that no significance may be attached to the omission of the word 'first' and that the principle remains as strong as before. Section 1(2) provides that 'in any proceedings in which any question with respect to the upbringing of a child arises, the court shall have regard to the principle that any delay in determining the question is likely

16

to prejudice the welfare of the child'. It is good that the inevitably prejudicial effect of delay is now given statutory recognition.

Section 1 then goes on to set out further matters to which the court shall have regard when making, varying or discharging orders under Part IV of the Act (see Chapter 5) or under s 8 (see Chapter 3), provided in the latter case the application is opposed. These matters are set out in the form of a checklist:

1.—(3) ... a court shall have regard in particular to—
(a) the ascertainable wishes and feelings of the child concerned (considered in the light of his age and understanding);
(b) his physical, emotional and educational needs;
(c) the likely effect on him of any change in his circumstances;
(d) his age, sex, background and any characteristics of his which the court considers relevant;
(e) any harm which he has suffered or is at risk of suffering;
(f) how capable each of his parents, and any other person in relation to whom the court considers the question to be relevant, is of meeting his needs;
(g) the range of powers available to the court under this Act in the proceedings in question.

Whilst it may seem odd that lack of opposition to the making of an order under s 8 should apparently render consideration of such important matters inappropriate, this does reflect the underlying principle upon which the Act is based. This is that children should be brought up by their parents without interference by the State unless they are placed at risk. If this is accepted, it follows that parents should be left to reach their own agreements, where possible, although there is clearly a danger that the absence of opposition to an application under s 8 may denote lack of interest rather than agreement. The Act's failure to extend s 1(3) to such applications may preclude full investigation of the applicant's proposals for the child.

It is interesting to note that the child's wishes and feelings head the checklist and that it will apply to care proceedings under Part IV but not emergency applications under Part V.

2.2 Parental responsibility

The fundamental principle guiding the Law Commission was that the primary responsibility for bringing up children should rest with their parents and that the State should be ready to help parents discharge that responsibility, and should only intervene compulsorily, where the child is placed at unacceptable risk. The proposed reforms set out to redefine parental responsibility, clearly stating where it shall lie and its boundaries.

2.2.1 Definition

Sections 2–4 introduce a new concept of parental responsibility. This replaces the old idea of parental rights as set out in s 1 of the Guardianship Act 1973 and defined, together with parental duties, in s 85 of the Children Act 1975. Both these statutes are now wholly repealed.

Parental responsibility is defined in s 3(1) as 'all the rights' duties, powers, responsiblities and authority which by law the parent of a child has in relation to the child and his property' but also includes 'the rights, powers and duties which a guardian of the child's estate (appointed before the commencement of s 5, to act generally) would have had in relation to the child and his property' (s 3(2)). This is a reference, in particular, to a guardian's right to receive and recover in his own name, for the benefit of the child, any property to which the child is entitled (s 3(3)).

The Act does not list these rights and duties. The Law Commission considered that they would change at various stages in a child's life to meet his differing needs and circumstances. This accords with the principle established in the leading case of *Gillick v West Norfolk and Wisbech Area Health Authority* [1986] AC 112 where the age and maturity of the child was taken into consideration and it was decided that a parent could not prevent doctors giving medical advice or treatment where the child was mature enough to consent herself.

There are, of course, other statutory provisions which impose specific duties on parents or limit their rights in some way. A parent who fails to obtain essential medical assistance for his child, for example, commits an offence under the Children and Young Persons Act 1933, s 1. Parents also have a duty to ensure that their school age children receive adequate full-time education suited to need, aptitude and ability. It may also be implied from the Act itself that parental responsibility carries with it a general duty to safeguard and promote the welfare of a child since a specific duty to do

18

so is imposed on a person who has the care of a child but does not have parental responsibility.

For brevity, a person with parental responsibility will be referrred to in Chapters 2 and 3 as the 'responsible parent'. This term will include those who have acquired parental responsibility under the Act (see *2.2.2* below) whether or not they are actually a natural parent of the child.

2.2.2 Acquisition

The Report concluded that no basic changes were needed to the present principles for acquisition of parental responsibility as laid down in the Family Law Reform Act 1987, ie where the parents are married at or after the time of a child's conception, both share parental responsibility; and where unmarried, the mother has parental responsibility automatically, whilst the father may subsequently acquire it. The Act, however, clarifies and simplifies those principles and procedures.

The Act first sets out the various ways in which parental responsibility may exist, or be acquired. It also points out that 'more than one person may have parental responsibility for the same child at the same time' (s 2(5)). The acquisition of parental responsibility by another person does not automatically cause the responsible parent to lose his or her rights (s 2(6)).

It is important to note that parental responsibility is not a bundle of rights and duties capable of transfer or surrender. Parental responsibility cannot be delegated but a responsible parent can arrange for someone else, including another responsible parent, to take over particular responsibilities (s 2(9), and (10). An obvious example would be for a parent to arrange for someone else to look after a child while away on holiday. Note that a responsible parent who has delegated part of his responsibility remains liable for any failure to meet all or any part of it (s 2(11)).

Section 2(1) states the basis for parental responsibility within a marriage:

Where a child's father and mother were married to each other at the time of his birth, they shall each have parental responsibility for the child.

The common law rule making a father the legal guardian of his legitimate child is abolished (s 2(4)) and parents will share parental responsibility even after a divorce although orders under s 8 (see Chapter 3) may govern particular aspects of the child's upbringing.

Section 2(2) deals with unmarried parents:

Where a child's father and mother were not married to each other at the time of his birth—
   (a)   the mother shall have parental responsibility for the child;
   (b)   the father shall not have parental responsibility for the child unless he acquires it in accordance with the provisions of this Act.

The natural father of a child (the 'putative father' in the old terminology) has no parental responsibility, therefore, unless he acquires it under the Act.

Note, however, that these sections must be construed by reference to s 1 of the Family Law Reform Act 1987 which extends the references to a child whose father and mother were married to each other at the time of his birth to include those children legitimated under ss 1 or 10 of the Legitimacy Act 1976 (ie children of void marriages or those whose parents subsequently marry); those otherwise treated in law as legitimate and children adopted under Part IV of the Adoption Act 1976. The time of birth extends back to the date of the insemination resulting in the birth; or where there was no insemination (eg in intra-vitro fertilisation) the date of conception. Section 2(1) would therefore apply to a child whose parents divorce between the date of insemination and birth.

An unmarried father, ie one who is not married to the mother of the child in question (although he may, of course be a married man), may acquire parental responsibility under the Act either by court order or by agreement (s 4). The right to apply for a court order was introduced in the Family Law Reform Act 1987, recognising for the first time a parental role, short of custody, for unmarried fathers. The idea of a formal agreement between unmarried parents is new and recognises the fact that many more children are now raised outside matrimony. Cohabiting couples and unmarried parents who live apart but maintain a good relationship will be able to share parental responsibility by agreement.

Any agreement must be made in the prescribed form and manner. This will be specified by the Lord Chancellor in regulations to be made under s 4(2). The Report envisaged a simple paper procedure with a small standard fee, the agreement then being noted on the court records.

Such agreements and orders may be terminated by an order of the court on application by any responsible parent. The child himself may also apply, with the leave of the court, provided that he has sufficient understanding to make the proposed application (s 4(3) and (4)).

Non parents may also acquire parental responsibility under subsequent provisions of the Act. Thus a guardian appointed under s 5, a person obtaining a residence order under s 8, a local authority named in a care order under Part IV and an applicant granted an emergency protection order under Part V will all acquire parental responsibility. In some cases, however, its exercise will be restricted and they will not be able to make certain decisions, usually within the ambit of parental responsibility, eg consent to adoption.

2.2.3 Extent

Section 2 also defines the extent of parental responsibility and how it is to be exercised generally. Section 2(7) states that where one or more persons have parental responsibility for a child each may act alone and without the other or others in meeting that responsibility unless the consent of more than one person is required under other legislation. For example, married parents of a child under the age of 18 years are both required to consent to their child's marriage under the provisions of the Marriage Act 1949 unless there is a residence order in force (see Chapter 3).

The fact that a person has parental responsibility for a child does not entitle him to act in any way which would be incompatible with any order made under the Act (s 2(8)). For example, a parent retaining parental responsibility may not decide where a child shall live if the court has made a residence order under s 8 specifying that he shall live with someone else. Neither will he have freedom of action in respect of any other matter which is the subject of a court order under s 8 (see Chapter 3). Similarly, a person with parental responsibility will not be able to remove a child who is subject to an emergency protection order under Part V of the Act.

The fact that a person does, or does not have parental responsibility, will not affect any statutory obligation which he may have in respect of a child. The Act specifically refers to the statutory duty to maintain the child in this context. Neither will it affect the rights which he, or any other person, may have in relation to the child's property (s 3(4)). The Report pointed out that the right to inherit a child's estate, under the intestacy laws, is based upon being related to the child in a particular way and operates irrespective of who is bringing up the child. (A child will usually die intestate because a will may only be made by a person under the age of 18 years in limited circumstances.) It was felt that the legislation should reflect this. In the same way the child's right to inherit is unaffected by the incidence of parental responsibility.

2.3 Appointment of guardians

Here, the Report found that the common law and statute created a legal patchwork and that modifications were necessary to create a coherent legislative structure.

Of particular concern were problems created when a parent died having appointed a testamentary guardian who then had equal rights with the surviving parent. If the surviving parent objected or was considered unfit to have care of the child by the guardian, the matter could only be resolved by the guardian making an application to a court. The guardian's position was always insecure because a surviving parent could object to the appointment at any time. Furthermore, the law made little provision for the needs of divorced or separated parents. In such cases, parents with custody were often anxious to ensure that their children did not immediately return to the care of the surviving parent. It was considered that the potential conflict arising from these situations could only be damaging to a child following upon a bereavement.

The Act seeks to resolve these difficulties. Section 5 sets out the ways in which a guardian may be appointed to take the place of a deceased parent. Note that all previous statutory provisions for the appointment of guardians are repealed and from the date of implementation it will only be possible for an appointment to be made in accordance with the provisions of s 5.

A guardian thus appointed will have parental responsibility for the child concerned (s 5(6)). It was felt in the Report that the power to control a child's upbringing should go hand in hand with responsibility to look after him, or at least to ensure that he is properly looked after. It seems to be generally expected that guardians will take over the responsibility for the care and upbringing of a child if the parents die, and that they should therefore have full legal responsibility.

Two or more people can be appointed to act as guardians jointly (s 5(10)).

2.3.1 Order of court

The court may appoint a guardian under s 5 if—

  (a) the child has no parent with parental responsibility for him; or

  (b) a residence order [see Chapter 3] has been made with respect to the child in favour of a parent or guardian of his who died while the order was in force (s 5(1)).

Example 1

W, a widow, dies leaving a child, C.
W has not appointed a guardian for C.
The court may appoint a guardian under s 5(1)(*a*).

Example 2

D, a divorcee dies leaving a child, C.
D has not appointed a guardian for C.
C is the subject of a residence order in favour of D.
C's father is still alive.
The court may still appoint a guardian under s 5(1)(*b*).
Note that the court has power to appoint a guardian of its own volition in any family proceedings if it is considered that the order should be made. Similarly, guardianship can be terminated of the court's own volition.

2.3.2 Appointment by a parent or existing guardian

A parent with parental responsibility may appoint another individual to be the child's guardian in the event of his death (s 5(3)). In the same way, a guardian may appoint another person to take his place on death (s 5(4)).

An appointment will not take effect until there is no surviving parent with parental responsibility, or there was a residence order in favour of the appointer in force at the time of his or her death (s 5(7)). In these circumstances, the guardian and surviving parent will share parental responsibility and either may apply to court for the appropriate order under s 8 (see Chapter 3) in the event of a dispute as to any aspect of the child's upbringing.

Example 1

M, a married woman, dies having appointed G to be guardian of C, the only child of the marriage.
M's husband H has parental responsibility for C.
Under s 5(7) the appointment will not take effect until H's death.
If H then appoints a different guardian for C, both appointments will take effect on his death and the two guardians will share parental responsibility.

Example 2

M, a divorced woman, dies having appointed G to be guardian of C, the child of her former marriage.
C is the subject of a residence order in favour of M.
C's father F is still alive and has parental responsibility for C.
G's appointment will become effective on the death of M.
G and F will share parental responsibility.
If they cannot agree on a matter relating to C's upbringing, including where C shall live, either can apply for an order under s 8.
F could also seek the termination of G's guardianship under s 6(7).
Note: the position would not differ if M has been separated rather than divorced provided she still had the benefit of a residence order immediately prior to her death.

Example 3

M, a single woman, dies having appointed G to be guardian of her child, C.

M was cohabiting with C's father, F, at the time of her death. F has not bothered to acquire parental responsibility either by agreement or court order under s 4.

G's appointment will take effect on M's death.

Only G will have parental responsibility.

F's remedy will be to seek a residence order under s 8.

If the court grants this it will also be obliged to make a parental responsibility order in his favour under s 4 under the provisions of s 12(1).

Example 4

M, a single woman, dies having appointed G to be guardian of her child, C.

C's father, F, has parental responsibilty by court order made under s 4.

G's appointment will only take effect on F's death.

If M wished to avoid this she should have obtained a residence order under s 8 during her lifetime.

These examples illustrate that those advising parents, with regard to both proceedings under s 8 (see Chapter 3) and the appointment of a guardian, will have to be extremely careful if an unexpected outcome is to be avoided.

2.3.3 Manner of appointment

Guardians had, in the past, to be appointed by deed or will. The Act simplifies the procedure, possibly taking into account the reluctance of some people to make wills!

Appointments must now be in writing, signed and dated by the appointer or signed by another at the direction of the appointer in the presence of two witnesses who each attest the signature, s 5(5). This is simple and relatively uncomplicated, as are the provisions for alteration and revocation.

Section 6(1) provides that:

An appointment under s 5 subsection (3) or (4) revokes an earlier such appointment ... made by the same person in respect of the same child, unless it is clear ... that the purpose of the later appointment is to appoint an additional guardian.

A guardian may be appointed in family proceedings of the court's own volition, even though there has been no application for guardianship. Similarly, in family proceedings, the court may bring guardianship to an end of its own volition, s 6(7)(c). Under s 6(7), application can be made to the court to terminate guardianship by anyone with parental responsibility for the child (which, of course, includes a guardian) or by the child.

2.3.4 Revocation and disclaimer of appointments

An appointment may be revoked by written instrument, provided that it is signed and dated (s 6(2)), either by the appointer or by another person at his direction in the presence of two witnesses who each attest his signature. Note that an original appointment by will or codicil to a will does not have to be revoked by another will or codicil. It may be revoked in writing, provided that it is signed and dated. However, destruction of the original appointment with the intention of revoking is sufficient revocation (s 6(3)). This applies to an appointment which is not in a will or codicil. However, the Wills Act 1837, s 20 provides that a will or codicil may be revoked by destruction with the intent to revoke; and s 6(4) specifically provides that:

For the avoidance of doubt, an appointment ... made in a will or codicil is revoked if the will or codicil is revoked.

It is therefore important to bear in mind that revocation may occur by physical destruction or the execution of a new will, and also by marriage.

Within a reasonable time of first knowing of the appointment, a guardian may disclaim his or her appointment, by signing a written statement, s 6(5). This disclaimer, in order to be effective, must be recorded in accordance with regulations to be made by the Lord Chancellor.

There are no guidelines as to what may constitute a reasonable time. Section 1(2) provides that in any question relating to the upbringing of a child, delay in determining that question is likely to prejudice the welfare of the child. It is likely that s 6(5) will be interpreted accordingly.

Finally, any appointment of a guardian under this section may be brought to an end at any time by order of the court (s 6(7)) on the application of any person with parental responsibility for the child himself, or of the court's own volition. This means, presumably, any family court with powers under the Act.

2.4 Welfare reports

The Act enables a court considering any question with respect to a child to request a welfare report from a local authority or a probation officer (s 7(1)). It will then be the duty of that person or body to comply with this request (s 7(5)). A local authority may be asked to arrange for one of its own officers or another appropriate person to prepare the report. This allows the authority to ask a voluntary agency, such as the NSPCC, to prepare the report if it has been more closely involved with the family.

Section 7 applies to all proceedings under the Act, including care proceedings under Part IV and emergency applications under Part V. Under the previous law the availability and provision of reports was governed by different statutory enactments depending on the nature of the proceedings. Local authorities were responsible for providing reports in care proceedings, probation officers in their role as court welfare officers provided reports in family proceedings. Different rules applied with regard to content, disclosure and admissibility. These inconsistencies should now be eliminated.

Welfare reports will (unless otherwise directed by the court) be required to deal with specific matters to be set out in regulations to be made under the Act (s 7(2)). The court will, presumably, indicate any particular matters to be addressed in the report and may request that it be presented orally or in writing (s 7(3)).

Note, that the court may take account of any statement in a report and any evidence given in respect of matters it refers to, provided in either case that these are relevant, regardless of any enactment or rule of law which would otherwise prevent it from doing so. Thus a court could consider evidence that would otherwise be inadmissible as hearsay. This provision is not new but re-enacts with some amendment s 6(3A) of the Guardianship Act 1973 which is now repealed. Section 6(3A) allowed magistrates' courts, in certain

27

civil proceedings, to take into account matters otherwise inadmissible but subject to the proviso that copy reports were provided in advance to all parties. The Act does not make similar provision for advance disclosure but it is likely that this will be provided in rules of court.

Chapter 3

Family Proceedings

3.1 Comparison of old and new law

The Law Commission in its *Report on Guardianship and Custody* (Law Commission No 172), referred to below as 'the Report', had to consider flaws in existing legislation, and ways of improving the availability of orders relating to important issues for children. In the old law custody and access were regulated by a number of different enactments depending on the nature of proceedings before the court. This created complexities for practitioners and parties alike and it was necessary to select the correct procedure to provide the appropriate remedy. There were, in addition, limitations on the orders available dependent upon the status of the applicant and courts were restricted in the scope of orders they could make of their own volition.

The Report recommended that appropriate orders should be widely available, and that the courts' power to make such orders should not depend on the nature of the proceedings in each individual case but should be set out clearly in a single and consistent statutory code. The Act sets out to achieve this and should reduce the potential for confusion.

Part II creates a new set of possible orders to be called 'section 8 orders'. These will be available in all 'family proceedings' and will enable the court, on an application, or of its own volition, to regulate a child's residence and contact with others, to prohibit the taking of any specified steps with regard to the child without the leave of the court and to deal with any specific issues arising in the child's upbringing. These orders will replace existing provision for custody, access and custodianship orders under the Guardianship of Minors Act 1971, the Guardianship Act 1973 and the Children Act 1975, all now repealed. They will also be available in matrimonial and other proceedings.

The s 8 orders will have a wide scope not only in their content but in their availability. Anyone may apply for an order with the leave of the court, save for local authority foster parents who (unless they are related to the child), will need the authority's consent to ask leave to apply for a residence order if the child has lived with them for less than three years. The Law Commission considered it important that anyone should be able to apply for an order and that the only restrictions imposed should be those necessary in the interests of the child.

Section 8 orders (save for those relating to residence) are not available in respect of children subject to a care order. Part IV of the Act contains special provision relating to such children (see Chapter 5).

3.2 Definition of family proceedings

The Act defines 'family proceedings' in s 8 (3) and (4). These include all proceedings 'under the inherent jurisdiction of the High Court in relation to children' (including wardship proceedings) but not an application by a local authority under s100(3) for leave to invoke the court's inherent jurisdiction (see Chapter 15).

The term also includes all proceedings under Parts I, II and IV of the Act; proceedings under the Matrimonial Causes Act 1973; the Domestic Violence and Matrimonial Proceedings Act 1976; the Adoption Act 1976; the Domestic Proceedings and Magistrates' Courts Act 1978; the Matrimonial Homes Act 1983, ss 1 and 9; and the Matrimonial and Family Proceedings Act 1984, Part III.

3.3 Section 8 orders

The purpose of the new orders is to reduce, rather than increase, the opportunities for conflict and litigation in the future. The orders available under the previous law often appeared to create further conflict, particularly those which were open to wide interpretation. What, for example, did joint custody actually mean in practical terms? Both judges and solicitors often seemed to have difficulty in explaining the full effect of such orders to those affected.

The Act creates four new types of order, each available under s 8. These orders are to be known as section 8 orders and the term is also applied to any order which varies or discharges a section 8 order.

Section 8(1) defines each new order:

8.—(1) In this Act—

'a contact order' means an order requiring the person with whom a child lives, or is to live, to allow the child to visit or stay with the person named in the order, or for that person and the child otherwise to have contact with each other;

'a prohibited steps order' means an order that no step which could be taken by a parent in meeting his parental responsibility for a child, and which is of a kind specified in the order, shall be taken by any person without the consent of the court;

'a residence order' means an order settling the arrangements to be made as to the person with whom the child is to live; and

'a specific issue order' means an order giving directions for the purpose of determining a specific issue which has arisen, or which may arise, in connection with any aspect of parental responsibility for a child.

These section 8 orders will comprehensively deal with matters formerly requiring access orders, injunctions, custody and custodianship orders and other remedies previously available in the different family proceedings. Having all the remedies under one enactment with one procedure common to all, will greatly simplify cases where such orders are sought, particularly where more than one order is appropriate. It will mean that practitioners will no longer have to consider which type of proceedings are appropriate to obtain a required order; the same remedies will be available in all family proceedings.

Example

M and F are unmarried but cohabit.
They each have parental responsibility for their only child, C.
F has assaulted M.
M wishes to apply for court orders to protect herself and C.
M can apply for an injunction under the Domestic Violence and Matrimonial Proceedings Act 1976 and seek a s 8 order in the same proceedings.

31

In proceedings for divorce, nullity and judicial separation the court will now have a positive duty under s 41 of the Matrimonial Causes Act 1973 to consider whether it should exercise any of its powers under the Children Act 1989 in respect of any children of the family under the age of 16 (Sched 12, para 31). This replaces the old duty for the court to declare itself satisfied with the arrangements for the children of the family before a decree nisi could be made absolute. Under s 41, as amended, the court will have power to defer decree absolute if it is unable to make the required order under the Children Act 1989 without further consideration of the case.

Note that it is not the function of section 8 orders to remove parental responsibility from anyone who would otherwise have it under Part I of the Act (see Chapter 2). The orders simply determine particular issues in relation to a child's upbringing.

It is helpful to consider the four types of order in more detail in the light of the comments in the Report.

3.3.1 Residence order

The residence order is designed to be flexible. The Law Commission had the situation of separated or divorced parents very much in mind. It was considered necessary to devise an order which would recognise the time children could spend with each parent without causing unnecessary legal complications in its interpretation. For example, it was suggested that where a child is to spend part of his time with one parent (possibly in term time) and the remainder with the other (during the holidays) the solution would be a residence order in favour of both parents. Section 11(4) empowers the court to specify periods of residence in each household involved, if necessary.

There is, from the practitioner's point of view, potential for conflict in the approach advocated by the Law Commission. Whilst it is accepted that flexibility is an ideal, it is a sad fact that many separated or divorcing parents cannot mutually agree and often rely on a court to impose a solution upon them. If possible, this will represent a compromise between the parties although the court will always act in the child's best interests. If an order does not set defined limits and there is disagreement or lack of co-operation between parents this may place additional stress on children and lead to further litigation.

Residence orders do not operate to remove parental responsibility from anyone who would otherwise have it under the provisions of Part I. A residence order will, however, give parental responsibility to any other person who does not already have it while it remains in force (see 3.8 below). A residence order which provides for a child to live with one of two parents who share parental responsibility for him will lapse if they live together for a continuous period of more than six months (s 11(5)).

3.3.2 Contact order

This is not the same as the old access order, which provided for the parent without custody to have access to a child. A contact order is much wider. It contemplates a situation where the child stays mainly with one parent but visits (and may stay with) the other. While the child is visiting the other parent, he or she will exercise their parental responsibilities but must not do anything which is incompatible with any order which deals with the child's residence.

By way of example the Report suggests that having the child's hair done in a way which would exclude him from school would be incompatible, but taking him to a sporting event over the weekend (no matter how much the parent with whom he lives might disapprove) would not. Whilst this attitude respects the rights of both parents some may feel that the Law Commission is being a little unrealistic here in its conception of compatibility! It will remain for the courts to clarify specific issues. Note, that although the Law Commission was primarily concerned with parents, others will be able to apply for contact orders although in some cases it will be necessary to seek the leave of the court first.

It is anticipated that 'contact' will include telephone calls, letters, parcels and other forms of communication where visiting is impracticable although in most cases the order, if expressed as 'reasonable contact', will include all these. Contact orders between parents will lapse if they live together for a continuous period of more than six months (s 11(6)).

3.3.3 Prohibited steps order

The Report modelled these on the wardship jurisdiction where no important step could be taken without the court's leave. Rather than leaving the burden of deciding what constitutes an important step to the person seeking leave, a prohibited steps order, instead, enables the court to spell out those matters which are to be referred back to it for a decision. A court could, for example, make an order prohibiting a child's removal from the jurisdiction without leave where there is no residence order in force. (Where there is a residence order there is an automatic prohibition on removal, see 3.9 below).

3.3.4 Specific issue order

The Report intended the specific issue order to enable either parent to submit a particular dispute to the court for resolution in accordance with the child's best interests. It was to be made in conjunction with a residence or contact order although the Act does not, in fact, limit its use in this way. The order was not envisaged as a way of giving one parent the right to determine issues in advance, nor was it intended to be a substitute for a residence or a contact order. The Act reflects these considerations but note that it also makes the order available to persons other than parents subject to certain restrictions.

3.4 When the court may make a section 8 order

'In any family proceedings in which a question arises with respect to the welfare of any child, the court may make a section 8 order with respect to that child' on the application of a person who is entitled to apply or has obtained the leave of the court to do so. The court may also make an order of its own volition (s 10(1)(b)).

This gives the court very wide powers to make section 8 orders in a wide variety of proceedings. It will be interesting to see how full a use is made of this power. For further information on who may apply, see 3.6 below.

Section 10(2) provides that a court may also make a section 8 order with respect to any child on the application of a person who is entitled to apply, or who has leave of the court to do so. It is worded in the same way as s 10(1) but for the omission of the words 'in any family proceedings'.

Section 10(1) therefore enables any person entitled to apply or granted leave to do so to make an application in the course of any family proceedings already commenced. Section 10(2) enables an applicant to apply ab initio where there are no current family proceedings.

Example 1

W and H are married.
W files a petition for divorce.
H wishes to apply for a residence order in respect of their only child, C.
H will apply under s 10(1) in the family proceedings already commenced by W.

Example 2

W and H are married but living apart.
H wishes to apply for a contact order in respect of their only child, C.
H will apply under s 10(2).
W then wishes to apply for a residence order.
W will apply under s 10(1) as family proceedings have already been commenced by H.

The power of the court to make a residence order of its own volition considerably widens the scope of s 8. It will, for example, permit a court to make an order relating to a child who is not the subject of an application if any question arises as to that child's welfare in the course of family proceedings.

Example

F and M are the parents of two children, C and D.
F and M are unmarried and live apart.
F has parental responsibility for C and D by agreement.
C lives with M.
D lives with F.
M applies for a residence order in respect of C under s 10(2).
F makes no application in respect of D.
The court makes a residence order in respect of C but is concerned about the welfare of D.

Under s 10(1)(b) the court may make a section 8 order in respect of D of its own volition.

It may also make other section 8 orders in respect of C even though the original application sought only a residence order.

Courts will be able to make section 8 orders in care proceedings as an alternative to care or supervision orders whether or not an application has been made under s 10.

Example

C, a child lives with her parents.

AB Council is applying for a care order in respect of C.

C's grandmother, G, wishes to offer C a home but is considered unsuitable by AB Council.

The court may make a residence order in favour of G of its own volition if it disagrees with AB Council.

G could also apply for a residence order in the care proceedings although she may first need to apply to the court for leave (see 3.6 below).

3.5 When the court may not make an order

Section 9 sets out several restrictions on the making of section 8 orders.

3.5.1 Only residence orders for children in care

The first restriction is very clear:

8.—(1) No court shall make any section 8 order, other than a residence order, with respect to a child who is in the care of a local authority (s 9(1)).

There are separate provisions for children who are subject to care orders (see Chapter 5). The power to make a residence order in such cases is, however, interesting since it will result in the automatic discharge of the care order (s 91(1)). This provision clearly allows foster parents (subject to restrictions) to apply for an order in the same way as they were able to seek custodianship under the old law. It also allows others, not otherwise entitled to seek the discharge of a care order, to secure the child's discharge from care by other means: note also that a care order automatically discharges a s 8 order, (s 91(2)).

Example

C is the child of unmarried parents, M and F.

F does not have parental responsibility in respect of C.

C is the subject of a care order in favour of AB Council.

AB Council placed C with foster parents X and Y four years previously.

F has now married W and they wish to offer C a home.

X and Y have become attached to C and also wish to offer her a permanent home.

C's grandmother, G, wants C to live with her.

F can apply for a residence order.

G can apply for a residence order, but only with the leave of the court.

X and Y can apply for a residence order.

Neither F, G, X or Y could apply for the discharge of the care order under Part IV of the Act, but if any of their applications for a residence order succeed the care order will be automatically discharged.

The Act, therefore, gives relatives, who are able to offer a child a home after a care order has been made, an opportunity previously denied to them. However, it will still be necessary for them to seek the leave of the court in most cases and this will not be granted if the proposed application is likely to disrupt the child's life to an extent which would be harmful (see 3.6.2 below).

Parents will be able to apply for a residence order as an alternative to seeking the discharge of a care order under Part IV of the Act, but it is not clear what advantage they will gain, if any, from doing so.

3.5.2 No residence or contact orders for local authorities

Section 9(2) is equally clear:

(2) No application may be made by a local authority for a residence order or contact order and no court shall make such an order in favour of a local authority.

The Act refers in s 9(2) to both contact and residence orders which are thereby rendered inaccessible to local authorities. This section applies whether a child is in care or not and it therefore seems that local authorities may seek other section 8 orders in respect of children who are not in care. An authority may, for example, seek a specific issue order to provide for a child to be medically examined where there are no grounds to seek an emergency protection order under Part V. It would, however, be necessary to obtain the leave of the court first.

3.5.3 Some foster parents need local authority's consent to seek section 8 order

Section 9(3) imposes restrictions on the application to the court for leave to apply for s 8 orders by some foster parents. All foster parents will need to obtain the leave of the court to apply for a s 8 order unless they are entitled under the Act to apply. Further, if they have fostered the child within the preceding six months they will need the consent of the local authority before seeking the court's leave to apply, unless they are related to the child, or the child has lived with them for a period exceeding three years.

Section 9(4) goes on to provide that 'the period of three years . . . need not be continuous but must have begun not more than five years before the making of the application.'

The Act clearly intended to cover the situation where foster parents have had a child intermittently, but for what amounts in total to a comparatively long period. There is an attempt here to recognise the bonding which would have taken place between the child and the foster parents despite the breaks in the child's residence with them, which could have been caused by attempts at rehabilitation with parents.

However, it seems that foster parents who last had the child living with them, say, nine months before they wish to seek the leave of the court to apply for a s 8 order, may do so without the need to obtain the consent of the local authority. Additionally, note that the provisions of s 10(5) are that anyone who has had the child living with them for a three year period commencing not more than five years and ending not more than three months before the application is entitled to apply for a residence or contact order.

Example

C, a child is in care to AB council.
The local authority have placed C with Mr and Mrs P, foster parents.
Mr and Mrs P are not related to C.
C has been living with Mr and Mrs P for two years.
Mr and Mrs P would like to offer C a permanent home.
AB council decide to place C for adoption.
Mr and Mrs P apply to adopt but are considered unsuitable by AB council.
Because C is in care the only order which Mr and Mrs P can seek is a residence order.
Before Mr and Mrs P could seek the leave of the court to apply for a residence order, they must have the consent of AB council.

Example

C, a child is in care to AB council.
The local authority have placed C with C's older sister and her husband (Mr and Mrs X) as foster parents.
C has been living with Mr and Mrs X for two years.
Mr and Mrs X would like to offer C a permanent home.
Mr and Mrs X do not require the consent of the local authority and they may seek leave of the court to apply for a residence order.

Example

C, a child is in care to AB council.
The local authority have placed C with Mr and Mrs Z, foster parents.
C has been living with Mr and Mrs Z for three years.
Mr and Mrs Z would like to offer C a permanent home.
Mr and Mrs Z may seek leave of the court immediately to apply for a residence order.
If the court grants a residence order, then the care order will be automatically discharged.

Example

C, a child is in care to AB council.

The local authority had in the past placed C with Mr and Mrs Y, foster parents.

C had been living with Mr and Mrs Y for three years but for the past nine months has been living with his mother, M.

M is unable to look after C any longer and tells Mr and Mrs Y that she intends to ask AB council to place C with Mr and Mrs Y again.

Mr and Mrs Y would like to offer C a permanent home.

Mr and Mrs Y are not automatically entitled to apply for a residence order under s 10(5) because s 10(10) requires that the three year period must have ended within three months of the application.

However, they may seek leave of the court to apply for a residence order.

If the court grants a residence order, then the care order will be automatically discharged.

On considering whether to grant leave, the court will have regard to their connection with the child and to the risk, if any, that the application may cause disruption to the child's life to such an extent that he would be harmed by it, s 10(9).

3.5.4 Restrictions on prohibited steps and specific issue orders

Section 9(5)(*a*) forbids a court to make a specific issue or prohibited steps order 'with a view to achieving a result which could be achieved by making a residence or contact order'.

In other words, it seems that the specific issue and prohibited steps orders are regarded as formidable powers to be used sparingly and only where appropriate.

Section 9(5)(*b*) forbids a court to exercise its power to make a specific issue or prohibited steps order 'in any way which is denied to the High Court (by section 100(2)) in the exercise of its inherent jurisdiction with respect to children'.

Section 100(2) is discussed more fully in Chapters 14 and 15 but its essential purpose is to ensure that local authorities seeking some measure of control over a child do so by way of proceedings under Parts IV or V of the Act and not by invoking the wardship jurisdiction. Section 9(5)(*b*) applies the same principle to s 8 proceedings. A local authority may not, therefore, apply for a specific issue or prohibited steps order for the ultimate purpose of removing a child from home, preventing his return from local authority accomodation, placing him under supervision or otherwise acquiring any other form of parental control over him.

3.5.5 No section 8 orders for children of 16 or over

Section 9(6) prohibits the making of any section 8 order which is to have effect for a period which will end after a child has reached the age of 16, unless the circumstances are exceptional. Variation or discharge of an existing order is permitted. There are no clues as yet as to the sort of circumstances which may be considered to be exceptional although recent cases concerning medical treatment for mentally handicapped children over the age of 16 would certainly fall within this category.

3.6 Who may apply for a section 8 order

The Act creates two distinct categories of applicant: those entitled to apply and those who must first seek the leave of the court.

3.6.1 Persons entitled to apply

This category is sub-divided into those who may apply for any section 8 order and those who may only apply for residence and contact orders. The list below is not exhaustive as the Act gives the Lord Chancellor power to extend the category of those entitled to apply by rules of court (s 10(7)).

The following are entitled to apply for any section 8 order:

(a) any parent or guardian of a child (s 10(4)(*a*))—this will include the 'unmarried' father of a child whether or not he has parental responsibility;

(b) any person in whose favour a residence order has been made in respect of the child (s 10(4)(*b*)).

Example

G is the grandmother of a child, C.
C's mother is dead.

41

C's father, F, is alive but cannot look after C.
A residence order has been made in favour of G.
G and F each have parental responsibility in respect of C.
G and F cannot agree about C's education.
This has led G to restrict F's contact with C.
F is entitled to apply for a contact order, under (a) above.
G is entitled to apply for a specific issue order relating to C's education, under (b) above.

The following are entitled to apply for a residence or contact order but not a prohibited steps order or a specific issue order:

(a) any party to a marriage (whether or not subsisting) in relation to whom the child is a child of the family (s $10(5)(a)$)—this provision enables a step-parent to seek a residence or contact order in the same way as he could previously seek custody or access.

Example

M and S are divorced.
C is M's child by a previous marriage.
C lived with M and S during their marriage and is a child of the family.
S is entitled to apply for a residence or contact order even though he is not the father of C.

(b) any person with whom the child has lived for a period of at least three years (s $10(5)(b)$—this provision covers those previously entitled to apply for custodianship under the old law. To ensure that the connection with the child is a recent one, s $10(10)$ provides that the three year period need not be continuous but must not have begun more than five years before, or ended more than three months before, the making of the application.

Example

M is the mother of a child, C.
M is mentally ill and cannot look after C.
C has been living with kindly neighbours, X and Y, for four years.

During this period she has returned to the care of her mother, M, for periods amounting to nine months in total.

X and Y are entitled to apply for a residence order.

If C were to return to the care of M for a period exceeding three months, X and Y would not be entitled to apply unless C lives with them again.

(c) any person who,

—where there is a residence order in force, has the consent of each of the persons in whose favour the order is made;

—where there is a care order in force, has the consent of the local authority (but note, the court can only make a residence order in such circumstances, see 3.5 above);

—in any other case, has the consent of each person with parental responsibility for the child.

Example 1

M and F are divorced.

C, their only child, lives with M during term time and with F during the school holidays.

There is a residence order in force in favour of both parents.

C's grandmother, G, seeks more contact with C and has made certain specific proposals.

F will not agree to these but will allow the matter to be resolved by the court.

G is entitled to apply for a contact order with the consent of M and F.

If G cannot obtain the consent of both M and F she may only apply with the leave of the court.

Example 2

C is the subject of a care order in favour of AB Council.

C's grandmother, G, was previously unable to offer her a home but can now do so.

AB Council believes that it would be in C's best interests to live with her grandmother.

G is entitled to apply for a residence order with the consent of AB Council.

If a residence order is made in favour of G, the care order will be discharged.

Example 3

M and F are unmarried but live together as man and wife. They have one child, C.

F has parental responsibility in respect of C by agreement.

F's father, G, seeks greater contact with C and has made certain specific proposals.

M will not agree to these but will allow the matter to be resolved by the court.

G is entitled to apply to the court with the consent of M and F.

If G cannot obtain the consent of both M and F, he may only apply with the leave of the court.

3.6.2 Persons who must seek leave

Any person not falling within one of the above categories may only apply for a section 8 order with the leave of the court. This category is open-ended and could include, for example, a local authority seeking a specific issue order in respect of a child who is not in care, a grandparent seeking a contact order without the consent of the child's parents and a relative seeking a residence order in respect of a child in care against the wishes of the local authority.

The child, himself, may also seek leave to apply for a section 8 order, but the court may only grant leave if satisfied that he has sufficient understanding to make the proposed application. An older child may, for example, wish to seek an order permitting contact with a grandparent or a prohibited steps order to prevent a parent from following a particular course of action.

The inclusion of the child as a party able to seek leave is a considerable step forward in the recognition of children's rights although it remains to be seen how readily the courts will grant leave in such cases.

3.6.3 Considerations on application for leave

Where a person is applying for leave, and is not the child concerned, s 10(9) requires the court to have particular regard to:

(a) the nature of the proposed application for the section 8 order;

(b) the applicant's connection with the child;

(c) any risk there might be of that proposed application disrupting the child's life to such an extent that he would be harmed by it; and

(d) where the child is being looked after by a local authority—
  (i) the authority's plans for the child's future; and
  (ii) the wishes and feelings of the child's parents.

These considerations could clearly affect a grandparent's chances of obtaining leave to apply for a contact order in the face of strong parental opposition as in many cases this could clearly disrupt the child's life to a harmful extent. The criteria will also ensure the exclusion of those whose connection with the child is weak or tenuous. In this way the Act appears to offer unlimited access to the courts for those seeking section 8 orders, but not entitled to apply, and then ensures that only those applications which may benefit the child may proceed.

3.7 Supplementary provisions

Section 11 of the Act contains supplementary provisions in relation to section 8 orders. The Law Commission expressed concern about potentially damaging delays in determining issues concerning children, and suggested that responsibility for the progress of cases should not be left with the parties. The Report envisaged that courts would have the power to consider how best to proceed in the interests of the child's welfare and in the light of available information, where required steps had not been taken in the time specified. If, for example, a welfare report was not ready, the court could decide to set a return date or to ask for a progress report rather than a hearing. The Report pointedly refers to a case in which the Court of Appeal suggested that it would be better to do without a welfare report if it was necessary to wait for as long as nine months for one (*Re C (A Minor) (Custody of Child)* [1980] 2 FLR 163). Bearing in mind the general principle in s 1 of the Act that, in any proceedings in which a question as to a child's upbringing is to be determined, delay in determining that question is likely to be prejudicial to the welfare of the child, the court must get on with its decision-making and permit no dilatory tactics. Section 11 goes on to facilitate speedy determination of issues.

Section 11(1) instructs the court 'to draw up a timetable with a view to determining the question without delay' and 'to give such directions as it considers appropriate for the purpose of ensuring, so far as is reasonably practicable, that the timetable is adhered to'.

Section 11(2) permits rules of court to 'specify periods within which specified steps must be taken in relation to proceedings in which such questions arise' and to 'make other provision . . . for the purpose of ensuring, so far as is reasonably practicable, that such questions are determined without delay'.

Section 11(4) provides that:

Where a court has power to make a section 8 order, it may do so at any time in the course of the proceedings in question even though it is not in a position to dispose finally of those proceedings.

Under this provision, for example, a court may make an interim residence order in any family proceedings including care proceedings under Part IV (see Chapter 5).

Section 11(4) tidies up a loose end, simply providing that where a residence order is made in favour of two or more persons who do not themselves live together, the order may specify the periods during which the child is to live in the different households concerned.

It would be unrealistic to have a residence or contact order still in force where the child is to live with one parent if both parents have resumed cohabitation. So s 11(5) provides that where there is a residence order in force, as a result of which the child lives, or is to live with one of two parents who each have parental responsibility for him, the residence order shall cease to have effect if the parents live together for a continuous period of more than six months.

Section 11(6) provides that:

A contact order which requires the parent with whom a child lives to allow the child to visit, or otherwise have contact with, his other parent shall cease to have effect if the parents live together for a continuous period of more than six months.

Section 11(7) contains additional procedural provisions. A section 8 order may contain directions about how it is to be carried into effect; expressly impose conditions on the person in whose favour it is made or those with parental responsibility; be made for a specified period, or contain provisions for a specified period; and make such incidental, supplemental or consequential provisions as the court thinks fit.

3.8 Residence orders and parental responsibility

It could be very difficult if a parent or any other person, were to have an order for a child to live with him but no parental responsibility. Therefore, s 12 ties in parental responsibility with residence orders.

Section 12(1) specifically requires the court to make an order under s 4 giving parental responsibility to a father, when making a residence order in his favour, if he would not otherwise have it. This is intended to assist 'unmarried' fathers who do not automatically have parental responsibility and can only acquire it by agreement or court order. The court may not bring that s 4 order to an end while the residence order remains in force (s 12(4)). Discharge of the residence order will not automatically result in discharge of the parental responsibility order. It will continue in force unless discharged under s 4(4).

Example

> F is the father of a child, C.
> F is not married to C's mother and does not have parental responsibility.
> F applies for a residence order in respect of C.
> The court makes a residence order in F's favour and when doing so must also make an order under s 4 giving him parental responsibility for C.
> Three years later the residence order is discharged.
> F will continue to have parental responsibility for C unless the s 4 order is also discharged.

Section 12(2) gives any person in favour of whom a residence order is made (not being a parent or guardian of the child concerned, or already having parental responsibility for him) parental responsibility during the subsistence of the order.

The Act does not, however, go as far as to allow the parental responsibility given under s 12(2) to cover agreement or the withholding of agreement to an adoption order, or to an application under s 18 of the Adoption Act 1976 or s 18 of the Adoption (Scotland) Act 1987 freeing a child for adoption, nor does it permit the appointment of a guardian for the child (s 12(3)).

3.9 Removal from the jurisdiction and change of name

The Report considered the law as it then existed with regard to removal from the jurisdiction of children subject to court orders. Of particular concern was the standard clause included in all custody orders made in divorce proceedings prohibiting the child's removal from England and Wales without the consent of both parents or the leave of the court. This restriction, honoured more in the breach, required a parent with custody to apply for leave to take a child on a short holiday abroad if the non-custodial parent would not consent for any reason. Against the background of marital breakdown it is not difficult to envisage circumstances in which consent may be withheld for reasons not wholly connected with the child's welfare.

The need to seek leave was clearly onerous when only a short trip was proposed. At the same time there was the risk of a parent removing a child abroad permanently without the knowledge of the other parent or the court. The Act achieves a compromise.

Section 13(1)(*b*) generally prohibits the removal of a child subject to a residence order from the United Kingdom without the written consent of every person who has parental responsibility for the child, or the leave of the court; whilst s 13(2) makes an exception permitting a person in whose favour a residence order is made to take the child abroad for a period of less than one month. A parent who fears that a child may be removed abroad permanently on the pretext of a short holiday may apply for a prohibited steps order excluding the effect of s 13(2).

Where the question of the removal of the child from the jurisdiction is anticipated the court may give leave on making a residence order, either generally, or for specified purposes (s 13(3)).

The law with regard to change of name remains much as before but is stated with clarity. Where a child is subject to a residence order, no person may change that child's surname without the written consent of every person with parental responsibility for that child, or the leave of the court (s 13(1)(*a*).

3.10 Family assistance order

Section 16 of the Act makes new provision for advice and assistance for families. In any family proceedings, where the court has power to make an order under s 8 or Sched 1 of the Act (see 3.11 below), it may also make a family assistance order requiring a probation officer or an officer of the local authority to be made available to 'advise, assist and befriend' any person named in the order (s 16(1)). The power exists whether or not the court actually makes an order under s 8 or Sched 1, but may only be exercised in exceptional circumstances and with the consent of every person named in the order other than the child (s 16(3)).

The person to be advised, assisted or befriended may be the child, a parent or guardian, any person with whom the child is living and any person in whose favour a contact order has been made (s 16(2)).

The order may direct the person(s) named to take whatever steps are necessary to keep the officer concerned informed of their address and to enable him to visit them (s 16(4)).

An order will last for six months unless a shorter period is specified (s 16(5)).

Where there is a family assistance order and a section 8 order in force, the officer concerned may refer to the court the question of whether the section 8 order should be varied or discharged. This power could obviously be of use where a family assistance order has been made at the same time as a contact order which is clearly not working.

Example

M and F are the parents of a child, C, aged 12 years.

Their marriage breaks down and they divorce.

In the divorce proceedings the court makes a residence order in favour of M.

M and F cannot agree about contact.

M alleges that F is making unreasonable demands for contact and introducing C to undesirable people when he does see her.

49

F alleges that M is deliberately turning C against him.
C wishes to maintain contact with F and the court believes that this is in her best interests.
M and F accept the need for professional help and will agree to a family assistance order.
The court makes a contact order in favour of C and a family assistance order naming M, F and C.
S, a social worker, is appointed to assist the family.
After four months S forms the view that arrangements for contact are unworkable and that continued contact with F will only cause C further distress.
S may ask the court to consider whether the contact order should be varied or discharged.

Note that the family assistance order to some extent replaces the old matrimonial supervision order although its purpose is more specific and its duration shorter. There is no longer any power for a court to make a supervision order, or indeed a care order, in family proceedings of its own volition. The Act instead provides a procedure for appropriate cases to be referred to the local authority for investigation. It will then be up to the authority to decide whether to make an application (see 37 and 5.3.2 below). The new power to make a family assistance order should ensure that supervision orders, under Part IV of the Act, are not made in inappropriate circumstances. The object of a family assistance order is to help families to resolve immediate problems with children which arise from separation or divorce. It is intended that a supervision order will only be made when some element of child protection is necessary.

3.11 Financial relief

Section 15 of and Sched 1 to the Act primarily re-enact (with modifications and minor amendments) the provisions of the Guardianship of Minors Act 1971 and the Guardianship Act 1973, the Children Act 1975 and ss 15 and 16 of the Family Law Reform Act 1987, making provision for financial relief for children.

These provisions do not affect the courts' power in matrimonial proceedings under the Matrimonial Causes Act 1973 or the

Domestic Proceedings and Magistrates' Courts Act 1978 to make orders about children's maintenance. In proceedings under those Acts, the maintenance of the adults concerned is often inextricably involved with that of the child. The power to make orders in respect of both is therefore left in place.

Rather than compare the previous law with the provisions of the Act for, clarity, there is set out below in chart form a basic outline of the provisions in Sched 1 (1) and (2).

3.11.1 *Financial orders in respect of children under eighteen*

who may apply	possible orders	court empowered to make order	duration
in each case applicant may be parent, guardian or person in whose favour a residence order is in force with respect to the child	*Periodical payments* payble by either or both parents (i) to applicant for benefit of child (ii) to child himself	High Court County Court Magistrates' Court	term specified in order; age 17 or age 18 (see 3.11.2 below)
	Secured periodical payments payable by either or both parents (i) to applicant for benefit of child or (ii) to child himself	High Court County Court	term specified in order age 17 or 18 (see 3.11.2 below)
	Lump sum payment payable by either or both parents (i) to applicant for benefit of child or (ii) to child himself	High Court County Court Magistrates' Court	(see below 3.11.2)
	Settlement of property (i) to which either parent is entitled; and (ii) specified in the order	High Court County Court	
	Transfer of property (to which parent(s) entitled and which is specified in order) by either or both parents of child (i) to applicant for benefit of child; or (ii) to child himself	High Court County Court	

51

Note that for the purposes of this Schedule 'parent' includes any party to a marriage (whether or not subsisting) in relation to whom the child concerned is a child of the family and 'child' includes, where the application is under para 2 or 6, a person who has reached the age of 18 (para 16).

The power of a magistrates' court to revoke, revive or vary a periodical payment order under s 60 of the Magistrates' Court Act 1980 may not be exercised in relation to an order made under Sched 1.

Where the High Court or a county court makes an order for the settlement or transfer of property, or for the securing of periodical payments, it may direct that the matter be referred to one of conveyancing counsel of the court to settle a proper instrument to be executed by all the necessary parties (para 13).

Note that a periodical payments or secured periodical payments order may be varied or discharged by a subsequent order made on the application of any person by or to whom payments were to be made under the previous order (Sched 1, para 1(4)). Where a court makes a subsequent order under this paragraph, the court has the option (if the child is under 18) of ordering further periodical payments, secured periodical payments, or a lump sum payment. The court is prevented by Sched 1, para 1(5) from making more than one order for settlement or transfer of property against the same person in respect of the same child. Under para 1(5) further orders are possible until the child reaches the age of 18.

Example

M and F are the mother and father of C respectively.

C is 15 years old.

M is separated from F.

M has a residence order for C to live with her.

F pays £200 per month under Sched 1, para 1(2)(*a*) to M for the benefit of C.

F argues that he cannot afford to continue payments and applies to the county court under Sched 1, para 1(4) to vary.

The court may order a reduction of periodical payments to £100 per month, but now order that the payments be secured.

52

Example

M is the guardian of C and D, children aged 15 and 2, respectively.

F, the father of C and D, has been ordered by the court to settle the sum of £1,000 to M for the benefit of C under para $1(2)(d)$; and also to pay £50 monthly each, in respect of both C and D, under para $1(2)(a)$.

M needs more money for both C and D and applies to the court for variation of the children's monthly payments under s 4.

The court is empowered by para 1(5) to make a further order for periodical payments, secured periodical payments or a lump sum for C and D; and it can make a settlement or transfer of property order against F in respect of D. It cannot make a further settlement or transfer of property order, however, in respect of C.

When a court makes, varies or discharges a residence order, it can exercise any of its powers under Sched 1 even though no application has been made to it under the Schedule (Sched 1(6)).

3.11.2 Duration of orders for financial relief

An order for periodical payments under Sched 1, para $1(2)(a)$ or (b) may begin with the date of the application or any later date, and the order may not extend beyond the child's seventeenth birthday, unless the court thinks it right to specify a later date, in which case it may not run beyond the child's eighteenth birthday unless it appears to the court that the child is, or will be receiving instruction at an educational establishment or undergoing training for a trade profession or vocation, whether or not in gainful employment or that there are special circumstances which justify the making of the order (Sched 1, para 3(1)).

Example

F is the father of C.

When C was 13, F was ordered to pay £250 per month to C's mother for C.

C is now approaching 17, and wants to train as a teacher.

Normally, C's payments would cease at 17, but the court could extend the payments during C's training, eg until he is 21.

Example

F is the father of C, a severely disabled child of 16.
C lives with her mother, M.
F and M are separated.
M applies for a residence order in her favour.
In making the residence order, the court orders periodical payments by F to M for the benefit of C, using its power under Sched 1, para 1(6).
The periodical payments order could be specified to continue until C is 21.

3.11.3 Financial relief for persons over eighteen

Schedule 1, para 2 provides that, on an application by a person over 18, the High Court, county court, or magistrates' court may order either or both parents of the applicant to make periodical payments or a lump sum payment. The applicant must either be receiving instruction at an educational establishment, undergoing training for a trade profession or vocation (whether or not in gainful employment) or there must be special circumstances which justify the order.

There can be no application where there was a periodical payments order in force in relation to the applicant immediately before he reached the age of 16 nor when the parents of the applicant are living together in the same household.

It is difficult to understand why this provision seems to favour those who have separated or divorced parents, and prevents those who have parents who live together, but who otherwise may be unsupportive, from making an application for financial relief. It also leaves unanswered the situation of a young person who had a periodical payments order which expired at the age of 16, who later needs financial help to undergo further training after reaching 18. A further periodical payments order could be made under para 1(5) if an application were to be made while the child is still under 18, and the child himself could make an application for the revival of the payments under para 6(5) provided that he makes the application on or before his eighteenth birthday, (see below 3.11.6); but if there has been a two year gap in payments, and no application is made on or before the child's eighteenth birthday, further relief does not appear to be available under the Act. The liability to make periodical payments ceases upon the death of the payer (para 3(3)).

The Schedule provides too that:

Where an order is made under paragraph 1(2)(*a*) or (*b*) requiring periodical payments to be made or secured to the parent of a child, the order shall cease to have effect if the parents of the child live together for a period of more than six months, (para 3(4)).

Example

M is the mother of C aged 14.

M and F live apart.

F, C's father, pays £25 per week by an order under Sched 1, para 2(a).

M and F lived together for eight months.

F's liability to pay ceases.

If F and M part again, then M will have to reapply for another order.

3.11.4 Matters considered by the court in making financial relief orders under Schedule 1

Schedule 1, para 4 provides:

In deciding whether to exercise its powers under para 1 or 2, and if so in what manner, the court shall have regard to all the circumstances including—

  (a) the income, earning capacity, property and other financial resources which each person mentioned in sub-para (3) has or is likely to have in the foreseeable future;

  (b) the financial needs, obligations and responsibilities which each person . . . has or is likely to have in the foreseeable future;

  (c) the financial needs of the child;

  (d) the income, earning capacity (if any), property and other financial resources of the child;

  (e) any physical or mental disability of the child;

  (f) the manner in which the child was being, or was expected to be, educated or trained.

The people mentioned in sub-para (3) to whom (a) and (b) above apply are: any parent of the child; the applicant for the order; and any other person in whose favour the court proposes to make the order. Anyone with a residence order in respect of the child in force in their favour may apply for an order under this Schedule, in addition to parents and guardians. Remember, too, that this Schedule gives the court power, on making, varying or discharging a residence order, to make an order for financial relief of its own volition.

There is a safeguard written into the Schedule in para 4 (2) that when the court is deciding whether to exercise its power to order financial relief against a person who is not the mother or father of the child in question, it must have regard to:

(a) whether that person had assumed responsibility for the maintenance of the child and, if so, the extent to which and basis on which he assumed that responsibility and the length of the period during which he met that responsibility;

(b) whether he did so knowing that the child was not his child;

(c) the liability of any other person to maintain the child.

Example

M is a single woman, and the mother of C, aged 7.

F is the father of C, but has not bothered to acquire parental responsibility under the Act.

F has been paying £10 per week to M for the benefit of C since her birth.

M lives with X.

F now refuses to pay anything more for C.

X maintains C, and treats C as his own child.

M and X separate.

X then refuses to maintain M or C.

M applies to the court for periodical payments for herself and for C, payable by X.

The court in considering the application for financial relief for C will have to look at whether X had in reality assumed responsibility for C, and for how long, and also consider the liability of F to maintain C.

If M applies for a residence order in respect of C, the court could, of its own volition, order payments by F if, having considered all the circumstances, they feel it to be appropriate.

3.11.5 *Lump sums*

Schedule 1, para 5 enables an applicant to obtain a lump sum payment to defray expenses incurred in connection with the birth of a child, or in maintaining the child, and which were reasonably incurred before the making of the order.

Magistrates' courts are empowered to order up to £500 at the present time, the Secretary of State having power to enlarge that sum by order, from time to time.

The court has power to make a lump sum order when it discharges or varies an order for secured or unsecured periodical payments by a parent.

Note that although Sched 1, para 1(5) provides that the court may not make more than one settlement or transfer order against the same person in respect of the same child, the court can order more than one lump sum payment (para 5(4)).

Lump sums can be payable by instalments, and either the payer or the payee has power to apply for a variation of the number of instalments payable, the amount of any instalment payable, or the date upon which an instalment becomes due (para 5(6)).

3.11.6 *Variation of periodical payments*

The payer, payee, or the child himself, if over 16, may apply for the variation of a periodical payments order. The court has to look at all the circumstances of the case, including any change in the matters outlined in para 4 (see 3.11.4 above) which had to be taken into account in making the original order. The court has a wide discretion to suspend or reinstate payments and to post-date or backdate payments, provided that they do not go back earlier than the date of the application.

Example

M and F live together, then separate. M is the mother of C, aged 16.
C lives with M, and is still at school.

F, the father of C, pays £50 per month to M for the benefit of C.

M was largely supporting C, but has recently lost her job, and is in financial difficulties.

If M applies to the court for variation in January 1990, but the case is not heard until June 1990, the varied payments (if ordered) can be backdated as far as January 1990.

In December 1990, F has an accident which stops him working and he cannot meet his liability on the new increased order.

F may apply for a suspension of the payments until he recovers, then either the court can order a revival of the order in a specified period, or leave it for F or M to apply to reinstate the order when F is recovered.

Where an order for periodical payment ceases when the child in respect of whom they are made reaches 16, that child may apply for the revival of the order at any time thereafter until his eighteenth birthday (para 6(5)). The court may order revival of the payments where the child is receiving instruction at an educational establishment or undergoing training for a trade, profession or vocation, whether or not in gainful employment, or where there are special circumstances justifying an order. This would presumably cover a child needing financial help whilst studying and working part-time in a 'sandwich course' for example.

Example

C has received £50 per month from her father F, under a periodical payments order.

C has intended to leave school at 16 and work.

The court had directed the payments to cease when C was sixteen.

C decides to opt for further education and is accepted on a course where she can work part-time and have study release. She cannot manage on her part-time salary. She may apply to the court for revival of the periodical payments.

Where a parent liable to make secured periodical payments dies, their personal representatives (eg the executor or administrator of their estate) or the payee may apply for a variation or discharge of the order. The court will take into consideration when deciding the issue, the changes in circumstances, including the death of the parent (para 7(1) and (5)).

Paragraph 7(2) imposes a time limit on applications (presumably by the payee as well as the personal representatives of the deceased payer) to vary or discharge an order for secured periodical payments of six months from the date that representation is first taken out, after which time the leave of the court must be obtained. The reason for this is that in the administration of an estate, there should be a reasonable time limit in which the personal representatives can finalise the affairs of the deceased. Claims against the estate must, if possible be settled in order to allow the final distribution of the assets. Paragraph 7 therefore goes on to provide that the personal representatives of an estate shall not be liable for a distribution of assets of the estate after the six-month period on the ground that they should have taken into account the possibility that a court might have allowed a claim for variation by the payee after that time. The personal representatives are able to bring the matter before a court for a decision and then they are free to settle the affairs of the estate. Where acting in the estate of a person against whom an order for secured periodical payments has been made, it would always be advisable to finalise the liability of the estate for the secured payments within the required period and before distributing the estate's assets because, after the six months have passed, if the court grants leave, application could be made to vary the order and obtain part of the distributed estate.

Example

M is a single woman, and mother of C.
F, father of C, is liable to make secured periodical payments to M on behalf of C.
F dies, leaving all to B.
Y and Z are the personal representatives of F.
Within six months of first taking out representation Y and Z should bring the matter of the secured payments before a court. If they do not, and they go on to distribute the estate to B, M may apply to the courts for leave to claim part of B's inheritance to meet the secured payments.

Normally M should bring her action within the six month period but, if in these circumstances M did not know of F's death until after six months had elapsed, the court might well consider giving leave to claim against the estate, and although Y and Z would not be liable for distributing the estate, having failed to anticipate M's claim, B would suffer a reduction in his inheritance.

Paragraph 7(6) provides that in considering when the grant of representation was first taken out, a grant limited to settled land or trust property shall be left out of account. It further provides that a grant limited to real estate or personal estate shall be left out of account unless a grant as to the remainder has already been taken out or is made at the same time. This latter provision appears complicated, but, quite simply, if the grant of representation is for part of the estate but not the whole of it, then it will not be taken into account. Where two or more grants add up to the whole of the estate, it will be taken into account.

Example

Z dies in June 1990.
P and R are the personal representatives of Z. Wishing to deal with personal property only at that time, P and R take out a grant of representation limited to personal estate in September 1990.
In December 1990, they take out a grant limited to the real estate.
They have covered by those two grants the whole of the property, so the date when representation is first taken out is deemed to be December 1990. The earlier grant, relating only to part of the estate is not taken into account.

3.11.7 Financial relief under other enactments

There will be situations arising during the implementation of the Children Act 1989 where a residence order is made with respect to a child who is already the subject of an order for financial relief made under previous legislation. Paragraph 8 deals with these situations, providing that the payer under the previous order, or the person in whose favour a residence order is in force, may apply to the court for revocation or variation of the 'old' order. Variation could include an alteration in the sum payable, or the substitution of the name of the person with the residence order in their favour for that of the person named in the order.

Example

M is the mother of C.
F, C's father, was ordered in 1986 to pay £10 per week to M for the benefit of C under the 'old legislation'.
C goes to live with his grandmother, G.
G applies for, and is granted a residence order for C to live with her.
G may ask the court to vary the maintenance order so that F must now pay £25 per week to G for the benefit of C.

3.11.8 Interim orders

The court may order interim financial relief restricted to periodical payments only whilst awaiting the disposal of an application under paras 1 and 2. These payments can be backdated but only so far as the date of the application. Either or both parents may be ordered to pay at times and for whatever period the court thinks fit. The court may also give whatever directions it thinks fit (para 9(1) to (3)).

The interim order automatically ceases on the disposal of the full application, or the date specified by the court, whichever is the earlier; but note that the court is able to vary the date specified in the order (para 9(4)).

3.11.9 Maintenance agreement

The Act defines maintenance agreement in para 10(1) as:

any agreement in writing made with respect to a child, whether before or after the commencement of this paragraph, which—
(a) is or was made between the father and mother of the child; and
(b) contains provision with respect to the making or securing of payments or the disposition or use of any property for the maintenance or education of the child.

Where the maintenance agreement is subsisting, and either of the parties are domiciled or resident in England and Wales, then either party may apply to the court for an alteration of the agreement. If one of the parties to an agreement providing for continuation of payments after his or her death then dies, the personal representatives of the deceased's estate may apply for alteration of the maintenance agreement to the High Court or a county court within six months of first obtaining the grant of representation. Any such application, if not made within six months of the first grant of representation, requires the leave of the court.

Paragraph 11(4) provides that in considering when the grant of representation was first taken out, a grant limited to settled land or trust property shall be left out of account. It further provides that a grant limited to real estate or personal estate shall be left out of account unless a grant as to the remainder has already been taken out or is made at the same time. Simply explained, if the grant of representation is for part of the estate but not the whole of it then it will not be taken into account. Where two or more grants add up to the whole of the estate, it will be taken into account in assessing the six month period.

Paragraph 11(6) and (7) go on to provide that the personal representatives of an estate shall not be liable for a distribution of assets of the estate after the six-month period on the ground that they should have taken into account the possibility that a court might have allowed a claim by the payee for variation after that time. The personal representatives are able to bring the matter before a court for a decision and then they are free to settle the affairs of the estate. Where acting in the estate of a person who has entered into a maintenance agreement providing periodical payments, it would always be advisable to finalise the liability of the estate for the agreed payments within the required period and before distributing the estate's assets because, after the six months have passed, if the court grants leave, application could be made to vary the order and obtain part of the distributed estate.

To make an alteration, the court must be satisfied either that there has been a change (foreseeable or not) in the circumstances in the light of which the agreement was made or the agreement does not contain proper financial arrangements for the child (para 10(3)). The court may make such changes to the financial arrangements in the agreement by alteration or revocation as it considers just in all the circumstances. The alterations by the court have effect as though made by agreement between the parties and for valuable consideration (ie they are fully legally binding).

When inserting provision for periodical payments or increasing the rate of periodical payments, the court must have regard to the same matters in deciding the term for which the altered provision applies, as it would in making such orders ab initio under the Act (for details of matters to consider see 3.11.4 above).

The Act limits the power of magistrates to cases where both parties are resident in England and Wales, and at least one is resident in the justices' commission area. They can only make an order where there is no provision for periodical payments by either party, in which case they can insert one or if there is an existing provision for periodical payments, they can increase, reduce or terminate any of those payments (para 10(6)).

The provisions in this Act expressly do not affect the power of any other court in relation to actions regarding maintenance agreements under any other enactment (para (7)).

3.11.10 Enforcement of maintenance orders

Orders made by the magistrates' court are enforceable as a magistrates' court maintenance order under the Magistrates' Courts Act 1980 (s 150(1)). Notice must be given to the court by anyone liable to make payments, of any change of address; and failure to give this notice, without reasonable excuse, is punishable by a fine of level 2 (currently £100).

3.11.11 Financial provision for children living outside England and Wales

Where one parent lives in England and Wales and their child lives outside England and Wales with a parent, guardian or person in whose favour a residence order is in force the court may, on the application of one of the latter, make an order for periodical payments and/or secured periodical payments against the parent in England and Wales.

3.11.12 General notes

Proceedings under Sched 1 are family proceedings and therefore

63

the court has power to make orders concerning the upbringing and welfare of those children who are the subject of the financial application and also, in certain circumstances, in relation to other children of the same household who are not the subject of the application. The court also has the power to make some orders (with the exception of care and supervision) of its own volition. Should the court have matters drawn to its attention during a financial application which leads it to consider that care or supervision may be appropriate, it may ask the local authority to investigate the child's circumstances, and to report to the court.

The same orders for financial relief are available under the Act for the children of both married and unmarried parents.

Under the provisions of Sched 1(6) the court has power on making, varying or discharging a residence order, to also make a financial order of its own volition.

Chapter 4

Local Authority Support for Children and Families

4.1 Outline of previous law

Part III of the Act sets out the responsibilities of local authorities to children and their families. It covers children in need (as defined in the Act), disabled children, the under-fives and children being looked after by local authorities.

Under the previous law these matters were principally dealt with in the Child Care Act 1980 (CCA 1980) which is now repealed. Section 1 of that Act gave express statutory authority for preventative and rehabilitative work to diminish the need to receive or keep children in care. Local authorities were, however, left with wide scope to decide what services to provide. The provision of services for disabled children was covered by the relevant health and welfare legislation (the National Health Service Act 1977, the National Assistance Act 1948 and the Chronically Sick and Disabled Persons Act 1970) applying to the disabled of all ages and was not therefore geared to the particular needs of children.

Certain provisions of the old legislation survive unaltered; others have been replaced, supplemented or updated. The Act gives local authorities an umbrella power to provide services not only to prevent the admission of children into care but also to safeguard and promote their welfare generally, and in particular to promote their upbringing within their own families. Within this power local authorities will be able to provide services to children at home, at day centres or in residential facilities. They will also be able to offer financial assistance in exceptional circumstances. Whilst many of these services were available prior to the Act, they have never before been consolidated into a single child care statute.

The duty to receive children into care where there is no-one to care for them properly survives but the power to assume parental rights over such children by administrative resolution does not. Local authorities will, instead, have to apply for a statutory order under Parts IV or V of the Act if they want to retain a child in care against parental wishes. This reflects a change of emphasis in child care law in that the provision of care away from the family home is now to be viewed as a positive means of providing family support and reducing the risk of long-term family breakdown. Under the previous law, reception into care under s 2 of the CCA 1980 was often identified with parental failure and viewed as a last resort. The Act further develops this approach by introducing a concept of partnership with parents who must be consulted as part of the decision-making process. To this end parents will no longer have to give notice before withdrawing their children from voluntary care.

Whilst Part III of the Act sets out most comprehensively a local authority's duties to children and their families, nothing it contains will affect any duty imposed on an authority by or under any other enactment (s 30(1)).

4.2 Services for children in need

Under s 17(1) every local authority has a duty:

(a) to safeguard and promote the welfare of children within their area who are in need; and
(b) so far as is consistent with that duty, to promote the upbringing of such children by their families,

by providing a range and level of services appropriate to those children's needs.

4.2.1 Children in need

This is a new term in child care law. A child is considered to be in need, for the purposes of the Act, if:

(a) he is unlikely to achieve or maintain, or to have the opportunity of achieving or maintaining, a reasonable standard of health or development without the provision for him of services by a local authority under this Part [of the Act];
(b) his health or development is likely to be significantly impaired,

66

or further impaired, without the provision for him of such services; or

(c) he is disabled (s 17(10)).

The definition of disablement is taken from the National Assistance Act 1948 and covers a child who is blind, deaf or dumb or who suffers from mental disorder or is substantially and permanently handicapped by illness, injury or congenital deformity or such other disability as may be prescribed (s 17(11)). 'Development' means physical, intellectual, emotional, social or behavioural development, 'Health' means physical or mental health.

Every local authority has a duty under the Act to take reasonable steps to identify the extent to which there are children in need within its area (Sched 2, para 1(1)). A register must be kept of all disabled children (para 2).

Whilst there is no specific duty to assess the individual requirements of each child in need, the Act assumes that an assessment will be necessary and provides that this may be carried out at the same time as assessments required under other legislation, eg the Education Act 1981 and the Chronically Sick and Disabled Persons Act 1970 (Sched 2, para 3).

4.2.2 Nature of services

Section 17(1) gives local authorities a broad power to provide a wide variety of services for the benefit of children in need within their area. Certain services may be provided to all children and not just to those in need. Often where the Act seems to impose a duty on local authorities to provide a particular service, eg day care for pre-school children in need, this may amount to little more than a power in reality as each authority is given a discretion to decide what provision is appropriate within its own area. The duty in these circumstances is to provide a level of service appropriate to the needs of the area rather than the needs of individual children or their families.

Local authorities are now required to facilitate the provision by others (including in particular voluntary organisations) of services which they have power to provide under the Act and they may arrange for any person to provide such services on their behalf (s 17(5)). Under the previous law, local authorities were able to delegate to others the provision of advice, guidance or assistance under s 1 of the CCA 1980 and could place children in accommodation provided by voluntary organisations. Section 17(5) goes beyond this. It amounts to a direction to local authorities to involve the voluntary sector actively in the provision of services for children and would seem to reflect the political ideology of the government responsible for the Act.

The provision of day care for under-fives, after school and holiday activities for older children and assistance in kind or in cash to the families of children in need is covered in Part III of the Act. The provision of other services such as family centres, home helps and facilities for the disabled is covered in Sched 2, Part I of the Act and all paragraph references in this section of the text are to that Schedule. The Lord Chancellor has stressed that the services provided for in Sched 2, Part I are no less important than those mentioned in the main body of the Act. Nevertheless, it must be noted that the Secretary of State has power by order to amend any provision in the Schedule (s 17(4)) although he can only do so after a draft of the order has been approved by each House of Parliament (s 104(2)). The government cannot amend any provision in Part III of the Act in this way. Services specified in the Act include:

Day care   Every local authority will have a statutory duty to provide such day care for children in need within their area who are under the age of five and not yet attending school (s 18(1)) as is appropriate. This replaces the power previously contained in the National Health Service Act 1977, Sched 8, para 1, which is now repealed. Day care, in this context, means any form of care or supervised activity provided for children during the day, whether on a regular basis or otherwise. In making arrangements for the provision of day care, local authorities have a duty to consider the racial groups to which children in need belong (para 11).

Local authorities will have power to provide day care for pre-school children who are not in need as defined in the Act and may also provide facilities (including training, advice, guidance and counselling) for those who care for or accompany children while they are in day care (s 18(2), (3)).

After school activities   Local authorities will have a duty to provide appropriate care or supervised activities for school age children in need outside school hours or during the school holidays (s 18(5)). There is also a discretionary power to provide such facilities for children who are not in need (s 18(6)).

Review of day care services   The Act requires every local authority to review the provision of day care services within its area every three years (s 19). This requirement was inserted into the Act following concern that local authorities would interpret their duties and powers under s 18 in a less than generous spirit. The intention is to give authorities an overview of day care services for young children within their area. This should then enable them to identify any gaps in provision and plug these by directly providing services themselves or by encouraging the private sector to do so. Note that the duty to review day care services in accordance with s 19 is one of the provisions of the Act which applies to Scotland as well as England and Wales (s 108(11)).

The first review must take place within one year of the implementation of the Act. Review must be conducted jointly with the local education authority and should cover services provided by the local authority under s 18 and those provided by childminders and nurseries in the private sector for children under the age of eight. This information should be readily available as childminders and private nurseries are required to register with the local authority under Part X of the Act (see Chapter 11). The review should also take into account the provision made for this age group in both maintained and private schools, children's homes, hospitals and other similar establishments which do not have to register under Part X.

The authorities conducting a review should have regard to any representations they consider to be relevant, particularly those of the local health authority. These may include representations made by voluntary groups, employers and individual parents. The results of the review must be published as soon as reasonably practicable together with any proposals the local authority may have as a consequence.

Assistance in kind or cash   Local authorities will be able to provide assistance in kind or, in exceptional circumstances, in cash (s 17(6)) for the benefit of children in need. This is not an entirely new power. Under the previous law local authorities could give assistance in kind or cash to diminish the need to receive or keep a child in care (CCA 1980, s 1). The new power is less restrictive and the Act now specifies that such assistance may be conditional upon repayment in full or part (s 17(7)) unless the recipient is in receipt of income support or family credit under the Social Security Act 1986 (s 17(9)). Whilst loans were often made under the previous provision, there was no specific reference to repayment in the legislation. Local authorities will now have to consider the means of the child and each of his parents before providing any assistance or requiring repayment (s 17(8)). Note that assistance may be provided to the family of a child in need or to any individual member of that family for the purpose of safeguarding or promoting the child's welfare (s 17(3)). 'Family' in this context includes any person who has parental responsibility for the child or with whom he is living (s 17(10)).

Prevention of neglect and abuse   Local authorities must take reasonable steps, through the provision of services under the Act, to prevent children within their area suffering ill-treatment or neglect (Sched 2, para 4(1)). Note that the term 'ill-treatment' is defined by s 31(9) to include sexual abuse and non-physical forms of ill-treatment. The Act endeavours to ensure that children at risk do not escape notice by moving to a different area. Where a local authority believes that a child within its area is likely to suffer harm, but lives or proposes to live in the area of another local authority, it must inform the 'home' authority specifying the likely harm and, if possible, the child's present or proposed address (Sched 2, para 4(2)). Whilst many local authorities already operate such procedures on a voluntary basis, the imposition of a statutory duty to notify should rectify some of the shortcomings highlighted in recent child death inquiries.

Provision of accommodation for abusers   Where a child is suffering, or is likely to suffer ill-treatment within the home a local authority may assist the alleged abuser to obtain alternative accommodation (para 5). Assistance may take the form of an offer of alternative accommodation or a cash payment. Where cash assistance is given the provisions of s 17(7) to (9) will apply (see 'Assistance in cash or kind' above). It is not intended that local authorities should give long-term assistance with housing costs under this provision. It should, however, ensure that consideration is given to moving the perpetrator rather than the victim of child abuse wherever this is feasible.

Avoidance of proceedings Local authorities are required to take steps to reduce the need for legal proceedings to be brought in respect of children within their area, to encourage such children not to commit offences and to avoid the need to place them in secure accommodation (see 4.7 below). Proceedings in this context means applications for care or supervision orders, criminal proceedings, family or other proceedings which might lead to a care order, and wardship proceedings (Sched 2, para 7).

Provision for disabled children Local authorities must provide services for disabled children which are designed to minimise the effect of their disabilities and enable them to lead lives which are as normal as possible (Sched 2, para 6). This introduces into child care law the underlying philosophy of the existing legislation dealing with the disabled and chronically sick of all ages.

Services for children at home Local authorities are required to make such provision 'as they consider appropriate' for the following services to be available to children in need while they are living with their families (Sched 2, para 8):
(a) advice, guidance and counselling;
(b) occupational, social, cultural or recreational activities;
(c) home help (which may include laundry facilities);
(d) transport or assistance with travel expenses in order to take advantage of any services provided;
(e) assistance to enable the child and his family to have a holiday.

This list includes services previously available under other statutory provisions but collected together for the first time in child care legislation.

Family centres Local authorities are required to provide such family centres 'as they consider appropriate' for families within their area (Sched 2, para 9). A family centre is defined as a centre where a child, his parents or any person having parental responsibility for him, and any other person looking after him may:

(a) attend for occupational, social, cultural or recreational activities;

(b) attend for advice, guidance or counselling; or

(c) be provided with accommodation while receiving advice, guidance or counselling.

This may include at one end of the spectrum, a playgroup in which parents are involved and encouraged to develop parenting skills and, at the other, a specialist residential unit providing intensive family therapy in cases of child abuse.

Note that the Act does not limit the provision and use of family centres to children in need.

Maintenance of family home Local authorities have a duty to protect the interests of any child in need within their area, who is not being looked after by a local authority but who is living apart from his family (Sched 2, para 10). They must take reasonable steps to enable the child to live with his own family or to maintain contact with them, if this is considered necessary to safeguard or promote his welfare. This duty will apply, for example, to disabled children living away from home. Note also that local authorities have a separate duty to safeguard and promote the welfare of certain children who live away from home, regardless of whether they are children in need, under ss 85 to 87 of the Act (see Chapter 13).

4.2.3 Provision of information

The Act requires local authorities to publish information about their services and to take reasonable steps to ensure that this is received by those likely to benefit (Sched 2, para 1(2)). There is no corresponding duty to publish information where similar services are provided by other bodies but local authorities are encouraged to do so, particularly where voluntary organisations are involved.

4.2.4 Charge for services

A local authority may impose a reasonable charge for any service provided under s 17 or s 18 of the Act, other than advice, guidance and counselling (s 29(1)). Those expected to pay will be the child himself, if he is over the age of 16 years; his parents, if he is under that age; and any member of his family for whom a service is provided (s 29(4)). Recipients of income support or family credit under the Social Security Act 1986 will not be liable to pay any charge and nobody with insufficient means to pay the full charge should be required to pay more than may reasonably be expected of him (s 29(2), (3)). Any charge properly made for a service may be recovered summarily as a civil debt.

4.3 Provision of accommodation for children

Although Part III of the Act places an emphasis on the provision of services to enable children to remain in the family home, it is recognised that this will not always be possible. Whilst local authorities have always had a duty to provide accommodation for children in certain circumstances, the terminology of the legislation has now changed signifying a new approach. Children will no longer be received into care. Instead they will be provided with accommodation under s 20, a term less suggestive of parental failure. The broad power to provide accommodation for certain children in respect of whom no statutory duty would arise recognises the value of this service as a temporary measure and emphasises its positive as opposed to negative features.

4.3.1 Duty to provide accommodation

Local authorities now have a statutory duty to provide accommodation for the following categories of children:

Children in need Section 20(1) provides that:

(1) Every local authority shall provide accommodation for any child in need within their area who appears to them to require accommodation as a result of—
  (a) there being no person who has parental responsibility for him;
  (b) his being lost or having been abandoned; or

73

(c) the person who has been caring for him being prevented (whether or not permanently, and for whatever reason) from providing him with suitable accommodation or care.

This provision replaces the old duty to receive children into care under s 2 of the CCA 1980. Although different terminology is used, the duty to provide accommodation will arise in similar circumstances. Under the previous legislation local authority intervention had to be justified in the interests of the child's welfare. Section 20(1) does not impose a similar requirement but the limitation of the duty to children in need (as defined by s 17(10)) has much the same effect. One important difference is that the new provision will apply to children up to the age of 18 years (s 105(1)).

Where a local authority provides accommodation under s 20(1) for a child ordinarily resident in the area of another local authority, the child's 'home' authority may take over responsibility for providing accommodation within three months of being notified in writing of the situation (s 20(2)). There is power in the Act for this period to be extended by statutory order. The authority providing accommodation will also be able to recover from the home authority any reasonable expenses incurred in accommodating and maintaining the child (s 29(7)). Local authorities will be expected to resolve any questions as to a child's ordinary residence by agreement, failing which the Secretary of State will decide (s 30(2)).

Children over sixteen There is an additional duty to provide accommodation for children in need who have reached the age of 16 years and whose welfare is likely to be seriously prejudiced otherwise (s 20(3)). The effect of this provision is to give older children an independent right to be provided with accommodation, if their welfare is at risk, even though they have a home and whether or not their parents object (see 4.3.4 below).

4.3.2 Power to provide accommodation

Local authorities may provide accommodation for children and young people in the following circumstances:

74

To safeguard and promote a child's welfare   Local authorities have a broad power to provide any child with accommodation for this purpose even though a person with parental responsibility for the child is able to provide a home (s20(4)).

To assist young people A local authority may provide accommodation for young people between the ages of 16 and 21 in any community home which takes children over the age of 16 years if this would safeguard and promote their welfare (s 20(5)). Under this power local authorities could, for example, accommodate young people in training or further education who have no home because they were previously in care or are estranged from their families. (For further provisions regarding community homes generally see Chapter 7.)

4.3.3 Duty to consult child

Local authorities have always had a duty to ascertain and give due consideration to the wishes of a child in care, having regard to his age and understanding. There is now a similar duty to ascertain the child's wishes *before* accommodation is provided under s 20, so far as this is reasonably practicable and consistent with the child's welfare (s 20(6)).

4.3.4 Parental rights

Subject to certain exceptions, a local authority may not provide accommodation for any child under these provisions if any person who has parental responsibility for the child, and is willing and able to provide or arrange accommodation for him, objects (s 20(7)). A person with parental responsibility may remove the child from accommodation provided by or on behalf of a local authority at any time without giving notice (s 20(8)). These provisions reflect the voluntary nature of arrangements under s 20. Nevertheless, it is expected that local authorities will reach agreements with parents to cover important aspects of the child's care and it is likely that these will include arrangements for the child's return home.

A person with parental responsibility will lose the above rights if there is a residence order in force and the person or persons who have the benefit of that order (if there are more than one)

75

all agree to the provision of accommodation by the local authority (s 20(9), (10)). The same will apply if a person who has care of the child by virtue of an order made by the High Court in wardship agrees to the provision of accommodation.

Example 1

C, aged 6 years, is the child of M and F.

M and F are divorced.

They each have parental responsibility for C.

There is a residence order in favour of M.

M is unwell and unable to care for C.

M agrees that AB Council shall provide accommodation for C until she is well again.

F objects to this.

AB Council may continue to provide accommodation notwithstanding F's objection.

F cannot remove C from local authority accommodation but he can apply for a residence order under Part II of the Act.

The rights of a person with parental responsibility are similarly restricted where a child aged sixteen or over has himself agreed to be provided with accommodation by the local authority (s 20(11)). In these circumstances there is no right to object or to remove the child at any time.

Example 2

C, aged 16 years, has run away from home.

AB Council finds C within its area.

C has no accommodation or means of support and is sleeping rough.

AB Council believe that she will resort to prostitution if she is not helped.

C refuses to return home but will agree to go into local authority accommodation.

C's parents will not agree to this.

AB Council has a duty to provide accommodation for C under s 20(3) and may do so without the consent of C's parents.

It is important to ascertain who does and does not have parental responsibility for a child when considering the provisions of s 20. This concept, which is fundamental to the Act, is discussed in detail in Chapter 2. Residence orders are discussed in Chapter 3.

4.3.5 Children removed under emergency provisions

Every local authority has a duty to make provision for the reception and accommodation of children removed or kept away from home under an emergency protection order (s 21(1)). They must also receive and accommodate children who have been taken into police protection, if requested to do so (s 21(2)). The Act also extends this duty to certain categories of children detained as a result of criminal proceedings, ie children who have been arrested and would otherwise be detained in police custody under s 38, Police and Criminal Evidence Act 1984; children on remand under s 23(1), CYPA 1969; and children who are the subject of supervision orders imposing a residence requirement under s 12AA, CYPA 1969.

A person who obtains and removes a child under an emergency protection order may therefore demand accommodation from the local authority for the area in which the child is then located. If he decides not to place the child either in local authority accommodation or in a state hospital, any reasonable expenses of providing accommodation elsewhere are recoverable from the child's home local authority (s 21(3)). This also applies where a child is detained under s 38, Police and Criminal Evidence Act 1984.

Where a local authority provides accommodation under s 21 for a child who is ordinarily resident elsewhere and he is not placed in a community home provided or controlled by that local authority, or in a state hospital, any reasonable costs of accommodating and maintaining him are recoverable from his home authority (s 29(8)). Under this provision a local authority could, for example, recover the boarding-out allowance paid to foster parents.

It is expected that any dispute as to a child's ordinary residence will be resolved by agreement between local authorities but failing this the Secretary of State will decide (s 30(8)).

4.4 Duties of local authorities to children looked after by them

The Act sets out in detail in ss 22–25, and Sched 2, Part II, the duties of a local authority in relation to any child it is 'looking after'. This phrase replaces the term 'in care' and applies to children who are the subject of care orders and children provided with accommodation by local authorities (in particular under the Act but also in exercise of any other functions delegated to the Social Services Committee) for a continuous period of more than 24 hours (s 22(1), (2)). Where the term 'in care' is used in the Act it refers to children who are the subject of care orders and not those being looked after under voluntary arrangements.

The new provisions replace those previously set out in the CCA 1980. Whilst many duties survive unchanged or subject to slight modification, the Act also introduces important new duties. All paragraph references are to Sched 2, Part II, unless otherwise stated.

The following duties are laid down in the Act:

4.4.1 To safeguard or promote the child's welfare

Under s 22(3) local authorities have a general duty to safeguard and promote the welfare of any child they are looking after and to make reasonable use of facilities and services available to children living with their parents. An authority may act in a manner inconsistent with this duty if necessary to protect members of the public from serious injury, or to comply with a direction given by the Secretary of State in relation to a particular child who may pose a risk to public safety (s 22(6)–(8)).

This provision broadly corresponds with the previous duty under the CCA 1980 except that public interest can only now override a local authority's duty to a particular child where there is risk of serious injury.

4.4.2 To consult the child and parents

Local authorities must now ascertain the wishes and feelings of the child, his parents, any non-parent with parental responsibility and any other person considered to be relevant before making any decision concerning a child they are looking after, or proposing to look after, so far as this is reasonably practicable (s 22(4)). They must give due consideration to the wishes and feelings of the people consulted in making any decisions although in the child's case this will depend on his age and understanding. The child's religious persuasion, racial origin and cultural and linguistic background must also be taken into account (s 22(5)).

Under the previous law there was a duty to take into account the child's wishes and religious persuasion, but there was no specific requirement to consider parental wishes or racial, cultural and linguistic factors.

4.4.3 To provide accommodation and maintenance

As before, local authorities will have a duty to provide accommodation and maintenance for children they are looking after (s 23(1)). Accommodation may be with foster parents (who may be relatives or friends of the child approved for this purpose), in a community home, voluntary home or registered children's home or in a specialist unit provided by the government if a child needs special facilities (s 23(2)). Placements will be subject to regulations to be made by the Secretary of State under the Act. Schedule 2, Part II, para 12 specifies matters to be included in the regulations governing foster placements. These will cover, in particular, arrangements for the health, education, religious upbringing and supervision of foster children. Parts VI, VII and VIII of the Act specify the content of regulations which will govern the management of all three types of children's homes (see Chapters 7–9).

Children who are the subject of care orders may be placed with a parent, a non-parent who has parental responsibility or a person who had the benefit of a residence order immediately before the care order was made, but only in accordance with regulations to be made by the Secretary of State (s 23(5)). Schedule 2, Part II, para 14 specifies matters which are to be covered in the proposed regulations and mentions, in particular, requirements for consultation prior to placement, for supervision and medical examination and for removal of the child if the placement proves unsatisfactory.

The Accommodation of Children (Charge and Control) Regulations 1988 (SI No 2183), which only came into effect on 1 June 1989, govern placements with parents, guardians, relatives and friends under the previous law. It is likely that any regulations to be made under the Act will contain similar provisions. The main difference is that placements with relatives and friends will now be treated as foster placements and those caring for the child will become local authority foster parents. The regulations to be made under s 22(5) will only cover placements with parents or those who have or recently had parental responsibility, eg where a child in care is placed at home on trial as part of a rehabilitation process.

Local authorities will also have a general power to make other appropriate arrangements to accommodate a child but must exercise this in accordance with any regulations made by the Secretary of State under the Act (s 23(2)(f)). Schedule 2, Part II, para 13 specifies matters to be covered in such regulations. These include persons to be notified, records to be kept by local authorities and arrangements for supervision of the child.

Whilst the general range of accommodation which may be provided is wide, local authorities are required to give priority to placements which enable a child to remain with his family or people he knows. They should make arrangements for him to live with either a parent or a non-parent who has or recently had parental responsibility or with a relative, friend or other person connected with him unless this would not be reasonably practicable or consistent with his welfare (s 23(6)). Any accommodation provided should be near to the child's home and siblings should be accommodated together, if this is reasonably practicable and consistent with the welfare of the children concerned (s 23(7)). Accommodation provided for disabled children should not be unsuitable for their particular needs (s 23(8)).

4.4.4 To promote and maintain contact

Where a local authority is looking after a child it must endeavour to promote contact between the child and his family, unless this is not reasonably practicable or consistent with his welfare (para 15). The Act specifies that this means contact with his parents, a non-parent who has parental responsibility and any relative, friend or other person 'connected with him'. The Act does not define connection in this context. Given its ordinary meaning it could clearly encompass friends, former neighbours, school teachers and distant relations who do not come within the statutory definition of relative (see s 105 and glossary).

This provision reproduces a fundamental principle of the statutory *Code of Practice on Access to Children in Care* published in 1983 and now largely superseded by the Act. Note, however, that the wording of the Act does not impose an absolute duty on local authorities. Provided they have used their best endeavours they will not be in breach of their statutory duty if either parent or child steadfastly refuses contact, or if a parent's whereabouts are unknown.

The provisions of Sched 2, para 15 must be considered in conjunction with s 34 of the Act insofar as they relate to children who are subject to care orders. Section 34 imposes a positive duty on local authorities to allow such children contact with their parents and certain other specified people and the court is given power to make orders concerning contact (see 5.5 below). Different provisions apply to children who are simply provided with accommodation under s 20. In their case a contact order may be made but only under s 8 of the Act (see Chapter 3).

The power under the previous law to offer financial assistance to enable parents to visit has been extended to include relatives, friends or any other person connected with the child. Payments may also now be made to the child himself, or to any person on his behalf, to cover travelling, subsistence or other expenses incurred by him in visiting his family (para 16). To make a payment the local authority must be satisfied that the visit could not otherwise be made without undue financial hardship and that the circumstances warrant it.

To facilitate contact, local authorities are required to take reasonable steps to keep parents (and non-parents with parental responsibility) informed of where the child is living and they in turn must keep the authority informed of their whereabouts (para 15(2)). A parent who fails to comply with this requirement is guilty of an offence, punishable on summary conviction by a fine not exceeding level 2 on the standard scale, unless he can show that at the material time he was living with the child's other parent and had reasonable cause to believe that the other parent had informed the authority that they were both at the same address. (See Appendix 1 for standard scale currently applicable).

If one authority takes over responsibility for a child from another under s 20(2) of the Act (see 4.3.1 above), it must inform the child's parents and any non-parent with parental responsibility. The transferring authority must also ensure that it informs at least one of the people entitled to know. A parent is under no duty to inform the receiving authority of his address until he has been notified of the transfer.

If a child is the subject of a care order, a local authority may withhold information as to his whereabouts if there is reasonable cause to believe that disclosure would prejudice his welfare (para 15(4)). This does not apply to children being provided with accommodation under the provisions of s 20 since this would clearly be contrary to the voluntary nature of such arrangements.

4.4.5 *To appoint a visitor for certain children*

A local authority must appoint an independent visitor to visit, advise and befriend any child it is looking after if:

(a) the communication between the child and any parent of his (or any non-parent who has parental responsibility) has been infrequent, or

(b) he has not lived with, visited or been visited by any such person during the preceding 12 months and,

(c) in either case, this would be in the child's best interests (para 17(1)).

Under the previous law this duty only applied to children over the age of five years who were subject to care orders and accommodated in community homes. The duty now applies to all children being looked after by local authorities. Children with sufficient understanding to make an informed decision are now given the right to object to an appointment being made or continuing. This reflects the greater emphasis given to the rights of children throughout the Act.

A person appointed visitor must be entirely independent of the local authority but may recover his expenses from them. The Secretary of State will have power to make regulations defining who may or may not be appointed an independent visitor. Similar regulations existed under the previous law. An appointment may be terminated by either party serving written notice. Note that an independent visitor will no longer have the power to apply for the discharge of a care order on behalf of a child in care.

4.4.6 To notify a child's death

The Act imposes a new duty on a local authority to notify the Secretary of State of the death of any child it is looking after (Sched 2, para 20(1)). There is also a duty to notify parents (and non-parents with parental responsibility) so far as reasonably practicable. Under the previous law there was no specific duty to notify parents although the rules governing the conduct of community and voluntary children's homes made provision for this.

Local authorities continue to have power to arrange for a child's burial or cremation but must now obtain parental consent to such arrangements, where reasonably practicable. As before a child may not be cremated if this is contrary to the tenets of his religion. Local authorities arranging burial or cremation must, of course, comply with the general law relating to such matters (para 20(6)). Funeral costs may be recovered from any parent of a child under 16 as a civil debt (para 20(4)).

Local authorities may pay to any parent, non-parent with parental responsibility, relative, friend or other person connected with the child, expenses incurred in attending the child's funeral if the circumstances warrant it and the person concerned could not otherwise attend without undue financial hardship (para 20(1), (2)).

4.4.7 To advise and assist

Section 24(1) of the Act imposes a new duty on local authorities to advise, assist and befriend children they are looking after with a view to promoting their welfare when they leave the care of the local authority. The duty may involve preparing the child to return to his family or, in the case of an older child, to an independent life. Assistance may be in kind or, in exceptional circumstances, in cash. It may be given on condition that it will be repaid in full or in part. The means of the child and each of his parents must be considered before any assistance is given or repayment required.

Note that the Act also imposes on local authorities a duty to advise and assist young people previously in care. This is discussed in 4.6 below.

4.5 Powers of local authorities in relation to children looked after by them

The Act gives local authorities certain specific powers in relation to children they are looking after. Some of these powers have already been discussed above because they relate directly to statutory duties. For example, the power to pay visiting expenses where necessary to enable the child to maintain contact with his family and friends. Schedule 2, Part II contains the following additional powers:

4.5.1 To guarantee apprenticeship deeds

A local authority may guarantee any deed of apprenticeship or articles of clerkship entered into by a child it is looking after and, once it has done so, may enter into a similar obligation under a supplemental deed, even if it is no longer looking after the child (para 18).

There is a similar power to guarantee apprenticeship deeds entered into by young people qualifying for advice and assistance under the after-care provisions of the Act (see 4.6 below).

4.5.2 To arrange emigration

A local authority may arrange, or assist in arranging, for any child it is looking after to live outside England and Wales (para 19). If the child is the subject of a care order this can only be done with the prior approval of the court. In all other cases prior approval must be forthcoming from every parent or person with parental responsibility for the child. This differs from the power under the previous law which required the approval of the Secretary of State, and not a court, in all cases.

A court cannot give its approval unless satisfied that:
   (a) living outside England and Wales would be in the child's best interests;
   (b) suitable arrangements have been, or will be, made for the child's reception in his new country;
   (c) the child has consented to living in that country; and
   (d) every parent, or person with parental responsibility, has also consented (para 19(3)).

The child's consent may be dispensed with if he does not have sufficient understanding to give it provided that he is emigrating to live with a parent, guardian or other suitable person (para 19(4)).

Parental consent may be dispensed with if a parent cannot be found, is incapable of consenting or witholds his consent unreasonably. These grounds are similar to the grounds for dispensing with parental consent to adoption and the relevant adoption case law will provide useful guidance on interpretation.

Where a court grants approval, it may direct that its decision shall not have effect during the appeal period (para 19(7)). This will mean that the child cannot be sent abroad until the determination of any appeal, or the expiry of the appeal period if no appeal is made (para 19(8)).

Note that s 56 of the Adoption Act 1976, which requires authority for the adoption abroad of a British child, does not apply to children emigrating with court approval under these provisions.

4.6 After care

The Act makes provision for young people who were living apart from their families at the age of 16 to continue to receive some form of support up to the age of 21. In doing this it consolidates, modifies and extends provisions previously contained in the CCA 1980. The support given may include advice, friendship, accommodation, assistance and, in exceptional circumstances, financial aid.

4.6.1 Advice and friendship

Section 24 imposes a duty on local authorities to advise and befriend young people under the age of 21 who were at any time between the ages of 16 and 18 years either looked after by a local authority or accommodated by or on behalf of a voluntary organisation. There is an identical power, rather than a duty, to advise and befriend young people who were formerly accommodated in registered children's homes, privately fostered or accommodated for more than three consecutive months by a health authority, a local education authority or in a residential care home, a nursing home or a mental nursing home. Note that in the latter case the qualifying period of three months may begin before the child reaches the age of 16.

The duty or power only applies to young people who are no longer being looked after or accommodated in this manner and will only arise if a local authority is aware of the young person's presence within its area. A request for help must come from the young person himself and the local authority must be satisfied that he is in need of advice and friendship.

If the young person was not previously looked after by the local authority, it can only offer advice and assistance if the person or organisation formerly responsible for his care does not have the necessary facilities for advising and befriending him (s24(5)).

The Act contains provisions for notification to ensure that local authorities are aware of the existence of young people within their areas who might qualify for advice and assistance. Thus voluntary organisations and those in charge of registered children's homes have a duty to inform the relevant local authority where any child over the age of 16 is leaving their care and proposes to live in the area of that authority (s 24(2)). Health authorities, local education authorities and those in charge of residential care homes or nursing homes have a similar duty where accommodation has been provided for a consecutive period of at least three months (s 24(12), (13)). Local authorities themselves have a duty to notify where it appears that a young person whom they have been advising or befriending proposes to live, or is living, in the area of another local authority (s 18(8)). Local authorities will also be required to publish information about the services they provide under s 24 and they must take reasonable steps to ensure that this reaches those likely to benefit (Sched 2, para 1(2)).

4.6.2 Assistance

Where a local authority has a duty or a power to advise and befriend a young person it may also give assistance in kind or, in exceptional circumstances, in cash (s 24(6), (7)). Assistance may be conditional on repayment, in full or part, but no repayment may be required from any person in receipt of income support or family credit under the Social Security Act 1986 (s 24(10)). The means of the young person and his parents (if relevant) must be considered before any assistance is given or repayment required.

Cash assistance may be given by contributing to expenses a young person may incur in living near a place where he is, or will be, working or seeking employment or receiving education or training (s 24(8)(a)). It may take the form of a grant to enable him to meet expenses connected with his education or training (s 24(8)(b)). Where a young person is given financial assistance to undertake a course of education or training this may continue until he completes the course even if he is then over the age of 21 (s 24(9)(a)). Any interruption in his studies may be disregarded provided that he resumes them as soon as reasonably practicable (s 24(9)(b)).

Section 24 gives local authorities a power and not a duty to provide assistance. It is not intended therefore that they should take over responsibility for income maintenance in the long term; this remains the province of the Department of Social Security. Neither will they be expected to finance the education or training of young people who are, for example, entitled to grants from a local education authority although assistance given under s 24 may help to meet additional expenses incurred in these circumstances.

4.6.3 Accommodation

Under s 20(5) local authorities have a general power to provide accommodation for any young person between the ages of 16 and 21 in any community home which takes children over the age of 16 (see 4.3.2 above).

4.7 Secure accommodation

Section 25 of the Act re-enacts with minor amendments s 21A of the CCA 1980 which was the original statutory provision restricting the power of local authorities to place children in care in secure accommodation. The provisions apply to all children being looked after by local authorities although a parent or person with parental responsibility for a child accommodated on a voluntary basis (s 20 and see 4.3 above) may remove a child from secure accommodation at any time if they wish to do so (s 25(9)).

Section 25(1) provides that no child may be kept in accommodation provided for the purpose of restricting liberty unless:

    (a) he has a history of absconding, is likely to abscond from any other type of accommodation and if he absconds is likely to suffer significant harm; or

(b) he is likely to injure himself or others if he is kept in any other type of accommodation.

The Secretary of State is given power to make regulations specifying the maximum period a child may be kept in secure accommodation without the authority of a court and the maximum period which may be authorised by a court (s 25(2)). Under the Secure Accommodation (No 2) Regulations 1983 (SI No 1808) a local authority could not keep a child in secure accommodation for more than 72 hours consecutively or in aggregate in any consecutive period of 28 days without the authority of the juvenile court. Courts were able to authorise detention for up to three months initially but could extend this authority for further periods not exceeding six months on the application of the local authority. It is likely that similar time limits will be imposed in the new regulations and that they will permit only local authorities to apply for authority to keep a child in secure accommodation.

If a court then determines that the relevant criteria are satisfied it will be required to make an order authorising the child's detention in secure accommodation for a specified maximum period (s 25(4)). Authorisation will not prejudice the power of any court in England and Wales or Scotland to give directions relating to the child (s 25(8)). Interim orders can be made if an application has to be adjourned (s 25(5)). Section 1(1), (2) and (5) of the Act will apply to applications under s 25 (see Chapter 2). The welfare of the child will therefore be the court's paramount consideration and an order should not be made unless the court considers this would be better for the child than to make no order at all.

A court cannot exercise its power to restrict the liberty of a child who is not legally represented in the proceedings unless he has refused or failed to apply for legal aid, having been informed of his right to do so (s 25(6)).

Jurisdiction to hear applications under s 21 will no longer be limited to the juvenile court with right of appeal to the High Court. Instead the general provisions of the Act relating to jurisdiction, venue, parties, evidence and appeal will apply (see Chapter 14).

Note that the Secretary of State has power by regulation to provide that s 21 shall or shall not apply to a particular category of children, or that its effect shall be modified in their case, or that other specified provisions shall apply to children in that category (s 21(8)). Under the 1983 Regulations this power was exercised to exclude (inter alia) children detained indefinitely by court order after committing grave and serious offences, children detained in a place of safety by the police, children in the care of voluntary organisations and young people over the age of 16 years not in care but accommodated in community homes.

4.8 Review of cases

Section 26(1) gives the Secretary of State power to make regulations requiring the case of each child who is being looked after by a local authority to be reviewed. Section 20 of the CCA 1980 contained a similar power but was never fully implemented. Instead under transitional provisions local authorities were required to review the case of each child in care every six months.

Section 26(2) states in considerable detail the content of the proposed regulations. They will specify the manner and frequency of review, and the matters to be considered in each case. They may require local authorities:

(a) before conducting the review, to seek the views of the child, his parents, any non-parent with parental responsibility and any other person whose views may be relevant, particularly with regard to any matter which is to be considered in the review;

(b) to consider, in the case of a child subject to a care order, whether to apply for discharge of the order;

(c) to consider, if the child is in accommodation provided by the local authority, whether it complies with Part III of the Act;

(d) to inform the child, so far as reasonably practicable, of any steps he may take under the Act, eg to apply for a contact order or for the discharge of a care order;

(e) to make arrangements to implement review decisions, if necessary with other bodies providing the appropriate services;

(f) to notify the child, his parents, any non-parent with parental responsibility and any other person who ought to be notified of the result of the review and any decision taken as a consequence; and

(g) to monitor their arrangements for reviewing cases to ensure that they comply with the regulations.

4.9 Complaints procedures

Local authorities now have a statutory duty to establish procedures for considering representations, including complaints, about the discharge of any of their functions under Part III of the Act in relation to any child who is being looked after by them or falls within the category of a child in need (s 26(3)). Representations may be made by the child himself, a parent, a non-parent with parental responsibility, a local authority foster parent and any other person considered by the authority to have sufficient interest in the child's welfare. Prior to the Act the only requirement on local authorities to establish complaints procedures was contained in the *Code of Practice on Access to Children in Care* and was restricted to complaints about access facilities.

The Secretary of State may make regulations specifying how the proposed procedures shall operate and be monitored (s 26(5)(6)). All procedures will have an independent element in that at least one person who is not a member or an officer of the local authority will be required to participate in the consideration process and in any discussions which may follow as to what action should be taken (s 26(4)). The procedures must be given appropriate publicity so that those parties entitled to use them are aware of their existence (s 26(8)).

After a complaint or representation has been considered the local authority must have due regard to any findings and must, where reasonably practicable, notify the complainant, the child (if he has sufficient understanding) and any other person likely to be affected, of its decision in the matter, with reasons, and any action which it has taken or proposes to take (s 26(7)).

The investigation of a complaint under this procedure may not, of course, result in the outcome the complainant seeks. Another avenue which may be explored, therefore, is to bring the matter to the attention of the Secretary of State who is given power under s 84 to act in default where a local authority has failed, without reasonable cause, to comply with any of the duties imposed on it by or under the Act (see Chapter 12).

90

4.10 Contribution towards maintenance

Local authorities may recover a contribution towards the maintenance of certain children they are looking after from the parents of a child who is under 16 and from the child himself if he is over that age. The relevant criteria and procedure are set out in Sched 2, Part III which re-enacts with some modifications the provisions previously contained in Part V of the CCA 1980 (s 29(6)). All paragraph references are to Sched 2 unless otherwise stated.

No contribution may be required in respect of any period during which a child is allowed to live with a parent (para 21(5)). Neither do the contribution provisions apply to any child who is being looked after under:

(a) section 21 (see 4.3.5 above);

(b) an interim care order;

(c) s 53 of the Children and Young Persons Act 1933 (punishment of certain grave offences) (para 19(7)).

Whilst a local authority must always consider whether it should recover contributions in any appropriate case, it may only do so if this would be reasonable (para 21(2)). The Secretary of State has power to make regulations specifying matters to be taken into account in this regard (para 25(a)). A parent, receiving income support or family credit under the Social Security Act 1986, will not be liable to contribute (para 21(4)).

The procedure for recovering contributions laid down in the Act requires local authorities to serve contribution notices on those liable specifying an amount they consider appropriate and arrangements for payment (para 22(1)). The amount may be a standard rate fixed by the authority for all the children it looks after but must not exceed the normal allowance paid to foster parents or the amount that is reasonable for the contributor to pay, having regard to his means. If the parties then agree an amount, and this is confirmed in writing by the contributor, no further action is required and any overdue payments may be recovered summarily as a civil debt (para 22(7)). The agreed amount may differ from that originally specified in the contribution notice.

If no agreement is reached within one month of service of a contribution notice, or the contributor withdraws his agreement, the local authority may apply to a court for a contribution order

91

(para 23(1)). The court may not order a weekly sum greater than that specified in the contribution notice and must have regard to the contributor's means when fixing an amount (para 23(3)). A contribution order will be automatically discharged if the local authority serves another contribution notice and the parties then reach an agreement but the court must be notified of this (para 23(6), (7)). An order may be varied or revoked on the application of either party (para 21(8)). An appeal will lie in accordance with rules of court from any order made under these provisions (s 23(11)).

A contribution order will be enforceable as a magistrates' court maintenance order, ie by distress, attachment of earnings or imprisonment if other methods of enforcement are inappropriate and the contributor's failure to pay results from wilful default or culpable neglect (para 24(1)). Where the contributor lives in the area of another local authority, arrangements can be made for that authority to collect contributions, and take enforcement action if necessary on behalf of the authority entitled to receive payment (para 24(2)). The collecting authority must then pay over the contributions collected less an agreed amount for services rendered. Such arrangements can be made even if the contributor lives outside the jurisdiction of the English courts in either Scotland or Northern Ireland.

The Secretary of State has power to make regulations specifying matters which the local authority are to take into account when proposing arrangements for payment and procedures to be followed in reaching agreements with contributors and other local authorities (para 25).

Parents of a child over the age of 16 cannot be required to contribute towards his maintenance. The child may, however, be entitled to a grant from the local education authority if he is receiving further education. The Secretary of State has power to determine by regulations how such children shall be treated for grant purposes (s 30(4)). Under previous regulations they have always been treated as children of parents without resources and therefore entitled to receive a full grant.

4.11 Co-operation between authorities

Section 27 authorises a local authority to approach and request help from other bodies which may be able to assist it in the exercise of its functions under Part III of the Act. The bodies specified are:

(a) any local authority;
(b) any local education authority;
(c) any local housing authority;
(d) any health authority; and
(e) any other person or body authorised by the Secretary of State.

An authority approached for help should comply with any request if this is compatible with its own statutory or other duties and obligations and does not unduly prejudice the discharge of its own functions (s 27(2)). If a local authority responds to a request relating to a child or other person ordinarily resident in the area of another local authority, it may recover from that authority any expenses reasonably incurred (s 29(9)).

Section 27(4) specifically requires every local authority to assist any local education authority with the provision of services for any child with special educational needs within its area. Where there is an overlap betwen the functions of a local authority under Part III of the Act and the functions of a local education authority, the Secretary of State may determine by regulation which authority is to act (s 30(3)).

4.12 Consultation with local education authorities

Section 28 provides for full consultation between the local social services authority and the local education authority before any child who is being looked after by a local authority is placed in a residential school or a home with education provided on the premises. This provision is of particular relevance to handicapped children and others with special educational needs who are placed in homes which are also schools. The purpose of consultation is to ensure that the child's welfare and educational needs are fully considered and that there is proper liaison between the statutory agencies concerned.

Under s 28(1) the local authority must consult the local education authority for its area before making a placement, so far as reasonably practicable. The education authority must also be informed when arrangements are made for such a placement and when the child leaves the establishment (s 28(2), (3)). Where a child has special educational needs and is the subject of a statement under the Education Act 1981, the local education authority to be consulted is the one which maintains the statement (s 28(4)).

Note that local education authorities have a corresponding duty under s 85 to notify the local authority of any placements in residential schools which last or are intended to last for three months (see Chapter 13).

Chapter 5

Care and Supervision

5.1 Outline of previous law

Part IV of the Act contains new provisions for the making of care, supervision and related orders. Under the previous law there were diverse routes of entry into care by court order. A juvenile court could make a care or supervision order in care proceedings under s 1 of the CYPA 1969 provided that specified grounds were satisfied. Care and supervision orders could also be made in matrimonial, guardianship, adoption and wardship proceedings in exceptional circumstances. Juvenile courts exercising their criminal jurisdiction had power to make care and supervision orders in respect of children found guilty of criminal offences. In addition, local authorities had power to assume parental rights over children in care on a voluntary basis by administrative resolution under s 3 of the CCA 1980.

The preconditions for admission into care under the various statutory provisions differed. An interdepartmental working party set up by the government in July 1984 to review child care law was to able to identify 20 separate provisions leading to care under a court order with several different sets of criteria for the court to apply. There were, it noted, defects and anomalies in each of these (Review of Child Care Law, September 1985, para 2.4).

As a result of these findings a major recommendation in the Review was for 'a single procedure and a single composite ground under which local authorities may intervene compulsorily in the care and upbringing of children' (para 3.26). This was supported by the Government in its White Paper on The Law on Child Care and Family Services (January 1987), Cmnd 62) and the Children Act 1989 duly assimilates the grounds for making care and supervision orders in care and family proceedings, removes the

95

power to make care orders in criminal proceedings (see Chapter 16) and abolishes the power of local authorities to assume parental rights over a child by administrative action (s 108(7)).

5.2 New grounds

Section 31(2) of the Act provides that a court may only make a care or supervision order if it is satisfied—

(a) that the child concerned is suffering, or is likely to suffer, significant harm; and

(b) that the harm, or likelihood of harm, is attributable to—
  (i) the care given to the child, or likely to be given to him if the order were not made, not being what it would be reasonable to expect a parent to give to him; or
  (ii) the child's being beyond parental control.

In addition, s 1(5) provides that where a court is considering whether or not to make one or more orders under the Act with respect to a child, it shall not make the order or any of the orders unless it considers that doing so would be better for the child than making no order at all. This replaces a requirement originally proposed in the White Paper for the court to be satisfied that the order proposed is the most effective means available to the court of safeguarding the child's welfare. The difference in emphasis is clear. The original proposal imposed a positive duty on courts to scrutinise the alternatives to a care order. Section 1(5) is prohibitive and was inserted into the Act to prevent children being put in care 'because of inadequate home circumstances but without evidence that the order would improve the situation' (Lord Chancellor's speech to the House of Lords on the 2nd Reading of the Children Bill 1988, 6 December 1988).

'Harm' is defined in s 31(9) as meaning ill-treatment or the impairment of health or development. 'Development' means physical, intellectual, emotional, social or behavioural development. 'Health' means physical and mental health and 'ill-treatment' includes sexual abuse and forms of ill-treatment which are not physical. Apart from 'harm' all these terms appeared in the previous grounds for care proceedings under s 1(2)(a) of the CYPA 1969 but were never given a statutory definition.

Where the question of whether any harm suffered by a child is significant turns on the child's health or development, s 31(10) states that his health or development shall be compared with that which could reasonably be expected of a similar child. When this sub-section of the Act was debated in the House of Lords it was suggested that the term 'a similar child' in this context should be taken to mean a hypothetical child with similar characteristics and handicaps (if any). The standard of health and development against which the child must be measured is that which it is reasonable to expect and not the best that could possibly be achieved for the child. Thus removal from home will not be justified simply because other arrangements may cater better for a child's needs than the care offered by his parents.

Note that the wording of s 26(9) seems to limit its application to the assessment of harm which a child has actually suffered rather than likely harm although courts may choose to apply a similar hypothetical test.

Any harm or likelihood of harm to the child must result from shortcomings in parental care. This may be because a parent is unwilling, unable or incapable of providing reasonable care or because the child is beyond control and therefore unable to benefit from the care which is on offer to him. Under the previous law, being beyond parental control was one of the specific grounds for care proceedings. The concept has therefore survived in the new Act albeit in a slightly different form. The quality of parental care given, or likely to be given to the child must be measured against an objective standard. The casual link between harm to the child and parental shortcomings introduces into care proceedings considerations which were previously more relevant to the assumption of parental rights under s 3 of the CCA 1980. In care proceedings, however, it was always necessary for the court to find the care or control test satisfied and this inevitably involved some assessment of parental capabilities.

The new grounds were drafted to deal with two principal shortcomings of the previous law. First, the grounds for making a care or supervision order under s 1 of the CYPA 1969 were largely confined to an examination of the past and present defects in the development or well-being of the child. Anticipated risk was only covered in a very restricted manner, eg where another child in the same household had suffered harm or where the child was or was likely to become a member of the same household as a person convicted of certain offences. It was therefore often necesary to wait until a child had suffered actual harm before care proceedings could be instituted even though the parent's conduct or incapacities would have provided grounds for a parental rights resolution had the child been in voluntary care.

Conversely, local authorities were often powerless to prevent the removal of children from voluntary care, even if there was a strong likelihood that this would cause them harm, unless the child had been in care for a period of at least three years or the parent's condition or conduct fell within one of the grounds for assuming rights by resolution specified in s 3 of the CCA 1980.

It was for these reasons that local authorities increasingly resorted to the wardship jurisdiction of the High Court to protect children at risk. The inclusion of likely risk in the new grounds is intended to eliminate the need for wardship proceedings in these circumstances and the Act severely restricts local authority access to the jurisdiction (see Chapter 15).

Exposure to moral danger, non-school attendance and the commission of an offence, all previously grounds for care proceedings under s 1 of the CYPA 1969, are not included in the new Act. It is intended that non-school attenders will be dealt with by means of the education supervision order (see 5.7 below) unless it is clear that lack of education is affecting the child's development to the extent that care proceedings are justified. The offence condition in the CYPA 1969 was little used and is unlikely to be missed as it will still be possible for offenders who fall within the ambit of s 31(2) to be dealt with by civil proceedings if this is felt to be more appropriate. Exposure to moral danger whilst not expressly mentioned in the Act could clearly impair a child's health or development within the meaning of the new grounds.

It is important to note that the welfare principle as set out in s 1 of the Act (see 2.1 above) will apply to care proceedings. This states that the child's welfare must be the court's paramount consideration when determining any question with respect to his upbringing. Prior to this it had been unclear whether and to what extent the welfare principle (then enacted in s 1 of the Guardianship of Minors Act 1973) applied to care proceedings. Section 1(3) provides a checklist of matters to which the court must have particular regard when considering whether to make, vary or discharge an order under Part IV of the Act. These are dealt with in greater detail in Chapter 2.

The civil standard of proof will apply to care proceedings as before; the case must therefore be proved on the balance of probabilities. In simplest terms this means that the court must find it more likely than not that the facts are as alleged by the applicant and the facts as proved must be sufficient to satisfy the grounds in s 31(2).

Example 1–Actual harm

AB Council is applying for a care order in respect of a child, C, aged 3 years.

C has bruises and burn marks on her body which have been diagnosed as non-accidental injuries.

C's parents have no explanation for these injuries but do not admit causing them.

To make a care order under s 31(1) the court must be satisfied that:

(i) C is suffering harm within the meaning of s 31(9) (ie ill-treatment or impairment of health or development);

(ii) that any impairment of C's health or development is significant within the meaning of s 31(10) (ie when C's health is compared with that of a similar child of her age); and

(iii) that C is suffering harm because the care given to her does not meet reasonable expectations of parental care (ie injuries were caused by one or both of her parents or arose from their failure to protect her adequately); and

(iv) that it would be better for C to make a care order than to make no order at all.

When considering these matters:

(i) C's welfare must be the court's paramount consideration (s 1(1)); and

(ii) it must have particular regard to the matters listed in s 1(3) (which will include (inter alia) C's ascertainable wishes and feelings, her physical and emotional needs, the likely effect on her of any change in her circumstances, any harm which she is at risk of suffering, how capable her parents and any other person may be

99

of meeting her needs and other options available to the court under the Act).

Example 2–Likely harm

C, aged 8 days, is the child of M, an unmarried woman.
C's father is unknown.
C has remained in hospital since her birth.
M suffers from a mental illness and is considered unfit to care for C.
AB Council is applying for a care order.
To make a care order under s 31(1) the court must be satisfied that:

(i) C is likely to suffer harm within the meaning of s 31(9) (ie ill-treatment or impairment of health or development);

(ii) that the likely harm is significant (the test in s 31(10), as drafted, does not strictly speaking apply to the assessment of likely harm but will obviously assist).

(iii) that C is likely to suffer harm because the care likely to be given to her, if the order were not made, will not meet reasonable expectations of parental care (ie for a very young baby).

(iv) that it would be better for C to make an order than to make no order at all.

When considering these matters:

(i) C's welfare must be the court's paramount consideration (s 1(1)); and

(ii) it must have particular regard to the matters listed in s 1(3) (see Example 1 above).

5.3 Application for an order

5.3.1 Applicants

Section 31(1) specifies that an application for a care or supervision order can be made by a local authority or an authorised person. The police no longer have power to institute proceedings. This follows logically on the elimination of the 'offence condition' and also reflects the prevailing policy behind Part IV of the Act, which

100

is that care proceedings should usually be brought by local authorities (*Review of Child Care Law*, paras 12.15 and 12.20)

Section 31(9) defines an authorised person as 'the National Society for the Prevention of Cruelty to Children and any of its officers and any person authorised by order of the Secretary of State to bring proceedings . . . and any officer of a body which is so authorised'. Under the previous law the only body so authorised was the National Society for the Prevention of Cruelty to Children and it is likely that this will continue to be the case although the power exists to authorise other bodies.

An authorised person will now have to consult the local authority in whose area the child ordinarily resides before making an application for a care or supervisory order, if it is reasonably practicable to do so (s 31(6)). Whether it does so or not, the court will not entertain it's application if the child is already subject to a care or supervision order (including a supervision order made in criminal proceedings) or there are earlier care proceedings which have not yet been disposed of.

The Act not only identifies local authorities as the prime applicants for care and supervision orders in this way, it also states the circumstances in which they must give specific consideration to whether or not to institute proceedings (see s 37(2) discussed at 5.3.2 below and s 47(3) discussed at 6.13.2 below).

5.3.2 Jurisdiction

The court has no power to make a care or supervision order in respect of a child who is over the age of 17 years, or 16 years if married (s 31(3)). Section 29(1) of the CYPA 1963 which enabled the court to make an order if a child attained the age of 17 years after the commencement of proceedings no longer applies (s 108 and Sched 15). The proximity of the child's seventeenth birthday (and the likelihood of marriage) must therefore be taken into account when proceedings are considered.

An application for a care or supervision order may be made on its own or in any other family proceedings (s 31(4)). Section 8(3) defines 'family proceedings' to include proceedings under Parts I, II and IV of the Act and wardship, matrimonial, domestic and adoption proceedings (see 3.2 above). The purpose of this provision is to create a unified code of public and private law relating to children. If, therefore, a child is already the subject of family proceedings, an applicant for a care or supervision order may apply in those proceedings without leave but must still satisfy the above conditions. Applicants will be expected to state at the outset whether they seek a care order or a supervision order although the court will have power to make a care order on application for a supervision order and vice versa (s 31(5)).

A court hearing family proceedings in which a question arises as to a child's welfare may also take the initiative and direct the appropriate local authority to investigate a child's circumstances with a view to applying for a care or supervision order if this appears to be appropriate (s 37). The court cannot make a full care or supervision order unless a local authority or an authorised person applies for one and satisfies the statutory grounds. It can, however, make an interim care or supervision order pending the outcome of the investigation (see 5.3.7 below). The appropriate local authority to undertake the investigation is the one in whose area the child ordinarily resides or, if this is not readily ascertainable, the local authority in whose area any circumstances arose in consequence of which the direction was given. The local authority undertaking the investigation is specifically required by s 37(2) to consider whether it should:

(a) apply for a care or supervision order;
(b) provide services or assistance for the child or his family;
(c) take any other action.

Where it decides not to apply for an order it must give the court its reasons and details of any service, assistance or any other action it proposes to take within eight weeks of the date of the direction unless the court directs otherwise (s 37(3), (4)). It must also consider whether it would be appropriate to review the case at a later date and if so, a date must be fixed for that review (s 37(6)).

Example

A court is hearing an application for a residence order in respect of a child, C.
C resides in the area of AB Council.
The Court considers that this is a case in which a care order may be appropriate.

The court cannot make a care order of its own volition but can refer the case to AB Council for investigation under s 37. AB Council investigates the case and decides not to apply for a care order but to offer social work support and day-care facilities and to review the case after three months.

AB Council must report back to the court within 8 weeks and must give the court the reasons for its decision and details of the services to be offered.

AB Council must fix a date for the review.

5.3.3 Venue

The High Court, the county court and the magistrates' court are given concurrent jurisdiction in proceedings under the Act (s 92(7). The present jurisdiction of the juvenile court in care proceedings is, however, transferred to the domestic arm of the magistrates' court to be renamed the family proceedings court (s 92(1)(2)).

The Lord Chancellor will have power to specify by rules of court which proceedings may be initiated in which courts and the circumstances in which they may be transferred between courts (s 92(8) and Sched 11, Part I). It is intended that most applications for care or supervision orders will commence in the magistrates' court. The proposed rules will allow single justices to deal with the transfer of cases to higher courts operating criteria to be laid down by the Lord Chancellor (Sched 11, para 3).

The provisions relating to jurisdiction and venue are common to all proceedings under the Act and are discussed more fully in Chapter 14.

5.3.4 Parties

The Act does not specify who is or can be made a party to care proceedings. Instead rules of court made under s 93(2)(b) will specify those entitled to full party status and those who may only make representations to the court. Under the previous law the applicant and child were automatically parties to the proceedings. Parents were entitled to full party status if there was a conflict of interest between parent and child leading to an order for separate representation. Grandparents had a right to apply for party status if they could demonstrate a substantial interest in the child's

103

upbringing at any time before the commencement of proceedings provided that this was in the interests of the child's welfare. Foster parents, relatives or friends with whom the child had lived for a specified period and others who could demonstrate an interest in the child's welfare had the right to make representations to the court but not to participate fully in the proceedings.

It seems unlikely that any of the groups currently entitled to party status will lose it when the new rules are introduced and it is possible that this right will be extended to anyone whose legal position could be affected by the proceedings (White Paper, para 55). This could include anyone entitled to seek and actually seeking an order under Part II of the Act (see 3.6.1 above).

5.3.5 Timetable

A court hearing an application for an order under Part IV of the Act must have regard to the general principle set out in s 1(2) that delay in determining any question relating to a child's upbringing is likely to prejudice that child's welfare (see Chapter 2). In each case the court will have to draw up a timetable for the disposal of the proceedings without delay and will have power to give directions to ensure that the timetable is adhered to, so far as is reasonably practicable (s 32(1)).

It is envisaged that rules of court will be made under s 32(2) specifying time limits for certain steps in the proceedings and making other provision for speedy disposal. Any timetable drawn up by the court will have to take these rules into account. The Act makes similar provisions for the speedy disposal of family proceedings under Part II (see 3.7 above). The imposition of strict time limits is not, of course, new in civil law but the positive duty on the court to draw up and police a timetable is innovative in care proceedings.

5.3.6 Evidence and procedure

Section 96 contains provisions which relax the rules of evidence applicable to proceedings under Part IV in a number of ways. In particular, the Lord Chancellor is given power to provide for the admission of hearsay evidence including statements recorded on audio and video tape. The privilege against self-incrimination, which witnesses have long been able to claim, is abolished. Courts will be able to hear the unsworn evidence of young children as they may now do in criminal proceedings.

Procedure will be governed by rules to be made under s 93. Further rules may be made under s 144 of the Magistrates' Courts Act 1980 to enable magistrates' courts to sit in private when exercising their powers under the Act (s 97(1)). It will also be an offence to publish or broadcast any material intended or likely to identify a child involved in proceedings in the magistrates' court (s 97(2)). Under s 95 the court will have power to order the attendance of the child and to authorise a police officer or any other person to bring him to court if the order is not complied with.

These provisions are all contained in Part XII of the Act which is discussed more fully in Chapter 14.

5.3.7 Interim orders

Section 38 contains provision for the court to make interim care and supervision orders and to give directions for medical and psychiatric examination or other assessment during the course of proceedings. Under the previous law there was power to make an interim care order but not an interim supervision order. The power to give directions as to medical and psychiatric examination or other assessment is also new. The powers and duties of local authorities under care and supervision orders (whether interim or otherwise) are discussed below (see 5.4 and 5.6).

Under s 38(1) the court will be able to make an interim care or supervision order when:

(a) adjourning an application for a care or supervision order; or

(b) giving a direction under s 37(1) in family proceedings (ie for a local authority to investigate a child's circumstances, see 5.3.2 above).

It cannot make an order unless satisfied 'that there are reasonable grounds for believing that the circumstances with respect to the child are as mentioned in section 31(2)' (s 38(2)). Thus there must be sufficient evidence before the court to justify a reasonable belief that the grounds for a full order may exist.

The maximum duration of an interim care order proposed in

the White Paper was eight weeks with the possibility of 14 day extensions in exceptional circumstances. This formula has not been followed in the Act which provides instead for an initial interim order of up to eight weeks with extensions of up to four weeks (s 38(4)). If the initial order is for less than four weeks a second or subsequent order may last until the expiry of a period of eight weeks from the date of the first order, eg first interim order lasts two weeks, second order may last six weeks, subsequent orders may only last a maximum of four weeks in each case.

An interim order will cease to have effect if the application is disposed of before its expiry date.

Example 1

AB Council is applying for a care order in respect of a child, C.

On the first hearing the case is adjourned so that C's parents can obtain legal representation.

The court makes an interim care order for a period of two weeks.

On the second hearing the case is adjourned as all parties are not ready to proceed.

The court makes an interim care order for a period of six weeks.

On the third hearing the case is adjourned because adequate time cannot be allocated in the court list for the full hearing with convening a special court.

The court makes an interim care order for a period of four weeks.

A special court is convened two weeks after this to hear the case.

After a two day hearing the court decides not to make a care order.

The interim care order made on the third hearing will automatically expire.

Example 2

A court hearing an application for a residence order in respect of a child, C, considers that a care order may be appropriate.

The court directs AB Council to investigate the case under s 37.

The court makes an interim care order in respect of C for a period of eight weeks.

Two weeks after the direction AB Council applies for a care order and the case is fixed for hearing one week later.

At the hearing the court decides to make a residence order after all.

The interim care order will automatically expire.

If the order was made by the court when giving a direction under s 37(1), it will cease to have effect before its stated expiry date if the local authority completes its investigation and decides not to apply for a care or supervision order.

Example 3

A court hearing an application for a residence order in respect of a child, C, considers that a care order may be appropriate.

The court directs AB Council to investigate the case under s 37.

The court makes an interim care order in respect of C for a period of eight weeks.

Four weeks later AB Council informs the court that it has decided not to apply for a care or supervision order.

The interim care order will cease to have effect.

When considering how long an interim order shall last the court must consider whether any party who was, or might have been, opposed to the order was in a position to argue his case in full (s 38(10)). A short order may, for example, be justified to give an unrepresented party the opportunity to return to court quickly to contest a further interim order with the benefit of legal representation.

5.3.8 Medical and psychiatric examination

Section 38(6) provides that where the court makes an interim care or supervision order it may give 'such directions (if any) as it considers appropriate with regard to the medical or psychiatric examination or other assessment of the child'. It may do this when

107

it actually makes the interim order or at any time while it remains in force (s 38(8)). It will be possible to apply for a direction to be varied but the Act does not specify who may apply; this will be left to rules of court. A direction may authorise or prohibit examination or assessment or it may state that no examination or assessment shall take place unless the court subsequently directs otherwise (s 38(7)).

If the child is of sufficient understanding to make an informed decision he may refuse to submit to the proposed examination or assessment (s 38(6)). This provision takes into account the decision of the House of Lords in the case of *Gillick* v *West Norfolk and Wisbech Area Health Authority and Another* [1986] AC 112, in which it was accepted that a child under the age of sixteen years could give or withhold consent to medical intervention. The Act does not specify the age at which a child may be deemed to have sufficient understanding to make decisions of this nature. Courts will presumably take steps to ascertain the child's views before making a direction, wherever appropriate. Once a direction has been made it will presumably be for the doctor, psychiatrist or person carrying out the assessment to ascertain whether the child is able to make an informed decision about the procedure.

Local authorities will be able to use this provision if they require the medical or psychiatric examination of a child who is subject to an interim supervision order or where, for example, they wish to prevent a parent from having the child examined. They may also seek directions from the court to examine or assess a child who is in interim care, even though they have authority to consent to this, if the proposed examination is controversial in the context of the proceedings.

Parents and other parties will be able to seek directions to obtain 'a second opinion' in respect of a child in interim care whereas previously they have had to rely upon the local authority giving its consent. They will also be able to seek directions to prevent the local authority from having the child examined.

The court may order or prohibit examination of its own volition and the child or a guardian ad litem on his behalf may also seek directions. The power will, perhaps, be of greatest use in contested cases to provide for joint assessment or medical examination thereby minimising the number of intrusive procedures the child is required to undergo.

5.3.9 'Interim' residence order

The court may make a residence order under s 8 as an interim measure on adjourning care proceedings or giving a direction under s 37(1). The power to do so is contained in s 11(3) of the Act which applies to proceedings under Part IV. A residence order will name the person or persons with whom the child is to live. It is discussed in further detail in Chapter 3.

Where the court makes a residence order on an application for a care or supervision order it must also make an interim supervision order unless satisfied that the child's welfare will be satisfactorily safeguarded without this (s 38(3)). The provisions limiting the maximum duration of interim care and supervision orders do not apply to residence orders but will, of course, apply to any interim supervision order made under s 38(3) in respect of a child.

Section 38(6) which empowers the court to give directions as to medical or psychiatric examination or other assessment does not apply to residence orders, but it will apply if the court makes an interim supervision order at the same time. If a residence order only is made the court may still have power to order or prohibit medical examination or other assessment by means of a specific issue order or a prohibited steps order under s 8 of the Act. It may also make a contact order under s 8 naming persons with whom the child is to be allowed contact. See Chapter 3 for a full discussion of section 8 orders.

The residence order coupled with an interim supervision order will enable the court to place a child at home or with a relative, friend or other appropriate person while the case is proceeding with the added safeguard of a supervision order. Under the previous law the court could either make an interim care order and leave the local authority to decide whether the child should be placed at home or elsewhere, or make no order at all in which case there would be no statutory supervision of the child.

5.4 Care orders

A care order means an order placing a child in the care of a designated local authority (s 31(1)(*a*)). It includes an interim care order made under s 38 except where express provision to the contrary is made (s 31(11)). The local authority designated in the order must be the authority in whose area the child ordinarily resides, or where the child does not reside in the area of a local authority, the authority within whose area any circumstances arose in consequence of which the order is made (s 31(8)). These are the same criteria as applied previously. (See *R* v *Manchester Justices, ex parte Bannister* [1983] 4 FLR 77 for a judicial interpretation of 'ordinarily resides').

A care order cannot be made in respect of a child who has reached the age of 17 (or 16, in the case of a married child) (s 31(3)). Under the previous law it was still possible for a care order to be made after a child reached 17 provided that the proceedings had commenced before his seventeenth birthday.

The making of a care order in respect of a child who is the subject of any section 8 order discharges that order (s 91(2)).

5.4.1 Duration of care orders

A care order (other than an interim order) will continue in force until the child's eighteenth birthday unless it is brought to an end earlier (s 91(11)). Under the previous law there was provision for a local authority to apply for an order to be extended for one year in special circumstances and any care order made after a child's sixteenth birthday always lasted until he attained the age of 19 years.

A care order will be automatically discharged by the child's adoption or by the making of a residence order under s 8 (see Chapter 3). A care order may also be discharged by a court on application under s 39 (see 5.9 below).

5.4.2 Powers and duties of local authorities

It is the duty of a local authority named in a care order to receive the child into its care and to keep him while the order remains in force (s 33(1)). If the application for a care order was made by an authorised person and the local authority was not informed in accordance with s 31(6) (see 5.3.1 above) the child may be kept in the care of that person until received into local authority care (s 33(2)). The purpose of this provision is presumably to allow the local authority sufficient time to make arrangements for the child.

A care order gives a local authority parental responsibility for a child subject to certain limitations. It may not cause the child to be brought up in any religious persuasion other than the one he would have been brought up in if the order had not been made (s 33(6)(a)). It may not appoint a guardian for the child or consent to an adoption order or an order freeing the child for adoption or providing for his adoption abroad (s 33(6)(b)). These restrictions are carried over from the previous law.

Section 33(7) contains further restrictions which are new. While the child is in care no person may cause him to be known by a new surname or remove him from the United Kingdom without either the written consent of every person who has parental responsibility or the leave of the court. This provision does not prevent the local authority from taking or consenting to the child's removal abroad for less than one month and it does not apply to arrangements for the child to live outside England and Wales which are governed by Sched 2, para 19 (see 4.5.2 above). A child may therefore go on a family holiday abroad with his foster parents but he may not be known by their surname however longstanding the placement.

The term parental responsibility is new to care proceedings and is defined in s 3(1) as 'all the rights, duties, powers, responsibilities and authority which by law a parent of a child has in relation to the child and his property'. Part I of the Act specifies who may have parental responsibility in respect of a child (see Chapter 2).

Note that a person with parental responsibility will not lose it if a care order is made but will not be entitled to act in any way which is incompatible with the order (s 2(8)). He will, in effect, retain a somewhat limited form of parental responsibility.

While the order is in force the local authority will be in the driving seat. It will 'have the power . . . to determine the extent to which a parent or guardian of [a] child may meet his parental responsibility' but it 'may not exercise this power unless . . . satisfied that it is necessary to do so in order to safeguard or promote the child's welfare' (s 33(3)(b) and (4)). A local authority may therefore prevent a parent from undermining its decisions but the Act builds in certain safeguards to ensure that this power is used sparingly and only where it is justified in the interests of the child.

Other rights which a parent or guardian may have in relation

111

to a child under other statutory provisions are also preserved, eg the right to consent or withhold consent to adoption or to the child's marriage (s 33(9)). Furthermore, a parent or guardian who has actual care of a child, while a care order is in force, may do whatever is reasonable in all the circumstances for the purpose of safeguarding or promoting the child's welfare (s 33(5)).

Whilst these safeguards may appear to enhance the status of parents while a care order is in force, the real power nevertheless resides with the local authority, as it must if the order is to be effective in protecting the child and promoting his welfare.

Example

C is subject to a care order in favour of AB Council.

AB Council determine that it is in C's best interests to attend a weekly boarding school.

C's parents do not agree with this decision.

C is allowed to stay with her parents each weekend.

C's parents cannot refuse to send her back to the boarding school; this would not be 'reasonable in all the circumstances of the case'.

If C became ill and required an emergency operation while in their care it would be reasonable for them to give consent.

Part III of the Act specifies the duties of local authorities in relation to children in care and how they are to be carried out (see ss 18–25 and Sched 2, Part II discussed at 4.4 above).

5.5 Parental contact

Section 34(1) enshrines in law for the first time a presumption of reasonable access to a child in care. It states that:

Where a child is in the care of a local authority, the authority shall (subject to the provisions of this section) allow the child reasonable contact with—
(a) his parents;
(b) any guardian of his;
(c) where there was a residence order in force with respect to the child immediately before the care order was made, the person in whose favour the order was made.

112

(d) where, immediately before the care order was made, a person had care of the child by virtue of an order made in the exercise of the High Court's inherent jurisdiction with respect to children, that person.

In an emergency an authority may refuse to allow the child contact with any of the above persons if it is satisfied that this is necessary to safeguard or promote the child's welfare (s 34(6)). In these circumstances, however, the refusal must be decided upon as a matter of urgency, it must not exceed seven days and the authority must follow the procedure set out in regulations to be made by the Secretary of State under s 34(6). After seven days, and in all non-urgent cases, the local authority must apply to the court for authority to refuse contact (s 34(4)). The child is also given the right to apply for such an order.

A court when making an order under s 34 may impose such conditions as it considers appropriate (s 34(7)). It could, for example, state that there should be no contact unless the local authority decides that a resumption would be in the child's interests. Contact may also be resumed, without an express condition to this effect, by agreement between the local authority and the person previously denied contact. Regulations to be made by the Secretary of State under s 34(8) will specify the circumstances in which such an agreement may be reached and any conditions that may be imposed.

Any of those mentioned in s 34(1) may apply to the court for a contact order (s 34(3)). This includes the natural father of a child born outside marriage whether or not he has acquired parental responsibility by agreement or court order (see 2.2.2 above). The court may make whatever order it considers appropriate with respect to contact between the child and the applicant. Since the local authority may not deny contact to such persons without the authority of a court order, except as a short-term emergency measure, it is likely that many applications for contact orders will be requests to the court to define the frequency, nature and location of access.

The Act recognises that the child may benefit from contact with others apart from those who have or have had parental responsibility for him. Any other person may therefore apply for a contact order but only with the leave of the court. Note that the provisions of s 34 only apply to a child who is the subject of a care order. A person seeking contact with a child being provided with accommodation by a local authority under s 20 of the Act (see 4.3 above) can apply for a contact order under s 8, although in some cases it is necessary to obtain the leave of the court first (see Chapter3).

The child, himself, may also apply for an order authorising contact with any person named in the application. This may be particularly useful if the child wishes to maintain contact with a relative, sibling or friend not otherwise entitled to contact. Local authorities will have a responsibility to inform children in their care of their rights under the legislation including their right to apply for an order under s 34.

The court is also given power to make an order under s 34 of its own volition, when making a care order or in any family proceedings which relate to a child who is in care (s 34(5)).

Section 91(17) contains provisions to prevent a vexatious litigant from making repeated contact applications. If the court refuses to make an order under s 34 the applicant may make no further application for a period of six months unless he obtains the leave of the court. This prohibition applies to all proceedings under s 34, including applications to vary or discharge existing orders, but does not apply to local authorities. There is also a general power in s 91(14) for the court to prohibit any further applications without leave when disposing of any application for an order under the Act.

Example

C, aged 10 years, is the subject of a care order in favour of AB Council.

C's parents, M and F, visit her twice a week but M would like to see her more frequently.

C's grandmother, G, has been allowed to visit C once a week in local authority accommodation.

G would like contact to take place in her own home but AB Council will not agree.

C would like to see her older sister, S, but AB Council does not consider this to be in her best interests.

While she is in care C discloses that she has been sexually abused by F and makes it clear that she does not wish to see him.

114

AB Council believes that continued contact with F will cause C further distress.

AB Council may refuse to allow F to have contact for a period of seven days but must then apply to the court for authority to refuse further contact.

M can apply for an order specifying contact at more frequent intervals.

G can apply for an order specifying that contact shall take place in her own home but only with the leave of the court.

C can apply for a contact order naming S.

If M, G or C fail in their applications, they may make no further application for a period of six months without leave.

A contact order may be made at the same time as a care order (including an interim care order) or at a later date (s 34(10)). It is likely that many orders either allowing or refusing contact will be made at the same time as care orders as the court will have a positive duty, before making a care order, to consider the arrangements which the local authority have made, or propose to make for contact with the child, and to invite the parties to the proceedings to comment on these (s 34(11)). Local authorities will therefore be expected to agree arrangements for contact at an early stage. Indeed, under Sched 2, Part II, para 15 they will have a positive duty to promote contact between the child and his parents and 'any relative, friend or other person connected with him', so far as reasonably practicable and consistent with his welfare (see 4.4.4 above). This re-inforces a principle previously found in the government's Code of Practice, *Access to Children in Care* published in 1983. Regulations to be made by the Secretary of State will make provision for local authorities to notify any variation or suspension of arrangements agreed voluntarily and not under a court order (s 34(8)(c)).

The parties will be able to depart from the terms of any order under s 34 by agreement but only in accordance with regulations to be made by the Secretary of State (s 34(8)). The court may also vary or discharge any s 34 order whether permitting or refusing contact, on the application of the child, the local authority or the person named in the order (s 34(9)). If an application for variation or discharge is refused, the applicant may not re-apply for six months except with the leave of the court (s 91(17)). This restriction does not apply if the applicant for discharge or variation was a local authority.

The new statutory code for contact represents a significant departure from the previous law. This left the matter of access entirely within the discretion of the local authority in most cases and gave a parent the right to apply for a court order only if the local authority served notice terminating or denying access. A parent who was simply dissatisfied with the arrangements proposed by the local authority had no redress. Grandparents, relatives and others connected with the child had no right to apply to the court at all although the Code of Practice recognised that any consideration of access had to take into account the child's wider family. Access proceedings were entirely separate from care proceedings and it was not usual for the court to consider access arrangements when making a care order.

The new provisions should meet many of the criticisms previously voiced. In addition the new requirement in Part III of the Act for all local authorities to establish a procedure for considering complaints and representations should provide another forum for the consideration of contact (s 26(3) and see 4.9 above).

5.6 Supervision orders

A supervision order is an order placing a child under the supervision of a designated local authority or, in certain circumstances, a probation officer. The court cannot name a local authority in a supervision order unless the child lives, or will live, in its area and the authority agrees (Sched 3, Part II, para 9(1)). It cannot designate a probation officer unless the relevant local authority requests this because there is already a probation officer working with another member of the household (Sched 3, Part II, para 9(2)). Under the previous law a probation officer could not supervise a child under the age of 13 years. There is no such restriction in the new provisions.

The making of a supervision order automatically terminates any earlier care or supervision order which would otherwise continue in force (Sched 3, Part II, para 10).

Detailed provisions relating to supervision orders are contained in Sched 3, Parts I and II of the Act and all references are to paragraphs in that Schedule unless otherwise stated.

5.6.1 Duration of supervision orders

A supervision order will cease to have effect one year after the date on which it was made unless the supervisor applies to the court to extend, or further extend it (para 6). An order may not be extended so as to last more than three years in total and may not extend beyond the child's eighteenth birthday (s 91(13) and para 6(4)). Under the previous law the court could make a supervision order for three years at the outset. The new provisions ensure that the order is kept under the scrutiny of the court.

An order may also cease to have effect if certain steps are taken or orders made under the Child Abduction and Custody Act 1985, which provides for the recognition and enforcement of foreign custody orders.

5.6.2 Duties of a supervisor

While a supervision order is in force it is a supervisor's duty:
  (a) to advise, assist and befriend the supervised child;
  (b) to take such steps as are reasonably necessary to give effect to the order;
  (c) to consider whether or not to apply for discharge or variation where the order is not wholly complied with or may no longer be necessary (s 35(1)).

The previous law only required a supervisor to advise, assist and befriend. The new requirements give statutory force to accepted good practice. In addition, the Secretary of State is given power to make regulations concerning the exercise of local authority functions with regard to supervision orders (para 11).

5.6.3 Specific requirements

Courts may include specific conditions in supervision orders requiring the child or a person with responsibility for him ('the responsible person') to act in a particular way. 'The responsible person' in this context means anyone who has parental responsibility for the child and any other person with whom the child is living (para 1). Under the previous law it was only possible for the court to impose requirements on the child and not a parent. This was often unrealistic especially in the case of a very young child.

The responsible person must now comply with a supervisor's request for the child's address, if known, and if he is actually living with the child he must allow the supervisor reasonable contact (para 8(2)). A supervisor who is denied access to a child may apply for a search warrant under s 102 (see Chapter 18). The responsible person may also be required to comply with any directions given by the supervisor for him to attend at a specified place to take part in specified activities either with or without the child (para 3(1)(c) and (2)). A supervisor could, for example, require a parent to attend classes in child care or to bring the child to a family care centre but not for more than 90 days in total, or such shorter period as may be specified in the order (para 7(1)). This type of requirement cannot be included in an order without the consent of the responsible person. Other specific requirements which may be included in an order relate to:

Information The order may require the child to inform his supervisor of any change of address and to allow the supervisor to visit him at home (para 8(1)). It may require a responsible person to keep the supervisor informed of his address, if different from the child's (para 3(3)).

Compliance with supervisor's directions The order may require the child to comply with any directions given by his supervisor:

 (a) to live at a specified place or places for certain periods of time;
 (b) to present himself to a specified person or persons at times and places as stated; and
 (c) to participate in specified activities at certain times.

It is left to the supervisor to specify how and to what extent a child shall live away from home or participate in any particular activity under these provisions subject to an overall limit of 90 days in all (or such shorter period as the court may specify) (para 7). For the purposes of calculation, any day on which the child fails to comply with a supervisor's directions may be disregarded.

Whilst these provisions differ very little from those relating to intermediate treatment under the CYPA 1969, there is a new power to include a requirement that a responsible person take all reasonable steps to ensure that the child complies with a supervisor's directions (para 3.1(a)). Such a requirement may only be included in an order, however, with the consent of the responsible person.

Psychiatric and medical examinations The previous power to include a general requirement for the child to be medically examined in accordance with arrangements made by the supervisor has been replaced by a broader and more specific provision (para 4). This covers medical and psychiatric examination and requires the court to specify where any examination shall take place. It may also specify who shall conduct it (para 4). The order may provide for the child to be examined on one occasion or for examinations to take place from time to time as directed by the supervisor.

A child cannot be required to attend a hospital or a mental nursing home as an in-patient for the purposes of examination unless the court is satisfied, on the evidence of a registered medical practitioner, that:

(a) the child may be suffering from a physical or mental condition that requires, and may be susceptible, to treatment; and

(b) a period as a resident patient is necessary if the examination is to be carried out properly (para 4(3)).

Where a child has sufficient understanding to make an informed decision, a court cannot include a requirement for examination in a supervision order unless satisfied that the child consents. The court must also be satisfied that satisfactory arrangements have been, or can be, made for the examination.

When including an examination requirement a court may also, with consent, include a requirement that a responsible person take all reasonable steps to ensure that the child is examined in accordance with the order (para 3(1)(*b*)). This new power will obviously be extremely useful when a supervision order is made in respect of a young child who cannot be expected to present himself for examination.

Psychiatric and medical treatment The previous power to include a requirement that a child receive treatment for a mental condition has been extended to include medical treatment for a physical condition (para 5). A court, when making or varying a supervision order, will now be able to include a medical treatment requirement if:

(a) it is satisfied on the evidence of a registered medical practitioner, that the child's physical condition requires, and may be susceptible to treatment; and

(b) that satisfactory arrangements have been, or can be made, for the treatment; and

(c) that the child consents to the order, where he has sufficient understanding to make an informed decision.

The same conditions apply to the inclusion of a mental treatment requirement except that the doctor must be approved under s 12 of the Mental Health Act 1983 and the court must be satisfied that the child's mental condition does not warrant detention under that Act. Under the previous law the child's consent to a mental treatment requirement was only required if he was over the age of 14 years. The new provision gives formal recognition to the principle laid down in the *Gillick* case (see 5.3.7 above) that children under that age may have sufficient understanding to give informed consent.

The order must specify the period of treatment and whether the child is to be a resident or non-resident patient. The treatment must be by, or under the direction of, a registered medical practitioner who may be specified in the order. If the child is to be a resident patient the treatment must take place at a health service hospital. If the child is to be an out-patient the order may specify the place of treatment.

The doctor responsible for the treatment must make a written report to the child's supervisor if he is unwilling to continue with the treatment or he forms the view that:

(a) the treatment should continue beyond the period specified in the order;

(b) the child needs different treatment;

(c) he is not susceptible to treatment; or

(d) he does not require further treatment.

A supervisor must refer such a report to the court which may then make an order cancelling or varying the treatment requirement.

As with medical examination, the court may include, with consent, a requirement that a responsible person take all reasonable steps to ensure that the child receives treatment in accordance with the order (para 3(1)(*b*)).

5.6.4 Reimbursement of supervisor

Where a supervision order requires compliance with directions, any expenditure incurred by a supervisor for the purposes of those directions must be defrayed by the local authority named in the order (para 11(2)).

5.7 Education supervision orders

The Act abolishes the power to make a care order for non-school attendance. Instead there is a separate procedure for local education authorities to apply for an education supervision order (s 36(1)). Note, however, that it is still possible for an application to be made for a care or supervision order under s 31(1) where non-attendance at school is causing harm or likely harm to the child within the meaning of that section.

5.7.1 Grounds

A court can only make an education supervision order 'if it is satisfied that the child concerned is of compulsory school age and is not being properly educated' (s 36(3)). The Act defines a child as being properly educated 'only if he is receiving efficient full-time education suitable to his age, ability and aptitude and any special educational needs he may have' (s 36(4)). This definition corresponds almost exactly with the wording of s 1(2)(e) of the CYPA 1969, the former education ground. Unless there is proof to the contrary, a court will be entitled to assume that a child is not being properly educated:

(a) if he is not regularly attending a school at which he is a registered pupil within the meaning of s 39 of the Education Act 1944; or

(b) if his parent is failing to comply with a school attendance order made under s 37 of the Education Act 1944 (s 36(5)).

Thus it is open to a parent to prove that his child is receiving a proper education albeit not at school.

5.7.2 Applicant

Any local education authority may apply for an order but the child will usually be placed under the supervision of his 'home' authority,

121

ie the local education authority for the area in which he lives or will live. If he is a registered pupil at a school outside this area he may be placed under the supervision of the 'school' authority if both authorities agree to this (s 36(7)). Before making an application the education authority must consult the social services committee of the child's 'home' local authority (s 36(8), (9)). If the child is being provided with accommodation by a local authority (see s 20 and 4.3 above) that authority must be consulted.

5.7.3 Jurisdiction and venue

A court cannot make an education supervision order if a child is already in the care of a local authority (s 36(6)). A child provided with accommodation by a local authority under s 20 of the Act is not considered to be in care hence the need for prior consultation with that authority.

The general provisions of the Act relating to jurisdiction, procedure, evidence and appeals apply to applications for education supervision orders (see Chapter 14).

5.7.4 Effect of order

Certain types of statutory order will cease to have effect, or may not be made, once an education supervision order has been made. These are a school attendance order under s 37, Education Act 1944 and an education requirement in a supervision order made in criminal proceedings (Sched 3, Part III, para 13(2)).

While the order remains in force ss 37 and 76 of the Education Act 1944 (school attendance orders and pupils to be educated in accordance with parents' wishes) and ss 6 and 7 of the Education Act 1980 (parental preference and appeals against admission decisions) will not apply to the child (para 13(2)(b)).

5.7.5 Powers and duties of supervisor

It is a supervisor's duty:

    (a) to advise, assist and befriend, and give directions to
        (i)   the supervised child; and
        (ii) his parents;
in such a way as will, in the opinion of the supervisor, secure that he is properly educated (Sch 3, Part III, para 12(1)).

Parent, in the context of education supervision orders only, is defined in accordance with the Education Act 1944 to include a non-parent with parental responsibility or any person who has care of a child (para 21).

An education supervision order gives a supervisor wide powers to decide how and where a child shall receive his education. He may give directions at any time while an order is in force. Before doing so, however, he must, so far as reasonably practicable, ascertain the wishes and feelings of the child and his parents including in particular their wishes as the place at which the child should be educated (para 12(2)). When settling the terms of any directions, he must give due consideration to such wishes and feelings as he has been able to ascertain although in the child's case the weight he attaches to these will depend on the child's age and understanding (para 12(3)).

The order may require the child to keep the supervisor informed of any change of address and to allow the supervisor to visit him wherever he is living (para 16(1)). A parent must, if asked, inform the supervisor of the child's address if this is known to him. If he is living with the child he must allow the supervisor reasonable contact with the child (para 16(2)).

If his directions are not complied with the supervisor must consider what further steps to take in exercise of his powers under the Act (para 12(1)(b)). If the child persistently fails to comply with any direction the education authority must notify the 'appropriate local authority' (para 19(1)). This means the local authority for the area in which the child lives, or in the case of a child provided with accommodation by a local authority, that authority. The Act does not specify what the local authority must do once it receives a referral of this nature. It is intended, presumably, that it will investigate the child's circumstances and consider what steps, if any, it should take under the Act (see 5.7.7 below).

A parent who persistently fails to comply with a direction given under an education supervision order is guilty of an offence punishable on summary conviction by a fine not exceeding level 3 on the standard scale (para 18(1)). (See Appendix 1 for standard scale currently applicable.) It is, however, a defence for a parent to prove that he took all reasonable steps to ensure that the direction was complied with or that the direction was unreasonable or that he has complied instead with a requirement under an existing supervision order and it was not reasonably practicable to comply with both (para 18(2)).

Once an education supervision order is in force, a parent's duty to comply with ss 36 and 39 of the Education Act 1944 (duty to secure education of children and to secure regular attendance of registered pupils) is superseded by a duty to comply with a supervisor's directions (para 13(1)). The Secretary of State is also given power to make regulations modifying or displacing any other statutory provisions relating to education insofar as they may affect the operation of an education supervision order, if necessary or expedient. If an education supervision order and an ordinary supervision order (whether made in care or criminal proceedings) are in force at the same time, any directions made under the latter will take precedence in the event of conflict (para 14).

5.7.6 Duration of orders

An order will initially last one year but may be extended by the court on application of the education authority (para 15(1)). An application for extension can only be made within the last three months of the order and must be heard before the expiry date (para 15(2), (3)). An order can be extended more than once but no single extension may exceed three years (para 15(5)).

An order, whether extended or otherwise, will automatically cease to have effect on the making of a care order or on the child reaching school leaving age which is currently 16 years. An order can be made, or remain in force, while a child is being provided with accommodation by a local authority under s 20 of the Act (see 5.7.3 above)

5.7.7 Discharge of orders

The child, a parent or the education authority concerned may apply to the court for the order to be discharged (para 17(1)). There are no specific grounds for discharge but the general principles in s 1 of the Act will apply. The child's welfare will therefore be the court's paramount consideration and it will have to consider the 'checklist' of factors in s 1(3) (see Chapter 2).

On discharging an order the court may direct the local authority within whose area the child lives, or will live, to investigate the child's circumstances (para 17(2)). This is akin to the court's power under s 37 to order an investigation in family proceedings although para 17(2) does not specify the purpose of such an investigation or how it is to be conducted. If local authorities follow the procedures set out in s 37 they will consider whether they should apply for a care or supervision order, provide services or assistance to the child or his family or take any other action. These are presumably the matters a court would intend them to consider when ordering an investigation.

5.8 Section 8 orders

It is important to note that proceedings under Part IV of the Act fall within the definition of 'family proceedings' for the purpose of Part II. This means that the court may make a section 8 order, if appropriate, instead of a care or supervision order. Any person entitled to apply for a section 8 order or granted leave to do so may make an application in care proceedings. The court may also make an order of its own volition although no application has been made.

This considerably widens the options available to the court in care proceedings. For example, it will now be possible for the court to make a residence order in favour of a relative instead of placing a child in care. A residence order may be made whether or not the statutory ground in s 31(2) is satisfied. The order may be coupled with a supervision order (in which case s 31(2) must be satisfied) and/or any other section 8 order. Note, that it is not possible for a court to make a care order *and* a section 8 order. The only section 8 order which may be made in respect of a child in care is a residence order and this will have the effect of discharging the care order (s 9(1), 91(1) and see 3.5 above).

Example

AB Council are applying for a care order in respect of a child, C. C lives with her mother, M.
The court is satisfied that the grounds in s 31(2) apply but consider that it would be in C's best interests to live with her aunt, D.

125

D lives within the area of AB Council.

The court is concerned that C shall continue to have contact with her mother, M.

There is some dispute as to the school which C should attend. The court can make a residence order in favour of D, a supervision order designating AB Council to supervise C, a contact order in favour of M and a specific issue order relating to C's education.

For further discussion of s 8 orders generally, see Chapter 3.

5.9 Discharge and variation of care and supervision orders

5.9.1 Care order

A care order (including an interim care order) may be discharged by the court on the application of the child, any person with parental responsibility for him or the local authority named in the order (s 39(1)).

Note that a parent (including an unmarried father who has parental responsibility by agreement or court order) or guardian may apply for discharge under s 39 as they will retain parental responsibility even though a care order has been made. A non-parent, who had the benefit of a residence order immediately before the care order was made, is not entitled to seek discharge under s 39 as he will not retain parental responsibility. He may, however, seek a residence order under s 8, with the leave of the court (see Chapter 3). This avenue is also open to any other person connected with the child who wishes to secure his discharge from care. If a residence order is granted it will automatically discharge any care order in force (s 91(1)).

The court may substitute a supervision order for the care order even if the grounds set out in s 31(2) would not be satisfied at that time (s 39(4)). It also has the power to make an s 8 order (see 5.8 above). It may, for example, decide that the care order should be discharged but the child should live with a relative rather than the parent seeking discharge.

5.9.2 Supervision order

A supervision order (including an interim supervision order) may be varied or discharged by the court on the application of the child, any person with parental responsibility for him or the supervisor (s 39(2)). A person who is not entitled to seek variation but with whom the child is living, may apply to vary any requirement which affects him (s 39(3)). The court cannot substitute a care order for a supervision order but it can make an s 8 order (see 5.8 above). A local authority which wishes to replace a supervision order with a care order will therefore have to apply afresh under s 31. This was not the case under the previous legislation but accords with one of the fundamental principles of the Act that there should only be one route into care.

5.9.3 Grounds

There are no specific grounds for variation or discharge. The court will be bound by the general principles in s 1 (see Chapter 2). The welfare of the child will therefore be its paramount consideration and it will have to consider the matters listed in s 1(2).

5.9.4 Procedure

The general provisions of the Act relating to jurisdiction, procedure, evidence and appeals will apply to applications for variation and discharge (see Chapter 14).

5.9.5 Repeated applications

No further application may be made for the discharge of a care or supervision order, or for the substitution of a supervision order for a care order within six months of a previous application without the leave of the court (s 91(15)). This restriction does not apply to interim orders (s 91(16)).

There is also a general power in s 91(14) for the court, when disposing of any application under the Act, to direct that there be no further applications by any person named in the order without leave of the court. This power could be used in appropriate cases to prevent a parent from making repeated (and futile) applications for variation or discharge every six months.

5.10 Orders pending appeal

Under s 94 appeal lies to the High Court against any order made by a magistrates' court under the Act or the refusal to make an order. This brings the magistrates' court into line with the county court which will have concurrent jurisdiction under the Act. Under the previous law, appeals in care proceedings were heard by the Crown Court and the local authority (or NSPCC) bringing proceedings had no right of appeal except to the Divisional Court by way of case stated on a point of law. This has now changed and a local authority (or the NSPCC) has an equal right of appeal.

Section 40 gives the court power to preserve the status quo pending appeal. Thus a court may make a care order pending appeal, if a child is the subject of an interim care order at the time when the court dismisses an application for a full care order. There is a similar power to make a supervision order pending appeal if the child is the subject of an interim supervision order when the court dismisses an application for a care or supervision order. Orders pending appeal may be subject to whatever directions the court sees fit to include.

Where a court grants an application to discharge a care or supervision order it may defer the effect of its decision pending appeal. The care order or supervision order will then continue in force but subject to any conditions the court sees fit to impose.

Note that under s 40 there is no power to preserve the status quo pending appeal in favour of a parent. A care order will take effect immediately and cannot be deferred pending the outcome of an appeal.

An order pending appeal may last until the determination of any appeal. Where is it made for a shorter period and an appeal is made or an application made to the appellate court concerning a proposed appeal (eg for an extension of time for appeal), the appellate court may extend the order until the determination of the appeal. Where an order pending appeal is made but no appeal subsequently lodged, the order will cease to have effect once the time limit for appeal has expired. The Act does not state a time limit for appeal; this will presumably be specified in rules of court.

5.11 Guardians ad litem

The court now has a positive duty to appoint a guardian ad litem in specified proceedings, 'unless satisfied that it is not necessary to do so in order to safeguard the child's interests' (s 41(1)). The proceedings specified are:

(a) an application for a care or supervision order;

(b) family proceedings in which a court has given a direction for the local authority to investigate under s 37(1) and has made, or is considering whether to make, an interim order;

(c) an application for the discharge of a care order or the variation or discharge of a supervision order;

(d) an application to substitute a supervision order for a care order;

(e) proceedings in which the court is considering whether to make a residence order in respect of a child who is the subject of a care order;

(f) proceedings with respect to contact between a child who is the subject of a care order and any other person;

(g) proceedings under Part V of the Act (emergency protection and child assessment orders);

(h) an appeal against:

    (i) the making or refusal to make a care or supervision order or an order relating to contact under s 34;

    (ii) the making or refusal to make a residence order in respect of a child who is the subject of a care order;

    (iii) the variation or discharge or the refusal to vary or discharge a care or supervision order, or a residence order in respect of a child who is subject to a care order;

    (iv) the refusal of an application to substitute a supervision order for a care order; and

    (v) the making or refusal to make an order under Part V (emergency protection and child assessment orders);

(i) Any other proceedings which may be specified by rules of court (s 41(6)).

Under the previous law, a court was only required to appoint a guardian if this was necessary to safeguard the child's interests. There was only one situation in which the court had a positive duty to appoint and this was where it was considering an unopposed application to discharge a care or supervision order. The change of emphasis under the new law makes it likely that guardians will be appointed in most cases. It is difficult to envisage many cases in which appointment will be unnecessary. An example cited by the Lord Chancellor is that of the older child who has already instructed his own solicitor when the case first comes before the court.

5.11.1 Duties of guardian

Rules of court will govern the appointment of guardians and the manner in which they carry out their duty to safeguard the interests of the child (s 41(2)). These will have to be broader in scope than the previous provision under rule 16 of the Magistrates' Courts (Children and Young Persons) Rules 1988 in view of the enhanced role the guardian will be expected to play in pre-trial reviews and in interim applications for medical examination, contact and other specific directions. The proposed rules may, in particular, specify the assistance which a guardian may be required to give to the court, the manner in which the guardian will be required to participate in pre-trial reviews and when, and in what circumstances, a guardian will be expected to consider applying for variation or discharge of certain orders made in proceedings (s 41(10)).

The guardian will, presumably, be expected to prepare a report for the court and, where necessary, give evidence. Under s 41(11) the court may take account of statements in the guardian's report and evidence relating to it, regardless of any enactment or rule of law which would otherwise prevent this, provided that the statements and/or evidence are relevant to the question being considered. This provision will enable the court to receive information from the guardian which would otherwise be inadmissible under the rules of evidence.

Guardians will have a right of access to local authority records (s 42). This will include general social work records which relate to the child as well as records relating directly to an application under the Act. The right of access will extend to records held by a local authority although they may originally have been compiled by another agency. The guardian will have a right to take copies of any records he is entitled to examine. Any copies taken will be admissible in evidence to support statements made by the guardian in his report or in his oral evidence regardless of any enactment or rule of law to the contrary.

One of the earliest duties of the guardian will be to appoint and instruct a solicitor to represent the child and the proposed rules of court will make provision for this. Under s 41(3) the court will also have power to appoint a solicitor for the child where no guardian has been appointed or where the guardian has not appointed a solicitor but it appears to the court that it would be in the child's best interests to be legally represented. The court may also appoint a solicitor for the child if he wishes to be legally represented and has sufficient understanding to give instructions himself. A solicitor appointed by the court or by a guardian will be required to represent the child in accordance with rules of court, to be made under the Act (s 41(5)).

These provisions aroused some controversy when the bill was debated in Parliament as it was feared that the child might lose his right to separate legal representation in the proceedings. The Lord Chancellor stressed, however, that this was not the case. The child as a party to the proceedings will always be entitled to legal representation but it will be left to rules of court to specify exactly how this will operate in practice. Whilst the child's solicitor would be expected to act in accordance with the guardian's instructions in most cases, this would not apply if the child was of an age to give his own instructions and wished to do so. Neither is there any intention to prevent an older child from appointing a solicitor of his own choice at an early stage in the proceedings before the court has had an opportunity to appoint either guardian or solicitor. The guardian would not be expected to appoint a solicitor if one had already been appointed by a competent child or by the court.

Taken together the various provisions of the Act will greatly strengthen the power and influence of the guardian ad litem. He will play an important role in proceedings from a very early stage, he will have a statutory right of access to relevant social work records and he will be able to present a wide range of information to the court, regardless of the rules of evidence.

5.11.2 Guardian ad litem panels

The Secretary of State has power to make new regulations governing the establishment of panels from which the court may appoint guardians ad litem (s 41(7)). These will replace existing regulations and will be wider in scope. In order to make the panels less dependent upon individual local authorities, two or more authorities will be expected to jointly manage a panel. Some local authorities already operate this system voluntarily.

The regulations will also make provision for the training of guardians, for the monitoring of their work and for the payment of fees and allowances to panel members (s 41(9)). The government has indicated that these measures represent an interim stage in the development of guardian ad litem services. They will establish certain national standards and provide for greater uniformity in management. Once the Act is in place it is proposed that all aspects of family law and business should be subject to review, including the organisation and function of related welfare services.

5.11.3 The Official Solicitor

Although the courts will have to appoint guardians ad litem from the appropriate local panel, the Lord Chancellor will still have power to confer or impose duties on the Official Solicitor under s 90(3) of the Supreme Court Act 1981 (s 35(8)). This means that he may specify that the Official Solicitor is to act instead of a guardian ad litem in proceedings under the Act, including those relating to care and supervision orders which are heard in the High Court.

Chapter 6

Protection of Children

6.1 Outline of previous law

Part V of the Act contains new provisions for the protection of children. Under the previous law there were several overlapping statutory provisions authorising the removal of children to a place of safety. The most frequently used power was the place of safety order which could be granted by a single magistrate without prior notice and in the absence of both parent and child (CYPA 1969, s 28(1)).

The place of safety order was felt to be unsatisfactory for a number of reasons. The criteria for granting an order were based upon the grounds for care proceedings generally and did not address the emergency nature of the application. The maximum duration of the order was 28 days and there was no opportunity for either parent or child to challenge the order in court at any time. It was unclear who had responsibility for the child while the order remained in force and the court had no power to define access or give directions for medical examination when making an order.

These shortcomings were recognised in the Review of Child Care Law and the emergency protection order (supplemented by a police power to remove children in an emergency) was proposed as 'a rationalised, simple procedure to protect children'.

The child assessment order was later proposed as a supplementary and less draconian power to be used when a child's immediate removal from home could not be justified. The idea was controversial. Many felt that the creation of a separate assessment order was unnecessary and confusing. The government was, however, won over to the idea and a child assessment order was

133

introduced into the Children Bill during the latter stages of the parliamentary process.

As a consequence there is now a range of options available to a local authority wishing to carry out an assessment or examination of a child at risk in the absence of parental co-operation. Where the child has been seen but it is impossible to discover whether he is suffering significant harm without an assessment, the child assessment order will be appropriate. Where it is impossible to gain access to the child or there are clear grounds for believing him to be at serious risk, an emergency protection order may be more appropriate. Where there is reasonable cause to believe that the grounds for a full care or supervision order will apply, an application may be made for an interim order with a direction for medical examination or other assessment (see 5.3.7 and 5.3.8 above).

6.2 Child assessment order

A court may make a child assessment order on the application of a local authority or authorised person if it is satisfied that:

(a) the applicant has reasonable cause to suspect that the child is suffering, or is likely to suffer, significant harm;

(b) an assessment of the state of the child's health or development, or of the way in which he has been treated, is required to enable the applicant to determine whether or not the child is suffering, or is likely to suffer, significant harm; and

(c) it is unlikely that such an assessment will be made, or be satisfactory, in the absence of an order . . . (s 43(1)).

An authorised person, in this context, means the NSPCC and any other body authorised to bring proceedings under s 31 (see 5.3.1 above).

The order will specify the nature of the assessment to be carried out and the date by which it is to begin. The assessment must be completed within seven days unless the court specifies a shorter period. If it is necessary for the child to be kept away from home for the purposes of the assessment, this must be expressly authorised in the order and the court must then give directions on the contact to be allowed between the child and his family during this period. The order does not authorise the child's removal from home under any other circumstances. If, as a result of the assessment, removal becomes necessary to protect the child, an application must be made for an emergency protection order (see 6.3 below).

A child assessment order imposes a duty on any person who is in a position to produce the child, to produce him to the person named in the order and to comply with any directions relating to assessment which the order may contain. The order may, for example, require the child to be produced to a named doctor at a specified location for the purposes of medical examination.

The order will authorise any person carrying out all or part of the assessment to do so in accordance with the terms of the order although a child of sufficient understanding to make an informed decision may refuse to submit to a medical or psychiatric examination or any other assessment (see 5.3.8 above).

It is intended that child assessment orders will be used in non-emergency situations. Applicants will therefore be expected to give notice of the application to the child, his parents, any non-parent with parental responsibility and any person with the benefit of a contact order, whether made under s 8 or s 34 (s 43(11)). Rules of court will specify the form in which an application is to be made and the circumstances in which those entitled to notice (or anyone else) may apply for an order to be varied or discharged (s 93(2) and s 43(12)).

The provisions of Part XI relating to evidence, jurisdiction, procedure and appeals will apply (see Chapter 14) and the court will be required to appoint a guardian ad litem for the child under s 41 unless satisfied that this is not necessary to safeguard his interests (see 5.11 above). The general principles set out in Part I of the Act will also apply but not the checklist in s 1(3) (see Chapter 2). If an application for a child assessment order is dismissed it will not be possible to apply again within six months without the leave of the court (s 91(15)).

Critics of the child assessment order were concerned about the overlap between the assessment order and the emergency protection order. It was feared that social workers would opt for the less draconian order, where inappropriate. This criticism is met by making the court the final arbiter of choice. Thus s 43(3) prohibits the court from making an assessment order if it is satisfied that there are grounds for making an emergency protection order and that such an order ought to be made. In these circumstances the

135

court may treat the application as an application for an emergency protection order.

The child assessment order is an innovation in child protection law and it remains to be seen what use will be made of it. It is likely to have most application in cases of neglect and emotional abuse where concern may be escalating but there is no significant incident to justify an emergency protection order. In such cases it may be impossible to proceed without an assessment and this can only be carried out under a court order if parents will not co-operate.

Example

Mr & Mrs J have one child C, aged 9 months.

S, a social worker employed by AB Council, has been visiting the family for one year.

C does not appear to be gaining weight and the parents have a poor understanding of her nutritional needs.

The parents will allow S access to the child but they refuse to see either the Health Visitor or a doctor and they will not take the child to the local Baby Clinic.

AB Council can apply for a child assessment order so that C can be medically assessed.

The order may provide for C to be admitted to hospital for this purpose, but not for a period exceeding seven days.

6.3 Emergency protection order

Section 44(1) of the Act contains three separate grounds for an emergency protection order. The first ground enables a court to make an EPO on the application of any person

if, but only if, it is satisfied that ... there is reasonable cause to believe that the child is likely to suffer significant harm if—
(a) he is not removed to accommodation provided by or on behalf of the applicant; or
(b) he does not remain in the place in which he is then being accommodated. (s 44(1)(a))

'Harm' in this context is defined in s 31(9) and means ill-treatment or the impairment of health or development (s 105(1)).

'Development' means physical, intellectual, emotional, social and behavioural development. 'Health' means physical and mental health. 'Ill-treatment' includes sexual abuse and forms of ill-treatment which are not physical.

Example 1

C, a child aged 10 years, lives with her father, F.
C's mother, M, has left the family home and her whereabouts are unknown.
C discloses that she has been sexually abused by F.
The disclosure is made to a social worker, W, employed by AB Council.
W can apply for an emergency protection order on behalf of AB Council in order to remove C from home.

Example 2

M gives birth prematurely to a child, C, in a hospital within the area of AB Council.
C is receiving special care because of her low birth weight.
M is considered unfit to care for C because of her long-term addiction to drugs.
It is feared that M will discharge herself and C from hospital and leave the area as soon as possible.
AB Council can apply for an emergency protection order to keep C in the hospital.

The second ground applies only to local authorities and allows them to apply for an emergency protection order where they are unable to gain access to a child at risk in the course of an investigation. In this case the court must be satisfied that:

(i) enquiries are being made with respect to the child under s 47(1)(b) [see 6.14 below]; and

(ii) those enquiries are being frustrated by access to the child being unreasonably refused to a person authorised to seek access and that the applicant has reasonable cause to believe that access to the child is required as a matter of urgency (s 44(1)(b)).

Note that under s 47(1)(b) a local authority has a duty to make enquiries whenever they have reasonable cause to suspect that a child who lives, or is found in their area, is suffering or is likely to suffer significant harm. This includes obtaining access to the child unless they are satisfied that they already have sufficient information about him (see 6.14.2 below).

Example

AB Council receives information from a neighbour concerning a child C, aged 4 years.

The neighbour reports overhearing a violent argument in C's flat during which a child was heard to scream and sob repeatedly.

Following this C was seen to have bruises and scratch marks on her face.

C's family is not known to AB Council.

S, a social worker employed by AB Council, makes enquiries to ascertain whether C is known to any other local agencies with a child care function without success.

S visits the family home but is refused access to C by her parents.

AB Council can apply for an emergency protection order.

The third ground is similar but applies to authorised persons, which in this context means the NSPCC and any other organisation which may be authorised to bring care proceedings under Part IV by order of the Secretary of State. An authorised person may apply for an emergency protection order where access to a child at risk is refused. The court may only make an order if satisfied that:

(i) the applicant has reasonable cause to suspect that a child is suffering or is likely to suffer, significant harm;

(ii) the applicant is making enquiries with respect to the child's welfare; and

(iii) those enquiries are being frustrated by access to the child being unreasonably refused to a person authorised to seek access and that the applicant has reasonable cause to believe that access to the child is required as a matter of urgency. (s 44(1)(c)).

Note that the second and third grounds require a reasonably held *suspicion* that a child is suffering, or likely to suffer, significant harm, together with the unreasonable refusal of access, whereas the first ground requires a reasonably held *belief.*

'A person authorised to seek access' means in the case of a local authority application, an officer of the authority or a person authorised to make enquiries on the authority's behalf (s 44(2)(b)). In the case of an application by the NSPCC it will mean a duly authorised officer of the society. The Act is silent on what will amount to an unreasonable refusal of access although an officer seeking access to a child will be obliged to produce some form of authorisation document, if requested to do so (s 44(3)). The absence of such a document would presumably justify refusal of access.

The new grounds enable the court to make an order where significant harm is anticipated but may not have yet occurred. Under the previous law a place of safety order could only be made for anticipated risk in very limited circumstances, eg where another child in the same household had suffered harm or where a person convicted of certain offences against children was or was likely to become a member of the same household. The introduction of the frustrated access grounds reflects the emphasis the Act places upon thorough and adequate investigation (see 6.14 below).

The general principles in s 1 of the Act apply to applications for EPOs. The welfare of the child must therefore be the court's paramount consideration (s 1(1)) and it should not make an order unless it considers that to do so would be better for the child than making no order (s 1(5)). Note that the checklist of factors in s 1(3) to be taken into account by courts in family and care proceedings (see Chapter 2) does not apply to emergency orders.

6.4 Effect of an EPO

6.4.1 Production of child

An EPO operates as a direction to any person who is in a position to produce the child to the applicant, to comply with any request to do so (s 44(4)(a)). It does not authorise the applicant to enter premises to search for the child unless a specific power is included to this effect (see 6.5.2 below). The order must name the child or, if this is not reasonably practicable, it must describe him as clearly as possible (s 44(14)).

6.4.2 Removal of child

The order authorises the child's removal to accommodation provided by or on behalf of the applicant or prohibits his removal from any hospital or other place in which he was accommodated immediately before the order was made (s 44(4)(b)).

Thus the applicant may seek authority to remove the child from an unsatisfactory home. Alternatively, he may wish to prevent parents or others from removing the child from, for example, a hospital where he is being treated, a relative's home where he has been living or from local authority accommodation provided under s 17 (see 4.3 above). Under the previous law a place of safety order could not be granted to prevent a child's removal from voluntary care although a local authority could, in certain circumstances, have prevented this by passing a parental rights resolution; a course of action no longer available under the Act.

Note, however, that the power to remove a child, or to prohibit his removal, must only be exercised if necessary 'in order to safeguard the welfare of the child' (s 44(5)(a)). This provision emphasises that removal is not to be automatic once an emergency protection order has been made. The applicant must continue to assess the situation and consider other options which may be as effective to protect the child. A local authority has, for example, the power to give assistance to an alleged abuser so that he or she may move to alternative accommodation (see 4.2.2 and Sched 2, para 5).

It is an offence to obstruct intentionally any person exercising the power to remove, or prevent the removal of, a child under an emergency protection order (s 44(15)). An offender will be liable on summary conviction to a fine not exceeding level 3 on the standard scale (see Appendix 1 for standard scale currently applicable).

6.4.3 Parental responsibility

The applicant will have parental responsibility for the child while the order remains in force (s 44(4)(c)). 'Parental responsibility' is defined in s 3(1) as all the rights, duties, powers, responsibilities and authority which by law a parent has in relation to a child and his property. In the case of an EPO, however, the exercise

140

of parental responsibility is restricted because of the short-term nature of the order. Section 44(5)(b) therefore stipulates that the applicant 'shall take and shall only take such action in meeting his parental responsibility as is reasonably required to safeguard or promote the welfare of the child (having regard in particular to the duration of the order)'. Note that the wording of this section not only limits an applicant's 'parental' powers but also imposes a positive duty on him to take action where necessary to safeguard and promote the child's welfare.

In practice this would presumably preclude an applicant from consenting to any course of action likely to have long-term consequences eg elective surgery or a change of schools, unless an immediate decision is necessary to safeguard or promote the child's welfare. Applicants exercising parental responsibility under an EPO will also have to comply with regulations to be made by the Secretary of State (s 44(5)(c)).

Example

S, a social worker employed by AB Council, has obtained an EPO in respect of a child, C.
S visits C's home and produces the order to C's mother, M.
S asks to see C.
M must produce C to S.
S may remove C to accommodation provided by or on behalf of AB Council if this is still necessary to safeguard C's welfare.
AB Council will have parental responsibility for C while the order remains in force, subject to certain limitations.
If M refuses to produce C, S may not enter the home to search for him.

6.5 Additional powers to trace children at risk

6.5.1 Order to disclose whereabouts

If an applicant does not have adequate information about a child's whereabouts but someone else does, the court may include in an EPO a direction to that person to disclose whatever information he has (s 48(1)). Disclosure will not be excused on the ground that it might incriminate the informant or his spouse but any statement

141

or admission thus made will not be admissible in evidence against either of them for any offence except perjury (s 48(2)).

6.5.2 Authority to search premises

An EPO may contain a provision authorising the applicant to enter named premises and search for the child (s 48(3)). Any person who then intentionally obstructs the applicant in exercising his power of entry and search commits an offence punishable on summary conviction by a fine not exceeding level 3 on the standard scale (s 48(7) and see Appendix 1 for standard scale). This should not be confused with the power to issue a warrant discussed at 6.5.4 below.

6.5.3 Authority to search for another child

If there is reasonable cause to believe that there may be another child on the same premises with respect to whom an EPO ought to be made the court may make an order authorising the applicant to search for that other child (s 48(4)). This order will then operate as an EPO if the other child is found on the premises and the applicant is satisfied that the grounds for an emergency order exist (s 48(5)). Where authority is given to search for another child, the applicant must notify the court of the outcome of the search (s 48(6)). An order made under s 48(4) must name the child, if it is reasonably practicable to do so. If he cannot be named it must describe him as clearly as possible, presumably by reference to age, physical attributes and other identifying features. It is an offence to obstruct entry and search if an order is made under s 48(4) (see 6.5.2 above).

Example

S, a social worker employed by AB Council, is granted an EPO in respect of a child, C.
The order contains a provision authorising S to enter C's home to search for the child.
S has reason to believe that there is another child at the same address who may also be at risk.
S does not know the name of this child.
The court may make an order authorising S to search the premises for the other child.

S finds C and the other child on the premises and is satisfied that the grounds for an EPO apply to both children.

The order to search for the other child will operate as an EPO.

S can remove both children.

S must notify the court of the action taken with regard to the other child.

6.5.4 Issue of a warrant

The court may issue a warrant authorising a police officer to assist any person attempting to exercise powers under an EPO, who has been refused entry to premises or access to a child (s 48(9)). This replaces the old power to grant a warrant under s 40, CYPA 1933 but is wider in scope. Any person may apply for the warrant and not just the applicant for the EPO. The warrant permits the use of reasonable force, if necessary.

Example

S, a social worker employed by AB Council, has been granted an EPO in respect of a child, C.

The order contains a provision authorising S to search C's home.

S is refused entry.

S fears that C may be removed from the home if she leaves.

S waits outside C's home while a colleague, W, applies to the court for a warrant authorising a police officer to assist S.

If the warrant is granted the police officer can force entry to the house, if necessary.

A warrant may be issued if difficulties are anticipated but have not yet occurred. Thus it will be possible for an application for an EPO and a warrant to be made simultaneously.

Example

S, a social worker employed by AB Council, seeks an EPO in respect of a child, C.

C's father, F, is a violent man who has threatened S before and thrown her out of the house on several occasions.

S can seek a warrant under s 48(9) when applying for the EPO.

Rules of court will specify the manner and form of application (s 48(12)). The warrant will be issued to a named officer who may be accompanied by the person who applied for the warrant unless the court directs otherwise (s 48(10)). Wherever reasonably practicable the warrant must name the child. If he cannot be named it must describe him as clearly as possible (s 48(13)).

6.6 Application for an order

6.6.1 Applicant

Any person may apply for an EPO. Most applications are likely to be made on behalf of local authorities, however, as they have a statutory duty under s 47 of the Act to investigate all reports that children are suffering or are likely to suffer significant harm (see 6.14 below). The Secretary of State will have power to provide, by regulation, for an applicant's responsibilities under the order to be transferred to the local authority in whose area the child ordinarily resides, if this is considered to be in the child's best interests (s 52(3)). This will apply whether the original applicant was another local authority, a person authorised to bring care proceedings under the Act or any other person.

6.6.2 Venue

Section 44(1) refers to an application for an EPO being made to 'the court'. For the purposes of the Act this may mean the High Court, a county court or a magistrates' court (s 92(7)) although the Lord Chancellor has power by order to specify which level of court shall deal with a particular category of proceedings under the Act. It is intended that magistrates will continue to hear the bulk of applications for emergency protection orders although this jurisdiction will be exercised by a newly formed family proceedings court rather than the juvenile bench as at present.

The Lord Chancellor will have power by order to specify circumstances in which single justices may make emergency protection orders. Under the previous law single magistrates had the power to grant place of safety orders at any time. The Cleveland Report recommended that all applications should normally be made in the first instance to the court and only to a single justice if no court was sitting or the application could not be heard within a reasonable time. The Act is silent on this matter but the Lord Chancellor may follow this recommendation.

6.6.3 Procedure and evidence

Under the previous law there were no specific rules governing procedure on an application for a place of safety order. Under the Act rules of court may now be made (s 52(1)). These will cover all proceedings under Part V of the Act and will specify how any application is to be made, who is to be notified and in what manner (s 52(2)). This is without prejudice to the general power to make rules of court contained in s 93 (see Chapter 14).

A court hearing an application for, or relating to, an order may take account of any statement contained in a report made to the court or any evidence given during the hearing provided it is relevant (s 45(7)). This applies regardless of any enactment or rule of law which might otherwise render such evidence inadmissible.

The proceedings will also be governed by the general principles set out in Part 1 of the Act but the checklist contained in s 1(3) will not apply (see Chapter 2).

6.6.4 Guardians ad litem

In all proceedings relating to emergency protection orders the court will have a duty to appoint a guardian ad litem unless satisfied that it is not necessary to do so in order to safeguard the child's interests. Section 41 which covers the appointment and duties of guardians and the provision of legal representation for the child (see 5.10 above) applies to all proceedings under Part V of the Act (s 41(6)(g)).

6.6.5 Appeals

There is no right of appeal against the making or refusal to make an emergency protection order, or against any direction made by the court in relation to an order (s 45(10)). It is possible, however, to apply for certain directions to be varied (see 6.7 and 6.8 below) and for the early discharge of an order (see 6.10 below).

6.7 Medical and psychiatric examination

The court may give 'such directions (if any) as it considers appropriate with respect to the medical or psychiatric examination or other assessment of the child' (s 44(6)(*b*)). The direction may take a negative form and specify that there is to be no examination whatsoever or no examination without the express consent of the court (s 44(8)). Note that a child who is of sufficient understanding to make an informed decision may refuse to submit to an examination or assessment ordered by the court (s 44(7)).

A direction may be given when the order is made or at any time while it is in force. It will be possible to apply for variation; rules of court will specify who may apply (s 44(9)).

Example

C, a child aged six years, has made allegations of sexual abuse against her father.
AB Council seeks an emergency protection order.
C displays no outward sign of illness or physical injury.
AB Council wishes to have C medically examined.
The court can give a direction for medical examination when making the emergency protection order or at any time while it remains in force.

It must be remembered that whilst a person granted an EPO will have parental responsibility for the child concerned, this will be limited to taking such action as is reasonably required to safeguard and promote the child's welfare, having regard to the duration of the order (see 6.4.3 above). Although consent to medical or psychiatric examination will be within the ambit of an applicant's parental responsibility where there may be an immediate need for treatment, the position is less clear where examination is required mainly for forensic purposes or as part of a long term treatment plan. In such situations, applicants will, presumably, request a medical direction from the court. Courts will also have power to give directions of their own volition. Where, for example, parents wish to have the child examined by a doctor of their own choice the court could give directions for a joint examination to save the child from repeated examinations of the same nature.

In the context of medical examination it is also important to note the court's power to direct that an applicant for an EPO may be accompanied by a doctor, nurse or health visitor when carrying out the order, if he so chooses (s 45(12)). This provision will be useful if it is feared that the child may require immediate medical assessment and treatment; in such situations the court could give directions under s 44(6)(b) and s 45(12).

6.8 'Parental' contact

The court may give 'such directions (if any) as it considers appropriate with respect to the contact which is, or is not, to be allowed between the child and any named person' (s 44(6)(a)). It may do so when making the order or at any time while it remains in force. As with directions for medical examination, it will be possible to apply for variation; rules of court will specify who may apply (s 44(9)).

Subject to any directions the court may give, the applicant will have a duty, once an EPO is made, to allow the child reasonable contact with

(a) his parents and any non-parent with parental responsibility for him;

(b) anyone with whom he was living immediately before the order was made;

(c) any person having the benefit of a contact order (see 3.3.2 above);

(d) any person who is allowed contact by virtue of an order under s 34 (see 5.5 above); and

(e) any person acting on behalf of any of the above (s 44(13)).

There is, therefore, a presumption in favour of contact. If circumstances warrant it, however, the court may suspend contact or impose appropriate conditions. It may state, for example, that contact shall only take place with the consent of the child's doctor or in the presence of a named third party.

147

Example

C, a child, has been sexually abused by her father, F, and does not wish to see him.

AB Council applies for an EPO in respect of C.

AB Council may request a direction prohibiting contact between C and F at the same time.

If no request is made, or the court refuses to make a direction, AB Council must allow reasonable contact between C and F.

No direction is made in respect of C's mother, M or her grandmother, G with whom C was living immediately before the order was made.

AB Council must allow M and G to have reasonable contact with C.

Three days after the order is made it emerges that M is exerting pressure on C to withdraw her allegation against F.

AB Council may ask the court to suspend contact or direct that it shall only take place in the presence of a named third party.

6.9 Duration of orders

The maximum duration of an EPO will be eight days (s 45(1)). If the eighth day falls on a public holiday (ie Christmas Day, Good Friday, a bank holiday or a Sunday) the order may last until noon on the first day which is not a holiday (s 45(2)).

Example

A court makes an EPO in respect of a child, C on Monday, May 22.

The order will ordinarily expire at midnight on Monday, May 29.

May 29 is a bank holiday.

The order will expire at noon on Tuesday, May 30.

An order may be extended for up to seven days but only if the applicant is a local authority or a person authorised to apply for a care order under the Act (s 45(4)).

The court may only extend the order if it has reasonable cause to believe that the child concerned is likely to suffer significant harm if it does not do so (s 45(5)).

An order may only be extended once (s 45(6)).

6.10 Application for early discharge

The White Paper proposed that parents should only have the right to challenge an EPO if an application was made for extension beyond eight days. The Act instead provides for a new right to challenge the order after 72 hours (s 45(8)(9)). This has clearly been inserted as a response to events leading to the Cleveland Inquiry. The intention is to provide a balance between the need to protect children from harm on the one hand and the need to give parents a right of challenge on the other. This balance was conspicuously absent from the previous legislation.

The right of challenge will be limited to the child, his parents, any non-parent with parental responsibility for him or any person with whom he was living immediately before the order was made (s 45(8)). A person otherwise entitled to apply for discharge may not do so if he was given notice of the proceedings (in accordance with rules of court) and was present at the hearing when the order was made (s 45(11)(a)). It is not clear from the Act itself how common an occurrence this will be since emergency applications, by their very nature, are usually made ex parte. Neither will it be possible to apply once an order has been extended under s 45(5). This is, presumably, because all relevant parties will have had an opportunity to be heard on the application for extension.

An application for early discharge, where possible, is the only method of 'appeal' against an EPO. There is no other right of appeal against either the making or refusal to make an order or against any direction given by the court (s 45(10)).

6.11 Duty to return child

An EPO gives the applicant power to remove or detain a child but he is not compelled to do so if the need no longer arises. There is instead a new and positive duty to return the child to his family at any time if it appears safe to do so (s 44(10)). This means that the applicant need not remove the child if this proves to be unnecessary. If, however, he does remove or detain the child he must keep the risk factor under constant review in the light of any changed circumstances.

If circumstances warrant it the child should be returned to the person from whose care he was removed. If this is not reasonably practicable he should be returned to a parent, a non-parent with parental responsibility for him or any other person whom the applicant (with the agreement of the court) considers to be appropriate (s 44(11)).

The order will remain in force until its normal expiry date even if the child is returned home early. The applicant may therefore remove the child again at any time (provided the order is still in force) if there is a further change of circumstances (s 44(12)).

Example

AB Council is granted an EPO in respect of a child, C.

C has been abused by her father, F.

C is removed from home.

Two days later, F is charged with an unrelated criminal offence and remanded in custody.

AB Council considers it safe to return C to the care of her mother.

Three days later F is released on unconditional bail.

AB Council can remove C from home again for the remaining period of the emergency protection order.

The discretion not to remove the child or to return him home at any time makes the EPO an extremely flexible remedy now that the court can give express directions regarding medical examination. A child may, for example, be medically examined under an order and only removed from home if the medical evidence warrants this.

A parent who believes that it is now safe for his child to return home, but cannot convince the applicant of this, will be able to apply for the early discharge of the order under s 45(8).

6.12 Police protection

The old police power in s 28(2) CYPA 1969 to detain a child in a place of safety for up to eight days without a court order is replaced by a new power to take a child into police protection for up to 72 hours. This is intended to be a short-term measure. The Act provides for the child to be transferred to local authority accommodation at an early stage. The police are not given parental responsibility and, if the child's continued detention is warranted, there is power to apply for an EPO on behalf of the local authority.

6.12.1 Grounds

Section 46(1) provides that where a constable has reasonable cause to believe that a child would otherwise be likely to suffer significant harm, he may—

(a) remove the child to suitable accommodation and keep him there; or
(b) take such steps as are reasonable to ensure that the child's removal from any hospital, or other place, in which he is then being accommodated is prevented.

A constable in this context may mean a police officer of any rank although the case must be inquired into by an officer specially designated for this purpose as soon as reasonably practicable (s 46(3)(e)). On completing the inquiry the designated officer must release the child unless he considers that there is still reasonable cause for believing that the child would be likely to suffer significant harm (s 46(5)).

6.12.2 Duties of constable

The Act imposes strict requirements on any police officer taking a child into police protection. As soon as reasonably practicable he must:

(a) inform the local authority within whose area the child was found of the steps taken and the reasons for taking them;
(b) give details of the child's present accommodation to the authority in whose area he ordinarily resides;
(c) inform the child (if he is capable of understanding) of the steps which have been or may be taken with reasons;
(d) take such steps as are reasonably practicable to discover the wishes and feelings of the child;

151

(e) secure that the case is inquired into by the designated officer;

(f) secure that the child is moved to accommodation provided by or on behalf of a local authority or designated as a refuge in accordance with s 51 (see 6.15 below) if he was otherwise accommodated on removal;

(g) take reasonable steps to notify the child's parents, those with parental responsibility for him and any other person with whom the child was living immediately before being taken into police protection of the steps which have been taken with reasons, and any further steps which may be taken.

6.12.3 Parental responsibility

While a child is kept in police protection neither the constable concerned nor the designated officer has parental responsibility for him. The designated officer must, however, do whatever is reasonable in the circumstances to safeguard or promote the child's welfare, having regard to the length of time he may remain in police protection (s 46(9)). This amounts to very limited authority to do whatever is essential for the child in the short term.

6.12.4 Parental contact

The designated officer must also allow the child such contact with his family as is both reasonable and in his best interests. Those to be specifically allowed contact are the child's parents, anyone who is not a parent but has parental responsibility, anyone with whom the child was living immediately before coming into police protection, anyone with the benefit of a contact order or entitled to contact by virtue of an order under s 34, and anyone acting on behalf of any of these individuals (s 46(10)). Once the child is moved into accommodation provided by or on behalf of a local authority, the designated officer will no longer be responsible for allowing contact. This duty will be transferred to the local authority.

6.12.5 Police application for an EPO

Police protection is intended to be a short-term measure. If the child's continued detention is warranted, the designated officer has power to apply for an EPO on behalf of the appropriate local authority, with or without that authority's consent or prior knowledge (s 46(7), (8)).

6.13 Accommodation and maintenance

Every local authority has a duty to make provision for the reception and accommodation of children removed under an EPO or taken into police protection (s 21).

If a child is not placed in accommodation provided by a local authority or in a state hospital, any reasonable accommodation expenses will be recoverable from the authority in whose area he ordinarily resides (s 21(3)).

If a local authority does provide accommodation under s 21 for a child ordinarily resident in the area of another authority, but this is not in a community home (see Chapter 7) or a state hospital, any reasonable expenses of accommodating and maintaining the child are recoverable from the home authority (s 29(8)).

6.14 Local authority's duty to investigate

Under the previous law a local authority had a duty to investigate whenever information was received which suggested that there were grounds for care proceedings. This is now replaced by an active duty to investigate any case where it is suspected that a child is suffering significant harm or is likely to do so. The Act specifies the nature of any enquiries and who must be consulted. It imposes a statutory duty on certain other agencies to assist. It provides for review of any decision not to take proceedings and it imposes a positive duty on local authorities to take action, where necessary, to safeguard or promote a child's welfare.

6.14.1 Investigation

Section 47(1) provides that where a local authority—

(a) is informed that a child who lives, or is found, in their area—
   (i) is the subject of an EPO; or
   (ii) is in police protection; or
(b) has reasonable cause to suspect that a child who lives, or is found in their area is suffering, or is likely to suffer, significant harm,

the authority shall make, or cause to be made, such enquiries as they consider necessary to enable them to decide whether they should take any action to safeguard or promote the child's welfare.

The police have a duty under s 46(3) to inform the relevant local authority when a child is taken into police protection. An applicant for an EPO does not have a similar duty under the Act although it is likely that rules of court to be made under s 52 will provide for this. Local authorities will also find out about many children removed under the emergency provisions of Part V when fulfilling their obligations to provide accommodation and maintenance for such children (see 6.13 above). If, in the course of enquiries, it appears that a child is ordinarily resident within the area of another authority, the investigating authority should consult that other authority which may then undertake the necessary enquiries in its place (s 47(12)).

A local authority which has itself obtained an EPO is under a similar duty to make enquiries to ascertain whether it should take any further action (s 47(2)).

6.14.2 *Nature of enquiries*

The Act is very specific about the nature and purpose of any enquiries. They must be directed, in particular, towards establishing:

(a) whether the authority should make any application to the court (eg for an EPO or a care or supervision order) or exercise any other powers it may have under the Act (eg to provide accommodation under Part III);

(b) whether any child who is subject to an EPO and not accommodated in local authority accommodation should be moved into such accommodation for the duration of the order; or

(c) whether the police should be asked to apply for an EPO under s 46(7) in respect of any child in police protection (s 47(3)).

The local authority must take such steps as are reasonably practicable to obtain access to the child unless satisfied that it already has sufficient information about him to decide what action, if any, to take (s 47(4)). A local authority may arrange for some one else to obtain access on its behalf. This could, for example, be an NSPCC officer or a health service professional. If access is refused or information about the child's whereabouts withheld, the local authority must apply for an emergency protection order, a child assessment order, a care order or a supervision order unless satisfied that the child's welfare can be satisfactorily safeguarded without so doing (s 47(6)).

If there are matters connected with the child's education which require investigation, the local education authority must be consulted (s 47(5)).

6.14.3 Duty to assist

Other local authorities, health authorities and local education and housing authorities will have a statutory duty to assist an investigating local authority unless it would be unreasonable to expect them to do so in all the circumstances of the case (s 47(10), (11)). The Secretary of State will have power to extend this duty to other persons or agencies. In the White Paper the government indicated that it intended to make legal provision for co-operation between statutory and voluntary agencies in the investigation of child abuse. It is therefore possible that certain voluntary agencies, such as the NSPCC, will be added to the list.

The statutory duty to co-operate must be considered in the context of the voluntary code for multi-disciplinary co-operation set out in the document 'Working Together' (DH, 1988). This provides a framework for different agencies to work together in the investigation and treatment of child abuse. The case conference, attended by representatives of each relevant agency, is part of the voluntary machinery but will obviously provide a forum for the exchange of information as required under the Act.

6.14.4 Duty to act

If, as a result of its enquiries, a local authority concludes that it should take action to safeguard or promote a child's welfare, it must do so, so far as this is within its power and reasonably practicable (s 47(8)). This provision imposes a greater obligation upon local authorities to act than the somewhat narrow duty under the previous law to bring care proceedings unless satisfied that

155

this was neither in the interests of the child nor the public (s 2(2), CYPA 1969).

6.14.5 Review

If, at the conclusion of its investigation, a local authority decides not to apply for a statutory order it must consider whether it would be appropriate to review the case at a later date. If so, a date must be fixed (s 47(7)). There is a similar duty to consider and fix a date for further review at the conclusion of a first or subsequent review.

It is important to remember in this context that investigation may lead to the inclusion of a child's name on the local Child Protection Register even though no application is made for a statutory order. Child Protection Registers are maintained as part of the non-statutory machinery for the protection of children. In most cases there is a procedure for review when a child's name has been on a register for a specified period. Any review under the provisions of s 47(7) will be additional to this but may well be carried out simultaneously.

6.15 Abduction and recovery of children

Sections 49 to 51 of the Act deal with the abduction and recovery of children who are in care or subject to emergency orders. Section 49 creates an offence of abduction which consolidates and updates the offences which previously existed under the Child Care Act 1980 and the CYPA 1969. Section 50 modernises and extends the existing law on the recovery of children who are abducted or otherwise missing from care or a placement under an emergency order. Section 51 recognises the valuable work carried out by certain organisations in providing safe houses for runaway children, by exempting them from criminal liability for abduction.

6.15.1 Offence of abduction

Under section 49 it is an offence to abduct a child who is in care, subject to an emergency protection order or in police protection. The offence is committed by any person who, knowingly and without lawful authority or reasonable excuse,

(a) takes such a child away from the responsible person; or
(b) keeps the child away from that person; or
(c) induces, assists or incites a child to run away or stay away.

The responsible person in this context means any person who for the time being has care of the child by virtue of a care order, an emergency protection order or the exercise of the police power of protection. It could therefore apply to any person with whom a child had been placed in such circumstances.

The offence is punishable on summary conviction by a term of imprisonment not exceeding six months or a fine not exceeding level 5 on the standard scale, or both. See Appendix 1 for standard scale currently applicable.

6.15.2 Recovery orders

Prosecution for abduction will not in itself lead to the recovery of a missing child. Under s 50, therefore, the court has power to make a recovery order where a child has been:

(a) unlawfully taken away or kept away from the responsible person; or
(b) has run away or is staying away from that person, or
(c) is missing.

Note that a recovery order may only be made in respect of a child who is in care, subject to an emergency protection order or in police protection. Other missing children may be protected by orders under s 8 of the Act (see Chapter 3) or by the exercise of the High Court's inherent jurisdiction.

It was possible to obtain a type of recovery order under the previous law but s 50 is wider in scope and spells out in a more comprehensive and understandable way the legal effect of an order. It is no longer possible to arrest a missing child without a warrant but the court can order any person with information about the child's whereabouts to disclose this.

Where a child is in care or subject to an emergency protection order, any person who has parental responsibility by virtue of the order may apply for a recovery order. In effect this will mean the local authority named in the care order or the person granted an emergency order. If a child is in police protection, application may be made by the designated officer (see s 46(3)(e) and 6.12 above).

A recovery order will:

    (a) operate as a direction to any person who is in a position to produce the child, to do so on the request of any authorised person;

    (b) authorise the removal of the child by any authorised person;

    (c) require any person who has information as to the child's whereabouts to disclose that information, on request, to a constable or an officer of the court; and

    (d) authorise a constable to enter specified premises and search for the child, using reasonable force if necessary, although authority to search will not be given unless there are reasonable grounds for believing that the child is on the premises.

An authorised person in this context means any person specified by the court, a constable or any person authorised to implement the recovery order by a person who has parental responsibility by virtue of a care order or an emergency protection order. A local authority or person with parental responsibility under an emergency protection order may therefore arrange for someone else to remove the child on their behalf once the order has been made. The power to search premises, however, is only exercisable by a police officer.

If a child is made the subject of a recovery order whilst being looked after by a local authority, any reasonable expenses incurred by an authorised person in enforcing the order are recoverable from the local authority (s 50(12)). A child is 'being looked after by a local authority' if he is subject to a care order, or being provided with accommodation by the authority under s 20 or s 21 of the Act (see Chapter 4).

No person may claim privilege against incriminating himself or his spouse if ordered to disclose information about a child's whereabouts. Any statement or admission made in complying with the order, however, will not be admissible in proceedings for any criminal offence other than perjury.

It is an offence to intentionally obstruct an authorised person who is exercising his power to remove a child under a recovery order. A guilty person is liable on summary conviction to a fine not exceeding level 3 on the standard scale (see Appendix 1 for standard scale currently applicable).

Section 50(13) and (14) extends the effect of recovery orders to Scotland and Northern Ireland.

6.15.3 Refuges for children at risk

Organisations which provide safe houses or refuges for runaway children at risk of serious harm may be exempt from criminal liability for abduction under s 49.

The exemption will only apply where a child is accommodated in a voluntary home (see Chapter 8) or a registered childrens' home (see Chapter 9) which has been formally certified as a refuge by the Secretary of State in accordance with regulations to be made under s 51(4). Where a local authority or a voluntary organisation arrange for a foster parent to provide refuge for runaway children, the Secretary of State may issue a certificate in respect of that foster parent.

The regulations will specify how certificates will be issued, when they may be withdrawn and the conditions which must be complied with while they are in force. It is likely, for example, that those providing refuge will be required to notify those reponsible for the child that he is safe but not disclose his whereabouts.

Safe houses in England and Wales may provide refuge for a variety of children. Some may have run away from their own homes, others may have left local authority accommodation or absconded from detention elsewhere in the British Isles. In view of this the Act extends the immunity against prosecution for certified refuges to offences under s 2 of the Child Abduction Act 1984 (abduction of a child from a person with lawful control), s 71 of the Social Work (Scotland) Act 1968 (harbouring of children who have absconded from residential establishments in Scotland) and s 32(3) CYPA 1969 (compelling, persuading, inciting or assisting a child to be absent from detention).

This important provision will enable voluntary organisations such as the Children's Society to help children who have run away from their own homes because they are being abused there. They will also be able to help children who have absconded with good reason from care or a placement under an emergency protection order although the Act does not prevent local authorities from applying for a recovery order under s 50 to discover the whereabouts of such children and to secure their return (see 6.15.2 above). It is

159

intended, however, that good practice and a commitment to inter-agency co-operation will make this unnecessary in most cases. In the exceptional cases where a local authority does seek a recovery order it is anticipated that the individual or organisation providing refuge for the child will be given an opportunity to make representations to the court before an order is made.

Chapter 7

Community Homes

7.1 Introduction

Part VI of the Act requires local authorities to secure that community homes are available for children who are looked after by them and provides for the management and conduct of these homes. These provisions re-enact with minor amendments Part IV of the Child Care Act 1980 which is now repealed.

There is one new provision. This deals with a lacuna identified in the White Paper 'The Law on Child Care and Family Services' (Cm 62). Under the previous law there was no provision for compensation to be paid to a local authority when premises used for a community home and provided by a voluntary organisation were disposed of or put to another use while the premises were still designated a community home. Local authorities will now be entitled to claim compensation for any sums expended during the time the premises were used as a community home. This change will be retrospective and will affect disposals occurring at any time after 13 January 1987, being the date of the White Paper.

7.2 Provision of community homes

Section 53 requires local authorities to make 'such arrangements as they consider appropriate' for securing that community homes are available for children they are looking after and for purposes connected with the welfare of children whether or not they are looked after by the authority. There is a wide discretion as to what arrangements may be made subject to the need to provide a range of accommodation suitable to the varying needs of different categories of children (s 53(2)). Two or more local authorities may jointly make provision (s 53(1)).

The term 'community home' covers residential accommodation provided, managed, equipped and maintained by a local authority and also accommodation provided by voluntary organisations (s 53(3)). A voluntary organisation is defined in s 105 as a body (other than a public or local authority) whose activities are not carried on for profit.

Community homes provided by voluntary organisations but managed, equipped and maintained by a local authority are designated 'controlled community homes' (s 53(4)). Those provided and managed by a voluntary organisation are designated 'assisted community homes' (s 53(5)).

7.3 Management and conduct of community homes

Schedule 4 contains detailed provisions for the management and conduct of controlled and assisted community homes. Paragraphs 1 and 2 deal with the instruments of management. Paragraph 3 apportions management duties between the local authority and the voluntary organisation providing the home. Paragraph 4 specifies the matters to be included in regulations governing all community homes.

7.3.1 Instruments of management

The Secretary of State has power by order to make an instrument of management governing the constitution of the management body of any controlled or assisted community home. This will specify how many managers may be appointed, who may appoint them and the criteria for selection. The local authority will be entitled to appoint two thirds of the management body of a controlled community home and one third of the managers of an assisted home. The remaining managers will represent the interests of the voluntary organisation and their particular role is to preserve the character of the home and to ensure that the terms of any trust deed relating to it are preserved. Note that an instrument of management cannot, in itself, alter the terms upon which any premises used as a voluntary home are held. If, for example, the use of the premises as a community home is not permitted under the terms of a trust deed by which the property is held, the trust itself must be varied if possible.

The Secretary of State may include any other appropriate provisions in an instrument of management. He may specify, in particular, the nature and purpose of the home, the number or proportion of places to be made available to local authorities or other named bodies and the charges that may be made. The instrument may be varied or revoked by order, after consultation with the voluntary organisation and local authority concerned.

7.3.2 Management duties

The Act distinguishes between the managers of a community home and the body responsible for management. The local authority is the responsible body for controlled community homes. The voluntary organisation which provides the home is the responsible body for assisted community homes. Schedule 4, para 3 specifies which functions may be carried out by the managers on behalf of the responsible body and which decisions cannot be delegated. Decisions relating to the employment of staff must be reserved to the responsible body. Other matters may be reserved if this is specified in the instrument of management or the responsible body serves a notice on the managers requiring this.

A voluntary organisation responsible for an assisted community home must, in addition, consult the local authority before engaging or terminating without notice the employment of any member of staff unless this requirement has been waived in the instrument of management or by the local authority concerned.

The managers of a home are required to keep proper records and accounts and to provide the responsible body with estimates of expenditure and receipts for the next accounting year.

7.3.3 Regulations

The Secretary of State is given power under Schedule 4, para 4 to make regulations for securing the welfare of children in all types of community homes. These will replace the Community Homes Regulations 1973 and may cover the placement of children and the conduct of homes. The regulations may, in particular:

(a) prescribe standards to which the premises must conform;

(b) impose requirements as to accommodation, staff, equipment, healthcare, record-keeping and facilities for religious instruction;

(c) provide for control and discipline;

(d) authorise the Secretary of State to give or revoke directions requiring a local authority or voluntary organisation to accommodate in the home a child looked after by a local authority for whom no places are ordinarily provided in that home or to take specified action in relation to a child who is accommodated there;

(e) provide for consultation with the Secretary of State as to applicants for appointment to take charge of the home;

(f) empower the Secretary of State to prohibit the appointment of a particular applicant in certain cases;

(g) require the approval of the Secretary of State to the provision and use of secure accommodation within a home and impose other requirements on its use (in addition to those imposed by s 25) including the need to obtain the consent of any local authority which is looking after a child concerned; and

(h) empower the Secretary of State to exempt a particular home or premises from any provision of the regulations.

7.4 Determination of disputes

Section 55 sets out the machinery for resolving disputes between local authorities and voluntary organisations providing community homes. It provides for referral to the Secretary of State who may resolve a dispute by giving such directions as he thinks fit to the local authority or the voluntary organisation concerned. A referral may involve the local authority specified in the home's instrument of management or any other local authority which has placed or wishes to place a child in the home. A dispute may be referred to the Secretary of State even if it relates to a matter which is reserved for the decision of the local authority or voluntary organisation under the provisions of Schedule 4 (see para 7.3.2 above).

The Secretary of State may not determine any disputes concerning religious instruction where any trust deed relating to a controlled or assisted community home reserves such matters to a bishop or other ecclesiastical or denominational body (s 55(5)).

7.5 Closure by Secretary of State

The Secretary of State has power under s 54 of the Act to direct that any premises cease to be used as a community home from a specified date if they are unsuitable for this purpose, or the conduct of the home does not comply with the regulations or is otherwise unsatisfactory. Written notice must be served on the responsible body. A direction may presumably be revoked if the defect complained of is remedied. Where the Secretary of State has given a direction which has not been subsequently revoked he may at any time revoke the instrument of management of the home concerned (s 54(2)).

7.6 Closure by voluntary organisation

A voluntary organisation which provides a controlled or assisted community home must give a minimum of two years' notice to the Secretary of State and the relevant local authority if it intends to withdraw that provision (s 56(1)). The home will cease to be a community home on the date specified in the notice. The home's managers may give notice to the Secretary of State that they are unwilling or unable to continue as managers until that date. If they do so, the Secretary of State may revoke the instrument of management and require the local authority to run the home as if it were a community home provided by them until the date specified for closure or such earlier date as may be substituted (s 56(4)).

7.7 Closure by the local authority

A local authority which wishes to withdraw the designation of any controlled or assisted community home must give a minimum of two years' notice to the Secretary of State and the voluntary organisation concerned (s 57(1)). If the managers are unwilling or unable to continue as managers until the date specified in the notice, the Secretary of State may revoke the home's instrument of management from an earlier date and the home will cease to be a community home (s 46(3)). This may only be done after consultation with the local authority and voluntary organisation concerned (s 46(4)).

7.8 Financial provisions on closure

Where a home ceases to be a controlled or assisted community home following the revocation of the instrument of management under ss 54, 56 or 57 of the Act or any premises used for a home are disposed of or put to another use at any time after 13 January 1987 the proprietor is liable to repay any increase in the value of the premises which is attributable to the expenditure of public money (s 58(2)–(4)). The proprietor in this context means the voluntary organisation which provided the home or, if the premises used for the home were not vested in the organisation, the persons in whom they are vested (s 58(6)).

Repayment must be made to the local authority or to the Secretary of State depending on the current designation of the home, its original status and the source of any funds expended on it (s 58(5)). The sum agreed shall be determined by agreement between the parties or failing this by the Secretary of State (s 58(8)). Agreement may be reached for any liability under s 58 to be discharged, in whole or in part, by the transfer of any premises (s 58(9)).

Note that s 58 applies regardless of any provision contained in a trust deed relating to a controlled or assisted community home or the provisions of any enactment or instrument governing the disposition of property by a voluntary organisation (s 58(10)).

Chapter 8

Voluntary Homes and Organisations

8.1 Introduction

Part VII of the Act provides for the registration and regulation of voluntary homes and for the welfare of children who are accommodated by or on behalf of voluntary organisations. A voluntary organisation, for the purposes of the Act, is a body (other than a public or local authority) whose activities are not carried on for profit.

The law in this area is largely unaltered and ss 59 to 62 and Sched 5 of the Act re-enact, with amendments, Part VI of the Child Care Act 1980 which is now repealed. Voluntary organisations are given duties similar to those imposed upon local authorities under Part III of the Act. Registration and regulation of voluntary homes is controlled by the Secretary of State but local authorities are responsible for ensuring the well-being of children being looked after by voluntary organisations. The power under the previous law for voluntary organisations to assume parental rights over children in their care by administrative resolution is abolished.

8.2 Provision of accommodation

Voluntary organisations do not always accommodate children in voluntary homes; they may place them with foster parents or in residential establishments provided by other bodies or individuals. Section 59 lists the different types of accommodation which may be used and empowers the Secretary of State to make regulations governing certain types of placements. The range of accommodation is the same as that available to a local authority under s 23 (see 4.4.3 above). A voluntary organisation may therefore place a child:

(a) with foster parents (who may be a family, a relative or any other suitable person);

(b) in a voluntary home;

(c) in a community home;

(d) in a registered children's home;

(e) in a specialist unit provided by the Secretary of State under s 82(5) of the Act if the child needs special facilities not available in an ordinary children's home.

It may also make any other arrangements which seem appropriate, subject to regulations to be made by the Secretary of State under s 59(3). The Secretary of State is also given power to make regulations governing foster placements and requiring voluntary organisations to set up review and complaints procedures (s 59(2)-(6)). It is intended that the regulatory framework governing placements by voluntary organisations will be as similar as possible to that governing local authority provision (see 4.4.3, 4.8 and 4.9 above).

The regulations may provide that any person who, without reasonable cause, contravenes or fails to comply with any regulation commits an offence punishable on summary conviction by a fine not exceeding level 4 on the standard scale (s 59(6)). (See Appendix 1 for the standard scale currently applicable.)

8.3 Registration

Section 60(1) provides that all voluntary homes must be registered with the Secretary of State. A voluntary home is defined as 'any home or other institution providing care and accommodation for children which is carried on by a voluntary organisation' (s 60(3)). It does not include a nursing home, a mental nursing home, a residential care home, a health service hospital, a community home, an institution provided, equipped and maintained by the Secretary of State or any home specifically exempted by regulation (s 60(3)).

Schedule 5, Part I contains detailed provisions as to registration. Application must be made by the persons intending to carry on the home and the Secretary of State may grant or refuse the application or approve it subject to appropriate conditions which may be varied from time to time. Registration may be cancelled if a home is not conducted in accordance with regulations made by the Secretary of State or is otherwise unsatisfactory. Any person who carries on a voluntary home which is not registered or contravenes any condition imposed on registration, without reasonable excuse, commits an offence punishable on summary conviction by a fine not exceeding level 5 on the standard scale (for non-registration) or level 4 (for breach of condition). See Appendix 1 for the standard scale of fines currently applicable.

There is an appeals procedure in respect of decisions concerning registration. The Secretary of State must serve notice of a proposal to refuse or cancel registration, to grant it subject to conditions which have not been agreed with the applicant, to vary an existing condition or to impose an additional one. The notice must give reasons for the proposal. The recipient must then be given a reasonable opportunity to make representations provided he notifies the Secretary of State within 14 days of his wish to do so. If the Secretary of State decides to adopt his original proposal, notwithstanding any representations, there is a right of appeal to a Registered Homes Tribunal which must be exercised within 28 days. The Tribunal may confirm or quash the decision, vary or cancel any existing condition or impose further conditions of its own.

The Secretary of State is required to notify a local authority whenever he registers or cancels the registration of a voluntary home within its area. This is to enable local authorities to carry out their supervisory duties in relation to children accommodated by voluntary organisations (see 8.6 below).

As part of the registration requirements, a person in charge of a voluntary home is under a duty to send to the Secretary of State each year such information relating to the home as may be prescribed by regulations. In the case of a home established after the commencement of the Act, the relevant particulars must be furnished within the first three months and thereafter on an annual basis. Failure to comply with these requirements, without reasonable excuse, is an offence punishable on summary conviction by a fine not exceeding level 2 on the standard scale. See Appendix 1 for the standard scale currently applicable.

8.4 Regulations

Schedule 5, Part II gives the Secretary of State power to make regulations for securing the welfare of children in voluntary homes.

169

These will replace and update the Administration of Children's Homes Regulations 1951 and will cover the placement of children and the conduct of homes. In particular, the regulations may:

(a) prescribe standards to which the premises must conform;

(b) provide for control and discipline;

(c) authorise the Secretary of State to impose a limit on the number of children accommodated;

(d) require him to be furnished with details of facilities provided for family visits;

(e) require him to be notified if there is a change in the person carrying on or in charge of the home or the premises used;

(f) impose requirements as to accommodation, staff, equipment, healthcare, facilities for religious instruction and the keeping of records; and

(g) prohibit the use of secure accommodation for the purpose of restricting the liberty of children.

Many of these matters were covered by the old regulations. The power to prohibit the use of secure accommodation is new. It reflects the prevailing view that the provision and use of such facilities in voluntary homes is inappropriate.

Contravention of any of the regulations, without reasonable excuse, will be an offence punishable on summary conviction by a fine not exceeding level 4 on the standard scale. See Appendix 1 for the standard scale currently applicable.

8.5 Welfare of children

Section 61 of the Act imposes on voluntary organisations duties similar to those imposed on local authorities under Part III. They have a duty to safeguard and promote the welfare of any child they are accommodating. They must make reasonable use of services and facilities available for children cared for by their own parents and they must advise, assist and befriend children with a view to promoting their welfare when they leave the care of the organisation.

Before making any decision with respect to a child they must ascertain the wishes and feelings of the child, his parents, any non-parent with parental responsibility and any other person considered relevant (s 61(2)). They must give such wishes and feelings due consideration, having regard in the child's case to his age and understanding and must also take into account the child's religious persuasion, racial origin and cultural and linguistic background (s 61(3)).

8.6 Duties of local authorities

Whilst the Secretary of State has power to register and regulate accommodation provided by voluntary organisations, local authorities are required to satisfy themselves that children in such accommodation are being properly looked after. This duty extends to children accommodated on behalf of the authority but outside their area (s 62(1)).

Every local authority must arrange for such children to be visited, from time to time, unless they are accommodated in voluntary homes which are also community homes (s 62(2), (4)). The Secretary of State is given power to make regulations specifying when and in what circumstances visits must be made to children accommodated within the local authority's area (s 62(3)). The regulations may also specify how a local authority is to carry out its functions under s 62.

Any person authorised by a local authority may enter, at any reasonable time, and inspect any premises in which children are accommodated by or on behalf of a voluntary organisation. He may inspect any child there and demand access to records kept under the regulations (s 62(6)). If the records are computerised, he may demand access to the computer and any associated apparatus or material in order to inspect and check its operation, if necessary with the assistance of the person responsible for operating the computer (s 62(8)). This is a new provision inserted to deal with practical problems which may arise from the increasing use of computerised records. Any person who intentionally obstructs a local authority representative carrying out an inspection commits an offence punishable on summary conviction by a fine not exceeding level 3 on the standard scale. See Appendix 1 for the standard scale currently applicable.

Where a local authority is not satisfied that the welfare of any child accommodated by or on behalf of a voluntary organisation is being satisfactorily safeguarded or promoted it must take such steps as are reasonably practicable to secure that the child's care is taken over by a parent, a non-parent with parental responsibility or a relative unless this would not be in his best interests (s 62(5)). It must also consider the extent to which it should exercise any of its own functions with respect to the child. This could mean offering services or accommodation under Part III, applying for a statutory order under Part IV or taking emergency action under Part V.

8.7 Disqualification

The Secretary of State is given power by regulation to disqualify certain people from carrying on or being employed in a voluntary home (para 8). The grounds for disqualification under the proposed regulations will be similar to those which apply to registered children's homes under s 65 (see 9.7 below) and private foster parents under s 68. The list includes people convicted of specified offences, those placed on probation or discharged conditionally or absolutely for the same offences and those whose own parental rights and powers have been taken over by a local authority.

Chapter 9

Registered Children's Homes

9.1 Introduction

Part VIII of the Act provides for the regulation and registration of private children's homes and for the welfare of children accommodated in them. The purpose of the provisions is to ensure that the same standards apply to facilities provided by private individuals or bodies as to those provided by local authorities and voluntary organisations.

The provisions are not new. They re-enact, with amendments, the provisions of the Children's Homes Act 1982 which has never been fully implemented. The effect of the amendments is to define more fully what constitutes a children's home for the purposes of the Act and to impose certain new duties on those running such homes similar to those imposed on voluntary organisations.

9.2 Definition of children's home

A children's home for the purposes of Part VIII, means 'a home which provides (or usually provides or is intended to provide) care and accommodation wholly or mainly for more than three children at any one time' (s 63(3)). The term 'home' includes any institution (s 63(9)).

The following types of accommodation are expressly excluded by the Act and the Secretary of State has power by regulation to add to this list (s 63(3)(b), (5) and (6)):

(a) a community home;

(b) a voluntary home;

(c) a residential care home, nursing home or mental nursing home;

173

(d) a health service hospital:

(e) a home provided, equipped and maintained by the Secretary of State; and

(f) a school (unless it is an independent school which is not approved under s 11(3)(*a*) of the Education Act 1981 and provides accommodation for no more than 50 children).

The Act also excludes certain other child care arrangements that might otherwise be caught by the definition in s 63(3). Thus, a child is not to be cared for or accommodated in a children's home when he is in the care of a parent, a non-parent with parental responsibility or a relative. In this context relative means a grandparent, brother, sister, uncle or aunt (whether of the full blood, half blood or by affinity) or step-parent (s 105).

Foster parents who foster more than three children will fall within the definition unless they are exempt under the terms of Sched 7 which imposes a usual fostering limit of three but specifies circumstances in which it may be exceeded. Schedule 7 applies to foster parents used by local authorities and voluntary organisations as well as those who foster privately. It specifies that the usual fostering limit of three may be exceeded if the children concerned are all siblings or if the local authority for the area in which the foster home is located grant an exemption. Schedule 7, para 4 sets out the matters to be taken into account by a local authority when considering whether to grant an exemption and specifies procedure for notification, variation and cancellation. The Secretary of State is given power by regulation to amplify or modify these provisions where children need to be placed with foster parents as a matter of urgency.

A foster parent will cease to be treated as such and will instead by treated as carrying on a children's home if he exceeds the usual fostering limit or where he is exempt, as above, he fosters any child not named in the exemption and thereby exceeds the usual fostering limit. A foster home will not be treated as a children's home, in any circumstances, if all the children concerned are siblings (Sched 7, para 5).

9.3 Registration

Section 63 (1) provides that 'no child shall be cared for and provided with accommodation in a children's home unless the home is

174

registered'. Note that a child is not treated as cared for and accommodated in a children's home if his parent or a person with parental responsibility for him also lives there or if the person who cares for him does so in a personal capacity while living and working in the home (s 63(7)).

Schedule 6, Part I contains detailed provision for registration. The procedure is very similar to that which applies to voluntary homes except that registration is with the local authority for the area in which the home is situated and not the Secretary of State. The register may be kept by means of a computer (s 63(1)). Application must be made by the person carrying on, or intending to carry on, the home and the local authority may grant or refuse the application, or approve it subject to conditions which may be varied from time to time. Regulations to be made by the Secretary of State will prescribe the manner in which an application is to be made, the particulars which must be supplied by the applicant and the requirements which must be fulfilled by the local authority. Particular provision will be made for premises to be inspected. A fee will be payable to the local authority. An application which has not been granted or refused within 12 months will be deemed to be refused.

Registration may be cancelled on the application of the person running the home. The local authority may also cancel registration if the home is not being run in accordance with 'the relevant requirements'. This means the requirements of Part VIII and any regulations made under Sched 6, para 10 and any conditions imposed on registration.

Any person who carries on a children's home which is not registered, or who contravenes any condition imposed on registration, without reasonable excuse, commits an offence punishable on summary conviction by a fine not exceeding level 5 on the standard scale (for non-registration) or level 4 (for breach of condition) (s 63(10) and Sched 6, para 2(3)). See Appendix 1 for the standard scale currently applicable.

There is an appeals procedure in respect of decisions concerning registration. The local authority must serve notice of a proposal to refuse or cancel registration, to grant it subject to conditions which have not been agreed with the applicant, to vary an existing condition or to impose an additional one. The notice must give reasons for the proposal. The recipient must then be given a reasonable opportunity to make representations provided he notifies the local authority within 14 days of his wish to do so. If the local authority decides to adopt its original proposal, notwithstanding any representations, there is a right of appeal to a Registered Homes Tribunal to be exercised within 28 days. The Tribunal may confirm or quash the decision, vary or cancel any existing condition or impose further conditions of its own.

If an application for registration is refused, no further application may be made for a period of six months from the date on which the applicant was notified of the refusal. If an appeal was lodged against the refusal, the six month time limit is calculated from the date the appeal was determined or abandoned, whichever the case may be. There is a similar prohibition on repeat applications for re-registration following cancellation.

Registration must be reviewed annually by the local authority. If the home is being conducted in accordance with all the relevant requirements, the registration will be confirmed for another year subject to payment of a specified fee. If the local authority is not satisfied it may give notice of cancellation and the appeals procedure will then apply.

9.4 Regulations

Schedule 6, Part II gives the Secretary of State power to make regulations for securing the welfare of children in registered children's homes. These will cover the placement of children and the conduct of homes. Paragraph 10 specifies that the regulations may, in particular:

(a) prescribe standards to which the premises must conform;

(b) impose requirements as to accommodation, staff, equipment, healthcare, record-keeping and facilities for religious instruction;

(c) provide for control and discipline;

(d) authorise the local authority to impose a limit on the number of children accommodated;

(e) make provision for the carrying out of annual reviews;

(f) require the local authority to be notified if there is any change in person carrying on or in charge of the home or the premises used;

176

(g) prohibit the use of secure accommodation for the purpose of restricting the liberty of children; and

(h) provide that contravention of or failure to comply with the regulations, without reasonable excuse, shall be an offence punishable on summary conviction by a fine not exceeding level 4 on the standard scale. (See Appendix 1 for the standard scale currently applicable.)

The Act seeks to provide, where possible, a uniformity in the matters to be addressed in regulations governing community homes, voluntary homes and registered children's homes. Thus the subject matter of the proposed regulations in each case is very similar although the particular requirements in each case may, of course, differ. It is likely, however, that all regulations will impose certain uniform standards to be met by all types of homes with regard to fundamental matters of child care as it would be unacceptable to impose different standards. The power to prohibit the use of secure accommodation is new and reflects prevailing opinion that the use of such facilities is inappropriate in privately-run children's homes.

9.5 Welfare of children

Section 64 imposes on the person carrying on a children's home, duties similar to those imposed on voluntary organisations under s 61 (see 8.5 above). These duties concern, in general, the need to safeguard and promote the child's welfare and to include the child, his parents and others whose views may be relevant in the decision-making process. Consideration must also be given to the childs's religious persuasion, racial origin and cultural and linguistic background when decisions are made.

There is a duty to make reasonable use of services and facilities available for children cared for by their own parents and a duty to advise, assist and befriend children with a view to promoting their welfare when they leave the home.

9.6 Duties of local authorities

Section 64(4) extends to registered children's homes, the provisions of s 62 which apply to voluntary organisations (see 8.6 above). Local authorities will therefore have a duty to satisfy themselves that children in registered homes are being properly looked after and will have power to enter and inspect premises for this purpose. If they are not satisfied, they must take reasonable steps to secure that a child's care is taken over by a parent or relative in appropriate cases and must also consider whether to exercise any of their own functions with respect to the child.

9.7 Disqualifications

Section 65 disqualifies certain people from carrying on, or being employed, in registered children's homes. The provisions extend to those involved in any way in the management of, or having a financial interest in, a registered home. The disqualification applies to anybody who would also be disqualified from being a private foster parent under s 68 (see 10.4 below). This list will include people convicted of specified offences, those placed on probation or discharged absolutely or conditionally for the same offences and those whose own parental rights and powers have been taken over by a local authority. The new grounds for disqualification are wider in scope than those contained in the Children's Homes Act 1982.

The local authority responsible for registering a home may waive disqualification after full disclosure has been made. Waiver must take the form of a written consent. If consent is refused, written notice must be served on the applicant, giving the local authority's reasons and the applicant may then appeal to a Registered Homes Tribunal. Procedure on appeal will be governed by Sched 6, Part I which also covers appeals relating to registration (see 9.3 above).

Any person who contravenes s 65, either because he is himself disqualified or because he has employed a disqualified person, commits an offence and is liable on summary conviction to a term of imprisonment not exceeding six months or a fine not exceeding level 5 on the standard scale (s 65(4)). (See Appendix 1 for the standard scale currently applicable.) Note that where a disqualified person is employed in a home, the offence is committed by the employer and not the employee. An employer will have a good defence if he can prove lack of knowledge and no reasonable grounds for believing that the employee was a person disqualified under the Act.

Chapter 10

Private Arrangements for Fostering Children

10.1 Outline

Where children in care are placed with foster parents, the local authority usually funds the fostering. In the case of a child in voluntary care, the fostering arrrangement is normally made after consultation with the child's parents.

Private fostering placements of children with foster parents are not generally arranged or paid for by local authorities.

For this reason, controls on private fostering arrangements are needed for the protection of the children involved. The Foster Children Act of 1980 is repealed, being replaced by the provisions of Part IX and Sched 7 of the Children Act, which maintains the old protective legislation but clarifying definitions and terms used, and setting out clearly the powers and duties involved.

10.2 Definitions

A privately fostered child is defined in s 66(1) of the Act as a child who is under the age of 16 (or if disabled, under 18 s 66(4)) and who is cared for and provided with accommodation by someone other than:

(1) a parent of his;
(2) a person who is not a parent of his but who has parental authority for him; or
(3) a relative of his (defined in s 105 as a grandparent, brother, sister, uncle or aunt, whether of the full blood or the half blood or by affinity, or step-parent).

To look after a child in the above circumstances is 'to foster a child privately' (s 61(1)(b)).

179

Obviously, parents quite often ask others to look after their children for short periods, varying from a few hours' babysitting to longer periods whilst they may be away from home for any reason. It is necessary to define at which stage this becomes 'private fostering' and incurs the protective provisions of this Act. Where a child is cared for and accommodated for a period of less than 28 days, and no longer period is intended, then this is not 'private fostering' (s 66(2)). Any longer arrangement, therefore, will impliedly come within the definition unless it falls within the exceptions to private fostering listed in Sched 8, paras 1–5 (see 10.3 below). The Act does not specify whether the 28 day period means any single period of this length, or a total of 28 days over a longer period. Since no longer period is mentioned (ie 28 days in each year), it seems clear that it means any single period of 28 days or more, where a longer period is intended.

10.3 Exceptions

There are a number of exceptions to the definition of private fostering listed in Sched 8, paras 1–5:

- children who are being looked after by a local authority (Sched 8, para 1);
- children cared for by a person in premises in which any parent or person with parental responsibility for the child or a relative who has assumed responsibility for the child's care is living (Sched 8, para 2(1)(a));
- children cared for in registered children's homes as defined in s 63, (ie, a home for more than three children where the child is not being accommodated by a parent, relative or person with parental responsibility for her and where the exceptions in s 63(5) (ie, community or voluntary homes, residential care, nursing or mental nursing homes, hospitals or certain schools do not apply);
- children cared for by voluntary organisations (Sched 8, para (2)(c));
- children in school receiving full time education (Sched 8, para (2)(d));
- children in any health service hospital (Sched 8, para (2)(e));

180

- children in residential care homes, nursing homes or mental health nursing homes, (Sched 8, para (2)(f));
- children in any other home or institution provided, equipped and maintained by the Secretary of State (Sched 8, para (2)(g)).

Also, the provisions of s 66(1) (private arrangements for fostering children) are subject to the requirements in s 63 of the Act (requiring registration of a home where more than three children are living with people who are not their parents or relatives and who do not have parental responsibility for them. Note that s 63(12) enables a person who fosters more than three children under the provisions of Sched 7, to do so without having to register as a children's home.

Situations may arise where a child is living in one of these places, but being cared for by a person who lives and/or works there in his or her private capacity (not as part of their duties in relation to the establishment). In these cases the exceptions will not apply (Sched 8, para 2(2)).

Those children who are in the care of a person under CYPA 1969, s 7(7)(b) and those who are under a supervision requirement within the meaning of the Social Work (Scotland) Act 1968, are also exempted from the private fostering regulations, Sched 8, para 3. Children detained or subject to guardianship under the Mental Health Act 1983 are exempt from these regulations, Sched 8, para 4.

Children placed for adoption by an agency under the Adoption Act 1976, s 1 or the Adoption (Scotland) Act 1978, s 1 or art 3 of the Adoption (Northern Ireland) Order 1987; or those who are protected under the adoption legislation are similarly exempted, Sched 8, para 5.

There is a duty imposed by s 67 on every local authority to satisfy themselves as to the welfare of all privately fostered children in their area and the Secretary of State is empowered to make regulations for such children to be visited by local authority officers at reasonable times to inspect the premises and the children there.

When the local authority is not satisfied that the welfare of a privately fostered child is being satisfactorily safeguarded or promoted, where it is in the child's interest, it is empowered either to take steps to have the child cared for by a parent, relative, or person with parental responsibility for the child, or to consider exercising its functions under the Act, s 67(5).

10.4 Prohibitions and disqualifications

Certain people may not be permitted to be private foster parents. The Secretary of State may make regulations under s 68 of the Act disqualifying certain people from privately fostering any child, or a specific child or children. It is anticipated that prohibition under these regulations could occur if a person had a history of certain criminal offences (eg, violence or offences against children); mental disturbance; had previously been prohibited from fostering; previously had his or her parental rights assumed by a local authority or any other circumstances rendering them unfit to take on the responsibility of fostering.

Apart from the powers of the Secretary of State a local authority has power under s 69 to prohibit a person from fostering on the ground that 'he is not a suitable person to foster a child' or that the premises to be used for the fostering are unsuitable or that 'it would be prejudicial to the welfare of the child to be, or continue to be accommodated by that person in those premises.' A potential foster parent may be prohibited from fostering any child or a specific child; and the prohibition may extend to any premises, or to specified premises (s 69(3)).

Prohibitions could also be coupled with requirements made under Sched 8, para 6, taking effect when the time specified for compliance with the requirement has expired and the requirement has not been complied with (s 69 (6)). Such prohibitions must be in writing giving the reasons and details of rights and time in which to appeal under Sched 8, para 8.

Unsuitability is a matter apparently for the discretion of the local authority and one has to look to the cases under former law to decide in which circumstances a person would be considered unsuitable. Mental illness, criminal convictions for violent or sexual crimes, offences against children or mode of life or habits such as serious drug or alcohol abuse may lead to a decision that the person is unsuitable. Poor hygiene or lack of physical space could lead to a decision that accommodation is unsuitable.

Once a local authority has made a prohibition they may also cancel it where it is considered no longer justified (s 69(4)).

Nobody may foster a child privately when they live in the same household as a prohibited person or live in a household where a prohibited person works unless they have disclosed any relevant facts and obtained written consent from the local authority (s 68(3)).

If the local authority is asked for its written consent and refuses to give it, it must give reasons in writing for the refusal and inform the applicant of their right to appeal under Sched 8, para 8.

10.5 Offences, defences and punishment

Failure to comply with a requirement to give notice or information without reasonable excuse is an offence, as is the provision of false information (s 70). Other offences created by s 70 include:

- refusal to allow a privately fostered child to be visited by a local authority officer (s 70(1)(*b*));
- obstructing a local authority officer exercising his authority under s 67(3) to inspect premises and children living there (s 70(1)(*c*));
- contravention of a prohibition under s 68 (s 70(1)(*d*));
- failure to comply with a requirement imposed by a local authority under Part IX of the Act (s 70(1)(*e*));
- accommodating a privately fostered child in contravention of a prohibition imposed by a local authority under Part IX of the Act (s 70(1)(*f*));
- knowingly advertising for private fostering without stating name and address (contrary to the requirements of Sched 8, para 10 (s 70(1)(*g*)).

It is a defence for a person alleged to have contravened s 68(3) (ie someone fostering privately whilst living in the same household as a disqualified person, see above at 10.4) to prove that 'he did not know and had no reasonable ground for believing that any person to whom s 68 (1) applied (ie a disqualified person) was living or employed in the premises in question. 'To establish the defence the court would have to be satisfied that either the accused did not know that the person in question was disqualified or that they did not know the disqualified person was employed or resident in the premises—the latter probably being rather difficult to establish in most cases.

The punishment on summary conviction of an offence under s 70(1)(*a*) is a fine not exceeding level 5 on the standard scale and for breach of 70(1)(*d*) or (*f*) it is a maximum fine of level 5 and/ or six months' imprisonment. Breach of s 70(1)(*e*) is punishable by a maximum fine at level 4. There is a lesser penalty for contravention of s 70(1)(*b*), (*c*) or (*g*) ie, a maximum fine of level 3.

Note too that proceedings for an offence of failing to give notice in the time required by any provision in Part IX of the Act must be brought within six months of the date that the relevant evidence came to the knowledge of the local authority (s 70(7)).

10.6 Powers of the local authority to impose requirements

Schedule 8 sets out in para 6 the matters in relation to which the local authority may impose requirements on any person who is, or intends to foster children privately.

These include:—

(a) the number age and sex of the children who may be privately fostered . . .;

(b) the standard of accommodation and equipment to be provided for them;

(c) arrangements to be made with respect to their health and safety; and

(d) particular arrangements . . . with respect to the provision of care for them, Sched 8, para 6(1).

Requirements may be made for a particular child, or class of child, para 6(2) or come into effect only when the children exceed a specified number, para 6(3).

The Secretary of State may make regulations as to notification which must be given to the local authority by persons arranging private fostering or undertaking private fostering, or parents of children who are intended to be privately fostered. The information to be notified will be determined by regulations, but may include commencement and cessation of private fostering, change of address, disqualifications, prohibitions and convictions of any offences, or the death of the child (Sched 8, para 7).

10.7 Appeals

Paragraph 8 of Sched 8 sets out the circumstances in which a person aggrieved by a requirement under para 6 or a refusal by a local authority of consent to foster privately under s 68, or a prohibition under s 69, or a refusal to cancel a prohibition, may appeal.

Appeal may also lie against a refusal to make an exemption as to the number of children to be fostered under Sched 7, para 4, or conditions or variations of these exemptions.

The court to which the appeal may be made is the magistrates' court, the county court and the High Court.

Appeal may be made within 14 days of the date of notification of the requirement, refusal or prohibition appealed against (Sched 8, para 8(2)); and the operation of a requirement is suspended pending an appeal (Sched 8, para 8(3)).

On allowing an appeal, the court may cancel or vary the original requirement or prohibition by allowing more time for compliance.

10.8 Special provisions for school holidays

Some children in private boarding schools remain there during the holidays, and if they live at the school for more than two weeks during the holidays, the situation is treated as one of private fostering under Sched 8, para 9; and Part IX of the Act (the controls on private fostering discussed above apply). The person who proposes to care for the children must notify the local authority of the estimated number of children staying on, and a duty arises to notify the local authority of the death of such a child, or where such a child leaves school (ie ceases to be privately fostered) during the holidays.

The local authority may grant exemption from the requirement to give notice for a special period, or indefinitely, and may revoke such an exemption by written notice.

10.9 Advertising

It is forbidden to advertise that a person will undertake private fostering, or will arrange for a child to be privately fostered, unless the published advertisement states that person's name and address (Sched 8, para 10).

10.10 Insurance of privately fostered children

It is forbidden to insure the lives of children fostered privately. The foster parent is deemed to have no interest in the child's life for insurance purposes, Sched 8, para 11.

Chapter 11

Childminding and Day Care

11.1 Introduction

Part X of the Act provides for the registration and regulation of child minding and day care services for children under the age of eight. Sections 71 to 79 and Sched 9 replace the Nurseries and Child-Minders Regulation Act 1948 which is now repealed. Part X of the Act applies to Scotland, as did the previous legislation.

The Act introduces a comprehensive code which specifies in greater detail than before the respective duties, powers and rights of the local authority and those providing child minding or day care services. Its purpose is to ensure that children are well cared for when in nurseries or under the care of child minders.

Whilst many aspects of the law remain as before, there are some important changes. Child minders will now have to register if they look after one or more children under the age of eight. Under the previous law, registration was only required in respect of children under the age of five. Those running nurseries or other facilities providing day care will have to register if they look after children under the age of eight for more than two hours in any day. Here the Act introduces some measure of deregulation as the previous law required local authorities to register all premises in which day care facilities were provided for more than two hours a day for children under school leaving age.

Where registration is required, however, the Act imposes tighter controls including the requirement that premises be inspected by the local authority each year as a condition of continuing registration. There is also a right of entry to premises where it is believed that children are being looked after in contravention of the Act. Under the previous law, a warrant was necessary in

187

these circumstances. Finally, there is a power to protect children in an emergency by applying to the court, ex parte, for cancellation of any registration under the Act.

11.2 Registration

Every local authority must keep a register of:
(a) persons who act as child minders on domestic premises within its area; and
(b) persons who provide day care for children under the age of eight on non-domestic premises for a total period which exceeds two hours in any day (s 71(1)).

The register may be kept by means of a computer but must be open to inspection by members of the public at all reasonable times (s 71(15)).

A child minder for the purposes of the Act is someone who looks after one or more children under the age of eight, for reward, for a total period which exceeds two hours in any day (s 71(2)). The most common form of child minding arrangement is where a person looks after a young child during the day while his mother is at work. Other less obvious types of arrangement could also fall within the ambit of the Act (eg where a child under eight is looked after for a relatively short period before and after school provided that the total period of care in any one day exceeds two hours).

The definition does not apply to a parent, relative, person with parental responsibility or a foster parent when looking after a child (s 71(4)). Neither does it apply to a nanny employed to look after a child by either a parent, a non-parent with parental responsibility or a relative who has assumed responsibility for the child's care. For the purposes of the Act a nanny is someone employed to look after a child wholly or mainly in the employer's home. Nanny sharing arrangements, an increasingly common feature of modern life, similarly excluded. Thus shared nanny will not become a childminder if she looks after the children of one employer in the home of the other (s 71(6)).

The term premises includes any vehicle eg a caravan. Domestic premises means those used wholly or mainly as a private dwelling.

11.2.1 Exemptions

Certain establishments which would otherwise fall within the ambit of s 71 are expressly excluded eg schools, play centres maintained or assisted by a local education authority, children's homes (community, voluntary and registered), health service hospitals, residential care homes, nursing homes and homes provided and maintained by the Secretary of State (Sched 9, paras 3 and 4). Registration is also unnecessary where premises are used to provide day care for under-eights for less than six days in any year eg an occasional creche, although the local authority must be given advance notice in writing (para 5).

11.2.2 Procedure

An applicant will have to lodge a statement containing information about himself and any person assisting, or likely to assist, in looking after children on the premises in question or living, or likely to live, there. The Secretary of State is given power by regulation to determine the exact form and content of these statements (para 1). Although it is the person providing day care facilities rather than the premises which must be registered, separate applications must be submitted for different premises even if the proprietor is the same (para 1(2)). There will be a prescribed fee to be paid on application. There will also be a fee to be paid each year after registration to cover the cost of inspection which must be carried out annually (see 11.8 below). Once registration is complete a certificate will be issued specifying the applicant's name and address, the address of any premises where day care facilities are provided and any requirements imposed under s 72 or 73 (see 11.3 below).

11.2.3 Refusal to register

A local authority may refuse to register an applicant if the premises to be used for child minding or day care are unfit for the purpose because of their condition, situation, construction, or size or because of the condition of any equipment used on the premises (s 71(11)). Registration may also be refused if any person living, or likely to be living, on the premises or employed, or likely to be employed there is unfit to be in the proximity of children under the age of eight (s 71(8),(10)). Where the application relates to day care facilities, a local authority may also refuse registration if any person looking after, or likely to look after any children on the premises is unfit to care for children under eight (s 71(9)).

Under s 77 there is a right of appeal against refusal to register (see 11.6 below).

11.2.4 Disqualification

The Secretary of State has power, by regulation, to disqualify certain people from registration (Sched 9, para 2). The criteria for disqualification will be similar to those which apply to registered children's homes under s 65 (see 9.7 above) and private foster parents under s 68 (see 10.4 above). The list will include people convicted of specified offences, those whose parental rights and powers have been taken over by a local authority at any time, those previously disqualified from private fostering and anyone previously refused registration under Part X or whose registration has been cancelled at any time (para 2(2)). A person who lives in the same household as a disqualified person, or in a household where such a person is employed, will also be disqualified unless he has disclosed the fact to the local authority and obtained their written consent (para 2(3)). A disqualified person cannot provide day care, be concerned with its management or have any financial interest in its provision unless he has disclosed the fact to the local authority and obtained their written consent (para 2(4)). The same applies where it is proposed to employ a disqualified person (para 2(5)).

Under s 77 there is a right of appeal if a local authority refuses to give consent following disclosure of any disqualification (see 11.6 below).

11.2.5 Offences

No person may provide day care for children under the age of eight on any premises within the area of a local authority unless he is registered by that authority with respect to those premises (s 78(1)).

A person who contravenes this provision without reasonable excuse commits an offence punishable on summary conviction by a fine not exceeding level 5 on the standard scale (s 78(1),(2)). (See Appendix 1 for the standard scale currently applicable.)

The law is a little kinder to unregistered child minders. They must be served with an enforcement notice by the local authority before criminal proceedings can be taken against them. The notice will have effect for one year from the date of service. An unregistered child minder who continues to look after children under the age of eight whilst an enforcement notice is in force, without reasonable excuse, commits an offence punishable on summary conviction by a fine not exceeding level 5 on the standard scale (s 78(3)–(6)). This will apply even if the child minder moves to another area but continues to contravene the Act (s 78(7)).

A person who acts as a child minder when disqualified by regulation (see 11.2.4 above) commits an offence punishable on summary conviction by a term of imprisonment of up to six months or a fine not exceeding level 5 on the standard scale or both (s 78(9)(*a*) and (12)).

The same penalty will apply to anyone who contravenes Sched 9, para 2(3)–(5) (see 11.2.4 above and s 78(9)(*b*)) unless:

(a) in the case of para (2)3, he can prove that he did not know, and had no reasonable grounds for believing, that a disqualified person was living or employed in the household (s 78(10)); or

(b) in the case of para (2)5, he proves that he did not know, and had no reasonable grounds for believing, that he was employing a disqualified person (s 78(11)).

11.3 Requirements for child minders

When registering a child minder, a local authority has a duty to impose whatever requirements it considers appropriate provided that these are also reasonable (s 72(1)). In particular, it must:

(a) specify the maximum number of children, or the maximum number within specified age groups, to be looked after (taking into account any other children who may be on the premises at any time eg the child minder's own children);

(b) require the premises and equipment used to be adequately maintained and kept safe;

(c) require a record to be kept of the names and addresses

191

of any child looked after, any person who assists in looking after such a child and any person living, or likely to be living on the premises; and

(d) require the child minder to notify the local authority of any changes in the information recorded under (c) above (s 72(2)).

Where a local authority imposes requirements in addition to those mentioned above, these must not be incompatible (s 71(5)). A local authority may impose a new requirement or vary or withdraw an existing one at any time (s 71(6)). There is a right of appeal under s 77 against the imposition, removal or variation of any requirement under s 72 (see 11.6 below).

The Secretary of State is given power, by regulation, to specify requirements which must be imposed in prescribed circumstances and also requirements which may not be imposed by local authorities (s 71(3)).

Any person who without reasonable cause contravenes, or otherwise fails to comply with a requirement under s 72 commits an offence punishable on summary conviction by a fine not exceeding level 4 on the standard scale (s 78(8)).

11.4 Requirements for day care facilities

A local authority has an identical duty to impose reasonable requirements when registering a person who provides day care facilities for young children (s 73(1)). The same specific requirements as to maximum numbers, safety of premises and record keeping must be imposed (see 11.3 above). In addition, the local authority must:

(a) specify the number of people required to assist in looking after children on the premises; and

(b) require the person registered to notify the local authority of any change in the facilities provided or the period for which they are available (s 73(3)).

Where the same person is registered for different premises within the same area, separate requirements must be imposed for each registration (s 73(2)).

Any additional requirements imposed may not be incompatible with those specifically mentioned in the Act (s 73(7)). As with child minding, there is a power to impose a new requirement or to vary or withdraw an existing one at any time (s 73(8)). There is also a right of appeal under s 77 against the imposition, removal or variation of any requirement under s 73 (see 11.6 below).

The Secretary of State is given power, by regulation, to specify requirements which must be imposed in prescribed circumstances and also requirements which may not be imposed by local authorities (s 73(3)).

Any person who without reasonable cause contravenes, or otherwise fails to comply with a requirement under s 73, commits an offence punishable on summary conviction by a fine not exceeding level 4 on the standard scale (s 78(8)).

11.5 Cancellation of registration

A local authority may at any time cancel the registration of a child minder or a person providing day care facilities if:

(a) the circumstances would justify them in refusing to register that person;

(b) the care provided is, in the opinion of the authority, seriously inadequate having regard to the needs of the child or children concerned; or

(c) that person has contravened a requirement imposed on him or failed to pay the annual fee for inspection (see 11.8 below) (s 74(1), (2)).

When considering the needs of any child the local authority must have regard to his religious persuasion, racial origin and cultural and linguistic background (s 74(6)).

A person providing day care facilities on different premises may have all his registrations cancelled if the circumstances would justify a refusal to register (s 74(3)). This will be the case even if the initial complaint leading to cancellation only relates to one set of premises.

A registration may not be cancelled on the ground that the premises are unfit if the local authority has imposed a requirement that certain repairs and alterations be carried out and the time limit for doing this has not yet expired (s 74(4)). This saving will only apply, of course, if the premises are unfit because the necessary work has not yet been carried out. If the cause is entirely unrelated the registration may still be cancelled.

Cancellation of registration must be made in writing (s 74(5)) and there is a right of appeal under s 77 (see 11.6 below).

11.6 Appeals

Section 77 sets out a procedure for appeal against the following steps which may be taken under Part X of the Act:

(a) refusal of registration under s 71 (see 11.2 above);

(b) cancellation of registration (see 11.5 above);

(c) refusal of consent after disclosure of disqualification under Sched 9, para 2 (see 11.2 above);

(d) imposition, removal or variation of any requirement under s 72 or s 73 (see 11.3 and 11.4 above); and

(e) refusal to grant any application for variation or removal of any such requirement.

The procedure incorporates a right to object to any of the above steps before they are actually taken as well as a right of appeal to the court afterwards. A local authority must follow the procedure set out in s 77 and cannot take any of the steps mentioned until the time limit for appeal has expired or, where any appeal has been made, its final determination (s 77(11)).

A local authority must serve written notice of its intention to take any of the above steps on the person concerned at least fourteen days before any action is taken (s 77(1)). The notice must give the authority's reasons and inform the recipient of his rights under s 77 (s 77(2)). If the recipient informs the local authority in writing of his desire to object he must be afforded an opportunity to do so (s 77(3)). An objection may be made in person or through a respresentative (s 77(4)).

If the local authority then decide to take the proposed step, regardless of the objection, they must send the person concerned written notice of their decision and he may then appeal against it to the court (s 77(5),(6)). Note that an aggrieved person has a right of appeal to the court under s 77(6) even if he did not exercise his right of objection at the relevant time.

The general provisions of the Act regarding jurisdiction, venue and procedure will apply to appeals under s 77 (see Chapter 14). The court in this context can mean the magistrates' court, the county court or the High Court and it is for the Lord Chancellor to determine by order which court will be appropriate.

Where the court allows an appeal against the refusal or cancellation of any registration it may impose requirements under s 72 or s 73 (s 77(9)). Where it allows an appeal against a requirement already imposed it may vary, rather than cancel it (s 77(9)). Any requirement imposed or varied in this way shall be treated as if it were imposed by the local authority concerned (s 77(8)).

11.7 Emergency protection of children

The procedure for cancellation of registration, or the variation, imposition or removal of a requirement, under s 77 is lengthy and inappropriate in cases where prompt action is needed to protect children from serious harm. Section 75 therefore provides a quick procedure for ex parte application to a court in an emergency.

The court may cancel registration, impose a new requirement or vary or remove an existing one if it appears that a child who is being, or may be looked after, by a registered child minder or in a registered day care facility (as the case may be), is suffering, or likely to suffer, significant harm (s 75(1)).

The application must be supported by a written statement of the local authority's reasons (s 75(3)). This must be served on the registered person, with notice of the order and its terms, as soon as reasonably practicable after the hearing (s 77(4)).

Any cancellation or variation, removal or imposition of a requirement made by the court under s 75 will take effect from the date of the order (s 75(2)). Any new requirement, or existing requirement which has been varied, will be treated for all purposes as if it had been made by the local authority although there will be no right of appeal under s 77.

11.8 Inspection

All premises requiring registration under the Act must be inspected by the local authority at least once every year (s 76(4)). Any person authorised by the local authority has a right of entry at any reasonable time and may inspect:

    (a) the premises;
    (b) any children being looked after there;
    (c) the arrangements for their welfare; and
    (d) any records relating to them kept in accordance with the Act.

Where any records are kept on computer there is a right of access to the apparatus and software used and a right to check its operation.

If necessary, an inspector may also request assistance from the person who is responsible for the records or in charge of the computer (s 76(5)).

A local authority proposing to carry out an annual inspection of registered premises must serve notice on the person concerned and require him to pay the prescribed fee. Registration will be cancelled under s 74 if payment is not made within 28 days (Sched 9, para 7).

Where a local authority has reasonable cause to believe that a child is being looked after on premises within their area in contravention of Part X, any authorised person may enter those premises and carry out an inspection at any reasonable time (s 76(2)). This power may be used where it is believed that children are being looked after by unregistered child minders or in unregistered day care facilities. Under the previous law it was necessary to obtain a warrant from the court for this purpose.

Any person exercising a power to inspect under s 76 must produce, on request, a duly authenticated document showing his authority to do so (s 76(6)). Any person who intentionally obstructs him will be guilty of an offence punishable on summary conviction by a fine not exceeding level 3 on the standard scale (s 76(7)). (See Appendix 1 for the standard scale currently applicable.)

11.9 Co-operation between authorities

A local authority may request the help of a local education authority in the exercise of any of its functions under Part X. Where it does so, the education authority should assist if this is compatible with its own duties and obligations and does not unduly prejudice the discharge of its own functions (Sched 9, para 2).

11.10 Application to Scotland

Part X of the Act applies to Scotland although some modification is necessary to take into account the different legislative framework and legal system (s 108(11)). Special provisions applying only to Scotland are contained in ss 77(10) and 79.

Chapter 12

Supervisory Functions of the Secretary of State

12.1 Outline of provisions generally

Part XI of the Act (ss 80/84) brings together the provisions relating to general matters such as research and training, and the giving of grants. It defines the powers of the Secretary of State in relation to registered children's homes, private foster homes, nurseries, residential care homes, mental nursing homes, nursing homes and premises in which children are being looked after by local authorities, voluntary organisations, or adoption agencies.

The Secretary of State has wide powers to enter and inspect premises, and any child living there. He may require access to records or to check the operation of any computer or apparatus used in connection with the keeping of records, and may initiate an enquiry into specified matters.

There is power for the Secretary of State to offer financial support for those undergoing child care training or for the preparation of material for child care training, and to offer grants to local authorities for secure accommodation in community homes. Grants may be offered to local authorities for secure accommodation in community homes and to voluntary organisations towards the establishment, maintenance or improvement of voluntary homes which were formerly assisted community homes.

The Secretary of State also has the power to conduct or to assist research into specified areas including adoption, accommodation of children in residential care, nursing or mental nursing homes. Local authorities have similar powers of research.

It seems that the provisions may have the effect of shifting a significant proportion of the burden of residential child care to voluntary organisations.

197

12.2 Inspection of premises and furnishing information

The premises liable to inspection are listed in s 80 as any:
- children's home;
- premises in which a child being looked after by a local authority is living;
- premises in which a child accommodated by a local education authority or voluntary organisation is living;
- premises in which a child accommodated by a health authority is living;
- premises in which a child is living with a person with whom he or she has been placed by an adoption agency;
- premises in which a child protected under Part III of the Adoption Act 1976 is living;
- premises in which a privately fostered child is living;
- premises on which any person is acting as a child minder;
- premises with respect to which a person is registered under s 71(1)(*b*);
- residential care homes, nursing or mental nursing homes required to be registered, and used to accommodate children;
- premises used to provide services for children under Part III of the Act;
- independent school providing accommodation for any child, s 80(1).

Information relating to any of these premises, or any child living there (including access to and inspection of records) under s 80(3) may be required by the Secretary of State from:
- a local authority;
- a voluntary organisation;
- a person carrying on a children's home;
- a person fostering privately or providing accommodation for a child on behalf of a local authority, voluntary organisation, local education authority or health authority;
- a local education authority providing accommodation for a child;
- a person teaching or working in an educational establishment where children accommodated by a local or education authority live;

- an occupier of premises in which any person acts as a child minder or provides day care for young children;
- anyone carrying on a residential care home or nursing home or mental nursing home accommodating children.

The person inspecting the home or premises may also inspect the children there (and examine the management of the home and the way in which the children are treated (s 80(6))).

Section 80(7) makes provision for access to computers, discs, and other apparatus for record keeping, and for assistance to be required from those in charge of the computer.

Section 80(8) gives a right of entry for inspection. Obstruction of entry is punishable on summary conviction by a fine not exceeding level 3 on the standard scale (s 80(10)). (See Appendix 1 for standard scale currently applicable).

12.3 Inquiries

Under s 81, the Secretary of State has the power to hold an inquiry into the functions of the social services committee of a local authority or of a voluntary organisation insofar as those functions relate to children. The functions of adoption agencies, residential and children's homes, nursing homes and places of detention of children under the CYPA 1969, s 53 (detention for certain grave offences) may also be examined.

Inquiries may be held wholly or partly in private (s 81(2) and and (3)).

12.4 Financial support by the Secretary of State

Under s 82(1), the Secretary of State has the power to defray or contribute towards:

(a) any fees or expenses incurred by any person undergoing approved child care training;

(b) any fees charged or expenses incurred by any person providing approved child care training or preparing material for use in connection with such training; or

(c) the cost of maintaining any person undergoing such training.

Not only can support be given to individuals, but to local authorities, in the provision of secure accommodation in community homes (s 82(2)) or to voluntary organisations towards the expenditure incurred by them in connection with the establishment, maintenance or improvement of voluntary homes which at the time the expenditure was incurred were or were designated as community homes (s 82(4)).

Finally, the Secretary of State may himself provide, equip and maintain homes for children in need of particular facilities and services specially provided in these homes and unlikely to be available in community homes (s 82(5)).

12.5 Research

Under s 83 the Secretary of State is empowered to conduct or assist in research into any other matter connected with his functions, or those of local authorities under the Act, the Children and Young Persons Acts 1933–1969, the Mental Health Act 1983, s 116, the Mental Health (Scotland) Act 1984, adoption of children or accommodation of children by local authorities or others in residential care homes, nursing or mental homes.

Local authorities are obliged to give the Secretary of State whatever particulars he may require (s 83(3)).

Information may be required from the clerk of each court as to proceedings relating to children (s 83(5)).

Each year, an abstract of the information gathered by the Secretary of State must be laid before Parliament (s 83(6)).

Representations and information from the Central Council for Education and Training in Social Work, local authorities and others must be considered to keep under review the adequacy of child care training (s 83(8)).

This is a means by which, hopefully, the Secretary of State can be kept informed of local and national needs, and should enable him to meet those needs in future with the minimum of delay.

12.6 Default power

Under s 84 the Secretary of State is given power to make a default order if satisfied that a local authority has failed, without reasonable cause, to comply with any duty imposed on it under the Act. The Secretary of State must give reasons when making an order and may include in it directions to ensure that the local authority fulfils its statutory obligations within a specified period. If a direction in a default order is not complied with the Secretary of State may apply to the High Court for an order of mandamus to enforce it.

Chapter 13

Welfare of Children living away from home

13.1 Introduction

Children may be accommodated away from home on a long-term basis in establishments provided by health authorities or local education authorities. They may also be placed in residential care homes or in nursing or mental nursing homes. Others may spend much of their childhood in independent boarding schools. In the past such accommodation has fallen outside the ambit of child care law and it was possible for children to languish in such establishments for many years, having little contact with their families, without a local authority even being aware of their existence.

Sections 85 and 86 of the Act seek to remedy this situation by imposing on local authorities a welfare duty to children living away from home on a long-term basis in accommodation which is not otherwise regulated under the Act. Those providing the accommodation are required to notify the relevant local authority of the child's presence so that it may fulfil its obligations under the Act. There is a corresponding duty to notify the local authority when the child leaves the accommodation.

Section 87 extends the welfare principle to children accommodated in independent boarding schools and enforces this by giving local authorities a right of entry and inspection.

These provisions extend new powers and duties to local authorities and are additional to the power given to the Secretary of State by s 80 to inspect such premises (see 12.2 above).

13.2 Children accommodated by health authorities and local education authorities

A health authority or a local education authority ('the accommodating authority') which provides a child with accommodation for a consecutive period of at least three months must notify the local authority within whose area the child was ordinarily resident immediately before being accommodated ('the responsible authority') (s 85(1), (3)).

If it is difficult to establish where the child was ordinarily resident, the responsible authority will be the local authority within whose area the accommodation is located.

The duty to notify will arise at the outset if an accommodating authority intend to accommodate a child for more than three months even though they may not already have done so.

Once a local authority has been notified, it must do what is reasonably practicable to determine whether the child's welfare is being adequately safeguarded and promoted while he is accommodated away from home and it must consider whether and to what extent it should exercise any of its' functions under the Act (s 85(4)). This could include the provision of services under Part III, an application for a care or supervision order under Part IV or an application for for a child assessment order or an emergency protection order under Part V.

An accommodating authority must inform the responsible authority when they cease to accommodate a child previously notified. If the child has returned home this will ensure that the local authority is aware of his presence within their area. If he is over the age of sixteen, this will enable them to fulfil any obligation they may have to offer him in advice and assistance under s 24 (see 4.6 above). This is especially important where a young person has no family support in the outside world.

Section 85 should ensure that the welfare needs of those children to whom it applies are not overlooked while their health and educational needs are being met by the appropriate agencies. At the same time there should be no unnecessary interference where parents are properly exercising their parental responsibility as the duty to notify will not arise, where children return to live with their families on a frequent and regular basis.

13.3 Children accommodated in residential care homes and nursing homes

Section 86 imposes a duty to notify in similar circumstances where a child is accommodated in any residential care home, nursing home or mental nursing home. In this case, however, the obligation to notify falls upon the person carrying on the home and the local authority to be notified is the one within whose area the home is located. Failure to notify without reasonable cause is an offence punishable on summary conviction by a fine not exceeding level 3 on the standard scale. (See Appendix 1 for standard scale currently applicable.)

The obligations of the local authority once notified are the same as those under s 85. In addition, a local authority has the power to enter any residential care home, nursing home or mental nursing home within its area to establish whether it has been notified of all children to whom s 86 applies. Any person who intentionally obstructs another in exercise of this power of entry commits an offence punishable on summary conviction by a fine not exceeding level 3 on the standard scale.

13.4 Children accommodated in independent schools

Section 87 was introduced into the Act following concern about the welfare of children accommodated in independent boarding schools. It extends to such schools elements of the welfare scheme which applies to children in private and voluntary homes under Parts VII and VIII of the Act. It requires local authorities to satisfy themselves about the social welfare of pupils in the same way as the schools inspectorate must be satisfied about educational standards.

An independent school in this context means a private school which provides education for five or more pupils of compulsory school age (Education Act 1944), s 114(1)). Note, however, that the new provisions in the Act do not cover independent schools with less than fifty boarders. These are categorised as children's homes under Part VIII (see Chapter 9) or registered care homes which are regulated under the Registered Homes Act 1984.

There are three main elements to the new provisions:

    (a) a new duty is imposed on the proprietor, or any other

person conducting an independent boarding school, to safeguard and promote the welfare of children accommodated in the school (s 87(1));

(b) all local authorities which have independent boarding schools within their area, are required to do what is reasonably practicable to determine whether the welfare of the children is adequately safeguarded and promoted while they are living at school (s 87(2)); and

(c) local authorities are required to notify the Secretary of State if they consider that the proprietor, or person conducting the school, is failing to discharge his welfare duty to any child or children under s 87(4). This will be a ground for complaint under s 71 of the Education Act 1944 and could lead to the school's removal from the register of independent schools and eventual closure.

The proprietor of a school, for the purposes of s 87, is the person or body responsible for the management of the school (Education Act, 1944, s 114(1)).

Any person authorised by the local authority has the right to enter any independent boarding school, at any reasonable time, to inspect the premises, children and records (s 87(5), (6)). Regulations to be made by the Secretary of State will govern the precise manner and extent of any inspection under this power but the Act expressly authorises the inspection of computerised records. There is a right of access to any computer, associated apparatus and software used for recordkeeping and the right to request assistance from any person in charge of the computer or its operation (s 87(8)).

Any person who intentionally obstructs another in exercise of any power conferred by s 87 or associated regulations commits an offence punishable on summary conviction by a fine not exceeding level 3 on the standard scale (s 87(9)). (See Appendix 1 for standard scale currently applicable). Note, that the wording of s 87(9) is wide and will cover refusal of entry, concealment of records, refusal to produce children for inspection and any other acts intended to hinder or obstruct the local authority.

Pupils who remain at boarding school for more than two weeks during a school holiday also fall within the protection of Part IX of the Act (Sched 8, para 9). They will be treated as privately fostered

205

children for this period and the relevant provisions of the Act will apply (see 10.8 above).

Chapter 14

Jurisdiction and Procedure

The provisions relating to jurisdiction and procedure are contained in ss 92–98 of the Act, together with Sched 11. Section 99 deals with legal aid, and the restrictions on the use of the High Court's wardship jurisdiction in s 100 is discussed in Chapter 15 below.

14.1 Courts having jurisdiction under the Act

It was recommended that the reform of the law relating to children should include the creation of a new family court, based on a hierarchical tier system. Each case should be able to move, where appropriate, from court to court within the hierarchy.

The new family court is not yet in being, but the Act creates a new concept 'the court' (ie the court which has power to make the various orders available under the Act) and defines it in s 92(7) as 'the High Court, a county court or a magistrates' court'. Before the Act some orders had only been available in some courts, or in certain proceedings, but not in others. Now, subject to some exceptions eg those restricting the power of magistrates' courts to make certain orders for financial relief (see Chapter 3) and orders relating to property belonging to or held in trust for a child or income from such property (s 92(4)), orders available under the Act may be made by 'the court'.

The county court and the magistrates' court will have a family proceedings division similar to that of the High Court. In the magistrates' court, the domestic court will now hear all family proceedings (which includes proceedings under the Act) and will be renamed the 'family proceedings court'. The magistrates sitting in the family proceedings court will be drawn from 'family panels' for which it is hoped that there will be special training. It is anticipated that the magistrates will be expected to read papers in advance of hearings, and to give reasons for their decisions, to bring them in line with the higher courts.

There is also provision in s 92(9) that the Lord Chancellor may order that the principal registry of the Family Division be treated as a county court for specified purposes of the Act.

14.2 Commencement of proceedings

Schedule 11 makes a beginning in establishing a framework for potential movement from one court to another within 'the court' by first permitting orders to be made by the Lord Chancellor requiring specified classes of proceedings to be initiated only in certain levels of court; specified classes of court; or particular courts (Sched 11, para 1(1)). Further orders may set out the circumstances in which specified proceedings may be only commenced in certain courts or classes or levels of court (Sched 11, para 1(2)–(4)).

14.3 Transfer of proceedings

Having created 'the court' (comprising the High Court, county court and the magistrates' court)—which is, perhaps, the first step towards the creation of a family court with a hierarchical tier system—it is necessary to be able to move cases to different levels within the court. The circumstances in which proceedings should move from one level in the court to another are not set out in the Act, but power is given to the Lord Chancellor to make orders relating to the transfer of proceedings under the Act, the Adoption Act 1976, and any other family proceedings save for those under the inherent jurisdiction of the High Court (Sched 11, para 2).

14.4 Hearings by a single justice

Occasionally it is impossible, particularly out of court hours, to convene a full bench for an urgent hearing. The Act therefore enables the Lord Chancellor to empower a single justice to make an emergency protection order, or to deal with any specified question

208

with respect to the transfer of proceedings to or from the magistrates' court (Sched 11, para 3).

14.5 Evidence

The Act relaxes the rules of evidence applicable in civil proceedings relating to children in several ways. It will be possible under s 96(1) and (2) for a court to admit the unsworn evidence of a child, where, in the opinion of the court he does not understand the nature of the oath, but does understand the duty to tell the truth. Before doing so, however, the court must be satisfied that the child has sufficient understanding to justify the reception of his evidence. This new provision brings the civil law in this area into line with existing criminal law.

The hearsay rule has long presented problems in proceedings involving children. The Act, in s 96(3)–(7), now gives the Lord Chancellor wide powers in specified civil proceedings to override the rules relating to hearsay and in proceedings relating to the upbringing, maintenance or welfare of a child and to admit hearsay evidence. Orders made under these provisions may be designed for specific purposes, or to operate within different levels of the court. An order could provide for certain types of hearsay evidence such as the statements of a child to be admissible in evidence whether made orally, in prescribed form or recorded by any prescribed method, for example, by audio or video tape-recording. There is power to repeal or amend any existing legislation relating to evidence as a consequence of any order made under the Act.

There has, in the past, been a willingness on the part of the courts to moderate the rules of evidence in civil cases concerning children, and in particular, the hearsay rule. Social workers, for example, have in the past been allowed to repeat to the court in cases involving the care, upbringing, or welfare of children, statements made by a child, without the necessity of calling that child to make those statements in court. On a strict interpretation of the rules of evidence this would not be permitted. However, recently, in the case of *Re H: Re K* [1989] FLR 296, the Court of Appeal held that hearsay evidence could only be admitted in civil proceedings (except in wardship) where the existing law recognises exceptions to the general rule. Wardship is an exception because it stems from the ancient jurisdiction of the High Court, pre-dating civil evidence rules. If, then, the law is to reflect the need to admit hearsay evidence in cases involving children, urgent legislative changes were required. As a result, s 96(3) was brought into force on 16 November 1989. Urgent consideration is being given to how the new power can be exercised. The orders made under this section will apply to present legislation, and subsequently apply to proceedings under the Act when the remainder of the Act comes into force.

The power to admit recorded statements will be of increasing importance in view of the increasing use of video-recording techniques in interviewing children. If the Lord Chancellor makes an appropriate order it is likely that video-recorded evidence will become as common a feature of proceedings under Part IV of the Act as it is now in wardship proceedings.

14.6 Self-incrimination

There is a general rule of privilege that a witness may refuse to answer any question or to give evidence on certain matters on the ground that it might incriminate that witness or their spouse. Section 98 applies to proceedings under Parts IV and V of the Act, removing the present privilege against self-incrimination. The courts will no longer be deprived of potentially important and useful evidence. In order to encourage open disclosure, such a witness is given an indemnity that the statement so made cannot be used against them or their spouse in proceedings for any offence other than perjury.

14.7 Court procedure

There will be rules of court made under s 93 governing procedure. The rules may prescribe in particular—

    (a) the way in which any application is to be made;

    (b) persons entitled to participate in proceedings (as parties or to make representations to the court);

    (c) documents, information and notices to be given;

    (d) application of enactments to tie in procedure on matters brought on complaint to the magistrates' court with those not brought on complaint;

    (e) preliminary hearings;

(f) service outside the United Kingdom;

(g) exercise of powers of the court outside the geographical jurisdiction;

(h) enabling an applicant to proceed ex parte in certain circumstances;

(i) authorisation of a single justice to exercise the powers of the court in specified circumstances;

(j) circumstances where a magistrates' court may order payment of costs.

14.8 Attendance of the child

Under the old law there was a duty to bring a child before the court in care proceedings. This has been replaced by the provisions of s 95. In proceedings under Parts IV and Part V of the Act, the court may order the child to attend court. A constable may be authorised to bring the child to court, and premises specified in the order may be entered and searched if necessary. There is power to order a person who may know where the child is to disclose their whereabouts and any person in a position to do so may be ordered to bring the child to the court.

14.9 Privacy

There are already provisions for the protection from publication of details of children's cases in the High Court and the county court but s 97(1) of the Act enables rules of court to be made under the Magistrates' Courts Act 1980, s 144, to allow a magistrates' court to sit in private in proceedings where it may exercise powers under the Act.

Section 97(2) prohibits the publication of any material which may identify the child as being involved in proceedings in which any power under the Act may be exercised. 'Publication' includes broadcasting by radio, television, or cable television, and 'material' includes any picture or representation (s 97(5)). Failure to comply with this section is an offence punishable by a maximum fine of level 4.

14.10 Transfers from England, Wales, Northern Ireland, Channel Islands and Isle of Man

It happens from time to time that cases need to be transferred from one geographical location to another and problems arise as a result. Section 70 empowers the Secretary of State to make regulations covering the transfer of cases. Section $70(1)(a)$ enables regulations to be made enabling prescribed orders made by Northern Ireland courts which appear to correspond with orders under the Act to take effect as though they had been made under the Act.

In a similar way, orders made by a court in England and Wales corresponding to provisions in force in Northern Ireland can take effect as if they had been made under Northern Ireland Law.

Under s 70(2) regulations may enable orders made by Channel Islands courts to take effect as though they had been made under the Act.

Regulations made under s 70 may make any consequential amendments to s 25 of the Children and Young Persons Act 1969 (transfers between England and Wales and Northern Ireland) and s 26 of the Children and Young Persons Act 1969 (transfers between England and Wales and the Channel Islands and the Isle of Man), and can modify any provisions of this Act to accommodate orders made outside England and Wales.

Chapter 15

Restrictions on the use of wardship

The High Court, as parens patriae, has jurisdiction over minors who owe allegiance to the Crown therefore including those resident within the United Kingdom, British Nationals, those physically present in England and Wales, and to some extent minors who are British Subjects resident abroad. Wardship proceedings, (which are part of the High Court's inherent jurisdiction) originated from the feudal exploitation of infants when a guardian was responsible for both the ward's physical well being and their estate, keeping the profits of the estate until the infant came of age (and often controlling the estate afterwards by arranging the infant's marriage). The wardship jurisdiction of the High Court developed over the centuries into a protection for infant and estate, vesting the custody of the ward in the High Court and thereby giving the court a supervisory role in the life of the child. No important step could be taken in the life of the child without the High Court's consent.

Under s 7 of the Family Law Reform Act 1969, the High Court had the power to place a ward of court in the care or under the supervision of a local authority. This meant, in effect, that where there was concern as to a child's welfare application could be made to ward the child, and the High Court had power to place that child in care where it was considered to be in the child's best interests to do so. Wardship came to be used, inter alia, as an avenue of appeal against magistrates' court decisions in care proceedings. It also meant that a child could be placed in care without the necessity of satisfying the court of the grounds laid down in the Children and Young Persons Act 1969.

After consideration in the Law Commission's *Review of Child Care Law* (Working Paper No 101 of 1987) it was decided to leave wardship mainly intact, save for the alterations to wardship and

213

to the High Court's inherent jurisdiction set out below, and to postpone any decisions as to an additional jurisdiction for the High Court in relation to children until the Act has come into force and its full effects can be seen. It will be remembered that (as part of 'the court') the High Court has full powers under the Act to make orders relating to children. The effect of the changes to the wardship jurisdiction therefore, is to ensure that the High Court can only make care or supervision orders to a local authority under the provisions of the Act on the grounds specified, and subject to the safeguards set out in the Act. There will be no other route to care or supervision.

15.1 Repeal of the power to make care or supervision orders in wardship

Section 100(1) repeals s 7 of the Family Law Reform Act 1969, removing the power of the High Court to place a ward of court in the care or under the supervision of a local authority. The effect of this is to force anyone seeking to place a child in the care or supervision of a local authority to apply for an order under the Act. 'The court', which has the power to make care and supervision orders, is defined in s 92(7) of the Act as the High Court, a county court or a magistrates' court. The High Court therefore has power to make a care or supervision order in family proceedings under the Act but not within other jurisdictions.

The court cannot make a care order of its own volition. In a case, for example, where the High Court in its wardship jurisdiction considers that care may be appropriate, it may then direct the local authority to investigate the child's circumstances, and if the statutory conditions set out in the Act are satisfied, it would seem possible for the High Court (as part of 'the court' in family proceedings) to make an interim care or supervision order, provided it has first received an appropriate application.

The use, or rather, misuse, of the wardship jurisdiction as an avenue of appeal against unpalatable magistrates' court decisions (for example, the refusal by the magistrates to make a care order requested by a local authority) has long been criticised, and the High Court may now be relieved of a considerable volume of work.

15.2 Restrictions on the High Court's inherent jurisdiction

Wardship is only part of the jurisdiction of the High Court. There also remains an inherent jurisdiction, which, in relation to children, under s 8(3) is within the definition of 'family proceedings'. Section 100(2)(*a*) forbids the exercise by any court of the High Court's inherent jurisdiction with respect to children by placing them in the care or under the supervision of a local authority, and s 100(2)(*b*) forbids the use of that inherent jurisdiction to place children in local authority accommodation.

No court may exercise the inherent jurisdiction of the High Court to confer on any local authority the power to determine any issue arising in connection with parental responsibility for that child (s 100(2)(*c*)). At times in the past, this inherent jurisdiction of the High Court has proved useful to fill in gaps in its statutory jurisdiction (see *Re SW (a minor) (Wardship jurisdiction)* [1986] 1 FLR 24, where a 17 year old girl was placed in the care of a local authority).

Section 100(3) to (5) goes on to provide that local authorities may apply with leave of the court for the exercise of the High Court's jurisdiction, but such leave is only to be granted where the result desired by the local authority can only be achieved by an order made in the exercise of the courts inherent jurisdiction, for which the local authority would be entitled to apply. It is difficult to envisage many circumstances in which a local authority would be unable to obtain an appropriate order from 'the court' under the Act.

A possible situation is that of the mentally handicapped young person in respect of whom the local authority seeks permission for sterilisation where, care proceedings are inappropriate (perhaps because of the young person's age) and when, before the Act, wardship would have met the legal requirements of the situation. Alternatively, a situation could occur where a child is in care, and the local authority wish to use the inherent jurisdiction of the High Court to resolve a specific issue upon which a ruling is sought. There is no power for the court to make a specific issue order in respect of a child in care (s 8(9)) and therefore the local authority may apply within the High Court's inherent jurisdiction because the remedy is not available under the Act.

Under s 100(2)(c) no child subject to a care order may be made a ward of court.

215

Chapter 16

Care and Supervision orders in criminal proceedings

16.1 Outline of previous law

Under the previous law, it was possible for a child who had committed an offence to be dealt with by care proceedings under the civil jurisdiction of the juvenile court, or alternatively, by criminal proceedings.

In care proceedings under s 1(2)(f) of the Children and Young Persons Act 1969, the court had power to make an order under that Act (including a care or supervision order) if satisfied that the child was guilty of an offence (excluding homicide) and was in need of care and control which he would be unlikely to receive unless an order were to be made.

In criminal proceedings, after a finding or admission of guilt, the court had power to make a care or supervision order in addition to other possible forms of disposal, although a care order could only be made if the offence was one which, in the case of an adult, would be punishable by imprisonment.

When the Children and Young Persons Act 1969 became law, it was intended that the age of criminal responsibility would eventually be raised from 10 to 14 years, so that all offenders under the age of 14 years would be brought before the courts in care proceedings. The separate power to commit a child to care in criminal proceedings reflected a fundamental purpose in the legislation which was to treat all children in trouble, whether as a result of their own actions, or those of others, as children potentially in need of care and protection.

The provisions of the Children Act 1989 represent a significant departure from this principle. The offence ground for care proceedings is abolished, together with the power to make a care

216

order in criminal proceedings. Instead, the courts will have the power to include in a supervision order made in criminal proceedings, a requirement that the child resides in local authority accommodation for a period of up to six months. There are limitations on the power to impose this requirement. The child must already be subject to a supervision order imposed in criminal proceedings at the time the offence was committed. It must be an offence which would be punishable by imprisonment in the case of an adult, and the circumstances in which the child was living must have contributed to its commission (see 16.3 below).

Despite these changes, it may still be appropriate for care proceedings to be brought in respect of a juvenile offender, but only if the grounds in s 31 are satisfied (see Chapter 5). It is not too difficult to envisage circumstances in which the grounds could apply since criminal conduct could clearly impair a child's development and may well result from inadequate parental care or control. It will be for the prosecuting authority to decide in each case, whether criminal proceedings are appropriate.

Section 5 of the Children and Young Persons Act 1969 makes it clear, however, that criminal proceedings are only to be instituted where other options (including new proceedings under the Children Act 1989) would not be adequate to deal with the case. There are other possible ways to deal with first offenders, or minor offences, eg by way of caution, which do not involve criminal court proceedings.

16.2 Abolition of the offence condition in care proceedings

Section 90(1) of the Act abolishes the court's power to make an order in care proceedings under s 1(2)(*f*) of the Children and Young Persons Act 1969 (the offence condition). This applies to the whole range of orders previously available in such proceedings. Presumably the additional provisions in s 3 of the Children and Young Persons Act 1969 relevant to s 1(2)(*f*) will also be redundant, although not specifically referred to in s 64. Sections 1 to 3 of the 1969 Act are in any event to be repealed in their entirety. The separate and specific mention of s 1(2)(*f*) would seem to suggest that s 64 of the Act may be implemented before the provisions of Part IV relating to care proceedings generally.

16.3 Abolition of power to make care orders in criminal proceedings

Section 90(2) abolishes the power of a court to make a care order under s 7(7) of the 1969 Act (ie in criminal proceedings), but retains the power to make a supervision order, or an order requiring parents to enter into a recognisance. The power of magistrates' courts to remit juvenile offenders for sentence to a juvenile court, unless they intend to deal with the matter by way of absolute or conditional discharge, fine or parental recognisance, is also retained.

16.4 Requirement in supervision orders for a child to live in local authority accommodation

Section 90(3) retains the power to include requirements in supervision orders in criminal proceedings (eg that the child must live in a specified place, comply with directions, or take part in specified activities) subject to amendments in Sched 12, Para 23 of the Act, which adds a new s 12AA to the CYPA 1969 (see Appendix 4).

Under the new s 12AA the court may make a new supervision order which includes a requirement that a juvenile offender reside in local authority accommodation for any period up to a maximum of six months if:

(a) a supervision order has previously been made in respect of that child or young person;

(b) that order imposed a condition under s 12(A)(3) CYPA 1969 or a residence requirement under s 12AA;

(c) the offence—
(i) was committed while that order was in force;
(ii) would be punishable by imprisonment in the case of a person over the age of 21; and
(iii) is serious in the opinion of the court; and

(d) the court is satisfied that the behaviour which constituted the offence is due, to a significant extent, to the circumstances in which the child was living (s 12AA(6)).

The new power to include a residence requirement in a supervision order, to some extent, replaces the 'criminal' care order abolished by s 90(2) although its scope and effect are very different. An offender may now only be removed from home where his home circumstances have in some way contributed to the commission of the offence. A residence requirement may also prohibit him from living with a named person (s 12AA)(4)).

Before imposing a residence requirement a court must consult the local authority concerned and obtained a social enquiry report which deals, in particular, with the child's home circumstances at the time the offence was committed (s 12AA(7)). Because the effect of such a requirement is to deprive a child of his liberty for a defined period, s 12AA(9) provides that a requirement may not be imposed on a child who is not legally represented unless legal aid has been refused on financial grounds, or there has been an opportunity to apply for legal aid which has not been taken up.

16.5 Remand to local authority accommodation

Schedule 12, para 26 substitutes a new s 23 of the CYPA 1969. A court will now have to make a remand to local authority accommodation where a child is remanded, convicted or committed for trial on a charge of homicide or a young person (construed for the purposes of this section as a person over the age of ten years) is charged with or convicted of one or more offences and not granted bail unless he is certified unruly.

This replaces the previous provision for juvenile offenders to be remanded to the care of local authorities in similar circumstances. Whilst local authorities will still have a duty to look after juvenile offenders on remand, they will no longer be treated as children in care.

The local authority designated to receive the child or young person will be the authority for the area in which he lives or where the offence (or one of the offences) was committed and a person acting on behalf of that local authority may detain the child.

Under the new s 23, CYPA 1969 the court retains the power to certify a child or young person unruly and he may not then be remanded to local authority accommodation. As before, a local authority may apply for a certificate of unruliness if a child on remand cannot safely be contained in local authority accommodation. Section 23 (as amended) states that a child who has been certified unruly may be remanded to a remand centre or to a prison. Note, however, that the Secretary of State has previously modified these provisions by order to prohibit the committal to prison of boys under the age of fifteen years and girls under the age of seventeen years (SI 1979 No 125 and SI 1981 No 81).

Chapter 17

Adoption

There is in progress at present a government review of adoption law. It is anticipated that after the report there will follow in due course measures for reform. The main body of the present law is in the Adoption Act 1976. Some sections of that Act have required immediate clarification. The Children Act 1989, in Scheds 10 and 15, makes a few changes to the current law, amending some of those sections and replacing others.

17.1 Orders available in adoption proceedings

Adoption proceedings are 'family proceedings' as defined in s 8(4)(*d*) of the Act. This means that the court (the High Court, county court or magistrates' court) may make any order in adoption proceedings which is allowed under the Act in such family proceedings. Under s 8, orders may be made as to contact with a child, the child's place of residence, specific issues and prohibited steps. These orders are therefore available in adoption proceedings. Unlike care or supervision orders, which must be made on the application of a local authority or authorised person, a s 8 order may be made by the court of its own volition, and therefore, at any stage in adoption proceedings, the court may make a s 8 order. If, in adoption proceedings, the court considers that care may be appropriate, then it will ask the local authority to investigate the circumstances in which the child is living and if an application for care is then made, the court will consider it. The court can no longer make a care order of its own volition in adoption proceedings, whatever the circumstances of the case.

221

17.2 Freeing a child for adoption

Under the Adoption Act 1976, application could be made to the court for an order freeing the child for adoption. Such an application could be made by an adoption agency or a local authority, but would require the consent of the parent or guardian of the child, unless the child was 'in the care of' a local authority or adoption agency. This was interpreted by the courts as in physical care, as opposed to the child being under the protection of a care order. Thus, a child placed in voluntary care with a local authority could be subject to an application for a freeing order without (theoretically) the need for parental consent. The Act has altered the concept of voluntary care. Now, where a parent places a child in local authority accommodation, the child may be removed by the parent quite easily, and there is no longer the possibility of the local authority assuming parental rights over the child. The only route into care is through an application to the court under Part IV of the Act. For this reason, the Act no longer refers to 'voluntary care' and '. . . a child in the care of an authority . . .' means specifically a child in respect of whom a care order has been made (s 105).

The only situation now where an adoption agency may apply for a freeing order without first obtaining parental consent is where the adoption agency is a local authority, and that child is subject to a care order to that local authority under the Act (Sched 10, para 6(1) and para 30(9)).

17.3 Birth records

The Adoption Act 1976, s 51, provided that those who were adopted before 1975 could have access to their birth records, but only after receiving counselling. There was a rather odd limitation in that the counselling had to take place in England, Wales or Scotland. Schedule 10, para 20 amends s 51 to permit counselling to take place anywhere in the United Kingdom, or with a suitable body providing counselling outside the United Kingdom. The question of suitability will be a matter for the Registrar General.

17.4 The Adoption Contact Register

From the need to facilitate contact when required between an adopted person and their birth parents and family, came the idea of creating a register in which the details of those who have had their children adopted, and of people who are themselves adopted, would be recorded. Schedule 10, para 21 adds a new section to the Adoption Act 1976, dealing with the new register, to be named the Adoption Contact Register. It is to be in two parts: part one of adopted people and part two containing the names and addresses of relatives.

An entry on the register is made only at the request of the person whose details are to be recorded, and a small fee will be charged for the service. Those requesting an entry in Part I of the register indicating that they are adopted and that they wish to contact a relative, must be over eighteen years of age, and must fulfil the conditions set out in Sched 10, para 4. There must be a record of that person's birth kept by the Registrar General and either information supplied under s 51 of the Adoption Act or sufficient information available to enable him to obtain a certified copy of a record of his birth.

The conditions for an entry in Part 2 of the register are: that a record of the adopted person's birth is kept by the Registrar General, that the person giving the notice is over eighteen years old and satisfies the Registrar General that he is a relative of the adopted person and that he has sufficient information to enable him to obtain a certified copy of the adopted person's birth (Sched 10, paras 5 and 6.).

There is permission in the Act for the register to be a computerised record. Entries in either part may be cancelled by the person who originally gave the notice. The procedure is that the Registrar will pass on to the adopted person, upon their making an entry in Part 1 of the register, the name and address of any relative recorded in Part 2 of the register. It will then be up to the adopted person to make such contact as he or she wishes.

17.5 Payments to adopters

Under the former adoption law, allowances could be made to benefit adopters and prospective adopters in need of financial assistance. Each arrangement for the payment of an allowance required the approval of the Secretary of State. The Act makes the payment of allowances easier in that now such payments will be subject to general regulations made by the Secretary of State. To assist adopters over the transitional period, Sched 10, para 25 provides that the existing schemes for payment will be replaced by allowances made under the new regulations.

17.6 Miscellaneous amendments to the Adoption Act 1976 and the Adoption (Scotland) Act 1978

There are quite a few amendments to the Adoption Act 1976 in conjunction with the Adoption (Scotland) Act 1978 to ensure that the work carried out by adoption agencies, including the orders made by the courts under parallel legislation in Northern Ireland is recognised in the United Kingdom. These include Sched 10, paras 2 (amending s 11 of the Adoption Act 1976, arranging adoptions and placement); 20 (amending s 51 of the Adoption Act 1976, disclosure of birth records); 30 (amending s 72 of the Adoption Act 1976, interpretation); 32 (amending the Adoption (Scotland) Act 1978, arranging adoptions and placement); 41 (amending s 45 of the Adoption (Scotland) Act 1978, adopted children register), and 46 (amending s 65(1) of the Adoption (Scotland) Act 1978 interpretation).

17.7 Guardians ad litem and reporting officers in adoption proceedings

Schedule 10, para 29 inserts a new s 65A in the Adoption Act 1976 relating to guardians ad litem and reporting officers. Section 65A enables the Secretary of State to establish and run panels from which guardians ad litem and reporting officers will be selected.

There are existing provisions for payment by local authorities of the fees and expenses of guardians ad litem. Section 65A reflects this arrangement and encourages the co-operation between local authorities and the panels in administrative matters and finance. However, note that the guardians ad litem are technically independent of local authorities, and should have as much autonomy as possible.

Chapter 18

Miscellaneous and General

18.1 Search Warrants

Under this Act there are several sections which give power to 'persons authorised by a local authority' to visit premises and inspect either the place itself, children resident there, or any records kept. This applies to local authority accommodation, children's homes (ss 62 and 64), children's homes run by voluntary organisations (s 62), private foster homes (s 67), domestic premises where child minding is carried on or day care provided (s 76) and other premises subject to supervision by the Secretary of State (s 80).

The Act provides for external inspection of homes and schools where children are being looked after, and creates a duty to take such steps as are reasonably practicable to ensure the welfare of the children being accommodated in those places. Section 86 permits the inspection of accommodation provided in residential care, nursing or mental nursing homes whilst s 87 provides for the inspection of accommodation and conditions in independent schools.

Schedule 3, para 8 provides that a supervision order may require the supervised child and the person responsible for him to allow the supervisor to visit them in the place where they live and to have reasonable contact. This will include providing information upon request as to any change of address.

There are specific provisions in the Act to enter and inspect premises and under s 33 of the Adoption Act 1976 the local authority has a duty to ensure that protected children are visited from time to time. In all these cases, situations may arise where the duly authorised officer goes to carry out an inspection, and meets with a lack of co-operation or deliberate obstruction.

225

Section 102(1) provides for the issue of a warrant by the court where there is a refusal of entry, or refusal of access to the child concerned, or the person attempting to exercise the powers given by the Act is prevented or likely to be prevented from doing so. If a warrant is issued, it authorises a police officer to assist the authorised person to exercise their powers, using reasonable force if necessary. Under s 102(2), all warrants must be addressed to and executed by a constable, but the person applying for the warrant (eg local authority officer, supervisor, etc) may go with the police officer to execute the warrant if they wish, provided that the court has not ordered otherwise. The court may direct that the constable concerned may be accompanied by a doctor, health visitor or a nurse to execute the warrant if he or she chooses (s 102(3)). The warrant should, where reasonably practicable, name the child concerned, or describe the child as clearly as possible (s 102(5)). There is also a power under s 50(3) to authorise a constable to enter and search any specified premises in order to recover a child who is absent or unlawfully taken from care.

18.2 Offences

Where any offence created by the Act is committed by a body corporate, and it is attributable to an action or the consent or connivance of a particular person who is an officer of that company, then that individual is liable to punishment personally (s 103). For example, where a company is running a school which has children staying over in the holidays, and fails to comply with the private fostering requirements of the Act (if that failure is attributable to an individual who is an officer of the company, eg the managing director) then he or she will be liable to personal punishment, as well as the company. Section 78 creates a number of specific offences.

(1) Failing, without reasonable excuse to register when providing day care for children under eight.

(2) Failing to register when acting as a child minder, having received an enforcement notice.

(3) Failing, without reasonable excuse to comply with the requirements of s 72 (child minders) or s 73 (day care) (see Chapter 11 above).

(4) Acting as a child minder when disqualified to do so; or

contravention of the provisions of Sched 9, para 2(3)–(5) or any regulations made under that Schedule (see Chapter 12).

The punishment for contravention of the requirements of s 72 or s 73 is a maximum fine of level 4. For contravention of the provisions made under Sched 9, para 2 and regulations made thereunder, the punishment is one of a maximum fine of level 5 and/or up to six months imprisonment. All offences under this section are punishable on summary conviction by a maximum fine of level 5.

18.3 Duration of orders

Section 91 deals with the effect and duration of orders under the Act. Most orders will last until the child in respect of whom they were made reaches the age of eighteen, unless they are discharged earlier by the court (s 91(7), (11) and (12)). Similarly, parental responsibility agreements made under s 4, and the appointment of a guardian under s 5 will remain in force until the child in respect of whom the agreement or appointment was made reaches eighteen, unless discharged earlier by the court (s 91(8)). There are, however, some orders which have their own special provisions. A Table showing the effect and duration of orders is shown in Appendix 2.

18.3.1 Section 8 orders

Usually, s 8 orders will cease when the child in respect of whom they were made reaches sixteen, unless, (in exceptional circumstances only), the court orders a longer period, s 9(6)–(7)). Section 8 orders may be made to have effect for a limited period, or contain provisions which have effect for a limited period (s 11(7)). A residence order made in favour of one of two parents each of whom has parental responsibility for the child, (and who would have been living apart at the time of the order), will cease to have effect if the parents then live together for a continuous period of at least six months (s 11(5)).

18.3.2 Contact orders

A contact order requiring the parent with whom a child lives to allow the child to visit or otherwise have contact with his other parent, shall cease to have effect if the parents then live together for a continuous period of at least six months (s 11(6)).

18.3.3 Financial orders

The financial orders have their own time limits, and there is insufficient space to set these out again here, but for further detail please refer to Chapter 3.

18.3.4 Supervision orders

Supervision orders cease to have effect on a child's eighteenth birthday. The period that an order may initially be made is one year, with possible extensions for up to a maximum total of three years. A supervision order made under the Act will supercede a care order or a previous supervision order made under the Act. However, it has no effect on a supervision order made in criminal proceedings, nor on an education supervision order (Sched 3, para 10).

18.3.5 Interim orders

Interim care and supervision orders will be of a duration set by the court. Section 38 sets out the considerations for the court in making interim orders. Section 38(4) provides that the first interim order may be for a maximum of eight weeks. Further orders may be for up to four weeks on each occasion (see 5.3.7 above). If the first order was for a period of less than four weeks, then the second order may be longer than four weeks, but may not extend beyond a period of eight weeks from the date of the first order.

18.4 Restrictions on repeated applications

Clearly it would not be in a child's interest to be the subject of repeated applications for orders under the Act. There are safeguards built into the Act to stop this happening. For instance, on disposal of an application for an order under the Act, the court may restrict or prevent subsequent vexatious applications by any named person. The court may rule that no further application may be made under the Act in respect of the child for an order of any specified kind without the leave of the court (s 91(14)). A six-month time limit on further applications may be made in specified cases.

In certain cases where the previous application has been for one of the following:

(a) discharge of a care order;

(b) the discharge of a supervision order;

(c) the discharge of an education supervision order;

(d) substitution of supervision order for care order; or

(e) a child assessment order

then under s 91(15) there can be no further application for any of these orders in respect of the child concerned without leave of the court until a period of six months has elapsed from the disposal of the last application. This provision does not apply to interim orders (s 91(16)).

Contact with child in care-restriction on applications Where a person has made an application under s 34 for contact with a child in care and the application has been refused by the court, then, unless six months has elapsed since the date of the refusal, no further application may be made in respect of the same child for such an order without the leave of the court (s 91(17)).

18.5 Legal aid

Legal aid will be available for proceedings under the Act. Being civil legal aid, it will be administered by the Legal Aid Board. Since delay in determining any question relating to the upbringing of a child, or the administration of a child's property or the income from it is likely to prejudice the welfare of the child (s 1(2)); and the welfare of the child is the paramount consideration for the court (s 1(1)); clearly, legal aid should in such cases be administered with as little delay as possible.

With this in mind, perhaps, s 99 amends the Legal Aid Act 1988, and empowers the Lord Chancellor to make such further orders as he considers necessary or expedient.

The effect of the amendments is to waive the test of merit in respect of those applicants for legal aid who are automatically parties to care or supervision proceedings, and for the child if he or she has applied.

Legal aid may also be granted on an emergency basis in care

and supervision proceedings, before the statement of means has been considered.

Local authorities (and other prescribed bodies) may not have legal aid for representation in proceedings under the Act (s 99(2)).

Proceedings for variation or discharge of supervision orders under s 15 of the Children and Young Persons Act 1969, or appeals under s 16(8) in respect of such orders, will now be included in s 19(5) of the Legal Aid Act 1988 dealing with the scope of criminal legal aid (s 99(3)).

Where a child seeks legal representation in respect of proceedings brought under s 25 of the Act (secure accommodation for restricting liberty), it must be granted (s 99(2)).

Chapter 19

Implementation and Transitional Provisions

19.1 Implementation

The Act received Royal Assent on 16 November 1989. The following provisions came into effect on that date:

s 96(3)   Power of Lord Chancellor, by order, to override the hearsay rule in civil proceedings concerning children (see Chapter 14).

Sched 12,   Child Care Act 1980 amended (in the interim and
para 35   until its repeal by the Act takes effect) to give unmarried fathers certain rights including, in particular, the right to apply for an access order where access to a child in care is refused or terminated.

s 89   Family Law Reform Act 1969, s 20, amended in relation to the carrying out of blood tests to establish paternity.

The following provision came into effect on 17 January 1990:

Sched 12,   Education Act 1981 amended so that local education
para 36   authorities who make and maintain statements of special educational needs under s 7 of the Act may arrange for a child to attend an establishment abroad and may pay or make a contribution towards the fees and other costs.

The government has stated its intention to bring the other provisions of the Act into force by October 1991.

231

19.2 Transitional provisions

When the Act is implemented it will be necessary to accommodate and integrate orders made under the previous legislation within the new statutory framework. Schedule 14 contains transitional provisions and savings designed to achieve this and all references to paragraph numbers in this Chapter refer to that Schedule. With the exception of those provisions mentioned above, it is assumed, for the purposes of this Chapter, that the entire Act will be implemented on the same date.

19.2.1 Pending proceedings

The Act will not affect any proceedings which are pending (ie have been commenced) when it comes into force with the following exceptions:

(a) Divorce and judicial separation—the repeal of s 42(3) of the Matrimonial Causes Act 1973 will have immediate effect and a court will not have power to declare a party to the marriage unfit to have custody of children of the family.

(b) Sexual offences—the repeal of s 38 of the Sexual Offences Act 1956 will have immediate effect and a court will not have power to divest a person of authority over a child in incest cases.

(c) Children beyond control—an order under s 3(1), CYPA 1963 directing a local authority to bring care proceedings in respect of a child who is beyond control will cease to have effect as soon as Part IV of the Act (care and supervision) is implemented.

(d) Hearsay evidence—an order made by the Lord Chancellor under s 96(3) overriding the hearsay rule in civil proceedings concerning children may apply to pending proceedings (para 1).

For the purpose of the remaining transitional provisions of Sched 14, any reference to an order made before the commencement of the Act (ie under the previous legislation) will include an order made in pending proceedings but after the Act came into force.

19.2.2 Custody and related orders

Here the transitional provisions preserve the effect of existing orders (with certain exceptions) but introduce modifications to bring them into the general scheme of the Act. The implementation of the Act will have the following effect on existing orders:

Declarations of unfitness Any declaration under s 42(3) of the Matrimonial Causes Act 1973 (party to a marriage unfit to have custody of a child of the family) or order under s 38(1) of the Sexual Offences Act 1956 (divesting a person of authority over a child in a case of incest) will cease to have effect (para 3).

Parental responsibility of parents Parental rights orders made under the Family Law Reform Act 1987, s 4(1) will be deemed to be orders under s 4 of the Children Act 1989 giving the father parental responsibility for the child (para 4). Parents who were married to each other at the time of a child's birth will share parental responsibility for that child where there is in force 'an existing order' (para 6(1)).

An existing order is an order determining custody, care and control, access or any matter relating to the child's upbringing (other than a care order) made under any of the following statutes:

The Domestic Proceedings and Magistrates' Courts Act 1978;
The Children Act 1978;
The Matrimonial Causes Act 1973;
The Guardianship of Minors Act 1971 and 1973;
The Matrimonial Causes Act 1965;
The Matrimonial Proceedings (Magistrates' Courts) Act 1960.

The fact that a parent has parental responsibility will not, however, entitle him to act in any way which would be incompatible with any existing order eg by removing the child from the parent who has a custody order (para 6(3)).

An unmarried father who has custody or care and control of his child under an existing order will also be deemed to have the benefit of an order under s 4(1) of the Act giving him parental responsibility and that order cannot be brought to an end at any time while he has care and control of the child under the original order (para 6(2), (4)).

Non-parents with custody or care and control A person who is not a parent or guardian but has custody or care and control of a child under an existing order will have parental responsibility for him as long as he continues to have custody or care and control under that order. This will not, however, entitle him to act in any way which would be incompatible with the existing order. It will entitle him to apply for any s 8 order (see Chapter 3) and also to apply for a contact order under s 34 if the child is taken into care (para 7).

Persons with care and control Where a person has care or control of a child by virtue of an existing order he may:

(a) appoint a guardian under s 5 of the Act, and the appointment will take effect on his death and will not be postponed until the death of the surviving parent unless the order also gave the surviving parent care and control (para 8);

(b) consent to another person applying for a residence or contact order under s $10(5)(c)(i)$;

(c) object to a local authority providing accommodation for the child under s 20;

(d) remove the child from that accommodation unless he is over sixteen and agrees to remain there;

(e) have the child placed with him while a care order is in force in accordance with s 24(4)–(6); and

(f) apply for a financial provision order under s 15(1) and Sched 1, (para 8).

Persons with access A person who has access to a child by virtue of an existing order:

(a) may apply for a contact order;

(b) may be named, with consent, in a family assistance order;

(c) is entitled to notice of an application for a child assessment order; and

(d) must be allowed reasonable contact with the child while an emergency protection order is in force (subject to any directions the court may give) or while the child is kept in police protection (para 9).

Enforcement of certain existing orders   Custody or custodianship orders made by a magistrates' court and previously enforceable under the Guardianship of Minors Act 1971, the Children Act 1975 or the Domestic Proceedings and Magistrates' Courts Act 1978 will be enforceable under s 14 of the Act (para 10).

Discharge of existing orders   The making of a residence order or a care order will discharge an existing order. Where a s 8 order (other than a residence order) is made while an existing order is in force, the existing order will take effect subject to the s 8 order (para 11(1)).

An existing order may be discharged in full or in part:

    (a) in any family proceedings relating to the child, or in which any question arises as to the child's welfare; and

    (b) on the application of any parent or guardian, any person named in the order or the child himself provided that he has been granted the leave of the court (para 11(3)–(5)).

If the application for discharge is opposed the court must consider the factors listed in s 1(4) of the Act (para 11(6)).

19.2.3 Guardians

Any appointment of a guardian which has taken effect before the Act comes into force will be deemed to be an appointment under the Act. Any appointment which has been made but has not yet come into effect at that time will take effect in accordance with s 5 and will therefore be subject to the new rules on guardianship which the Act imposes (para 13). For the purposes of the Wills Act 1837 any disposition in a will of 'the custody and tuition of any child' made before the Act comes into force will be deemed to be an appointment by will of a guardian for the child (para 14).

19.2.4 Children in care

Existing care orders   Children who are already the subject of care orders or parental rights resolutions under the previous legislation at the time the Act comes into force will be deemed to be children in care under the Act (para 15). This will apply whether the original care order was made in proceedings under the CYPA 1969 or in any other proceedings where the court is given power by statute to commit a child to care. It will not apply to care orders made in criminal proceedings under s 7 of CYPA 1969.

Where an existing care order was made in matrimonial, guardianship, custodianship, wardship or adoption proceedings and the court has given directions to the local authority, those directions will continue to have effect until varied or discharged by the court (para 16(5)). This is contrary to the general position under the Act where a court only has power to give directions to a local authority on specified matters.

A care order made under the CYPA 1969 when a child was over the age of seventeen will continue in force until the child reaches the age of nineteen even though the Act otherwise provides for all care orders to end at the age of eighteen (para 16(1), (2)).

Charge and control placements   A child subject to an existing care order, who has been placed under the charge and control of a parent, guardian, or person previously having custody or care and control of him under a court order, will be treated as a child placed under s 23(5) of the Act and the regulations made under the subsection will apply to the placement (para 17).

Access orders   An order for access to a child in care made under s 12C of the Child Care Act 1980 will take effect as a contact order under s 34 as soon as the Act comes into force (para 18). Where, immediately before the Act comes into force, a court has suspended an existing access order for seven days under s 12E of the Child Care Act 1980, that suspension will continue to have effect as if the Act had not been passed (para 19).

Children in voluntary care   A child in voluntary care under s 2 of the Child Care Act 1980, but not subject to a resolution under s 3 of that Act, will be treated as a child provided with accommodation by the local authority under Part III when the Act comes into force (para 20). If at that time he was placed under the charge and control of a parent, guardian or person previously having custody or care and control under a court order he will not fall within this category and will not be treated, for the purposes of the Act, as a child who is being looked after by a local authority.

Boarded out children   A child in care who is already living with foster parents or with a relative or friend (not being a person who previously had custody or care and control of the child under a court order) when the Act comes into force will be treated as a child who has been placed with local authority foster parents under the Act (para 21(1)).

The placement will, however, continue to be regulated by the Boarding-out of Children Regulations 1988 (if it is a placement with foster parents) or by the Accommodation of Children (Charge and Control) Regulations 1988 (if it is a placement with a relative or friend) for a period of twelve months after the Act comes into force (para 21(2)). After this period the relevant provisions of the Act and related regulations will apply to all placements of children in care. The twelve-months delay should give local authorities time to bring existing placements into line with the new provisions of the Act.

Advice and assistance   Young people under the age of twenty-one who were in care under the previous legislation and who left care between the ages of sixteen and eighteen will qualify for advice and assistance under Part III of the Act (para 22).

Emigration of children in care   Where the Secretary of State has received a request for consent to the emigration of a child in care under the previous law (CCA 1980, s 24) but has not made a decision on this at the time the Act comes into force, the old law will continue to apply (para 23).

Maintenance of children in care   Contribution orders (and other orders treated as contribution orders) made before the Act comes into force will have effect as if they were made under the Act (para 24).

19.2.5 Supervision orders

Supervision orders in care proceedings   Supervision orders made under s 1(3)(*c*) of CYPA 1969 (care proceedings) or s 21(2) of CYPA 1969 (on the discharge of a care order made in care proceedings) will be deemed to be orders under s 31 once the Act is implemented but will be modified in accordance with the new provisions (para 25).

Any requirement for the child to reside with a named person will remain in effect unless the court directs otherwise. Any other requirement imposed by the court, or directions given by a supervisor, will be deemed to have been made under the appropriate provisions of Sched 3.

Orders made under the old law for more than one year will be reduced unless a court directs otherwise. Thus, an order which has been in force for more than six months, will automatically cease to have effect six months after the Act comes into force unless it would have ended earlier than this in any event or it is extended by the court. An order which has been in force for less than six months on implementation will cease to have effect one year after it was made unless it would have ended earlier than this in any event or it is extended by the court. Note that under the Act a supervision order, even when extended by a court, cannot last more than three years in total.

Other supervision orders Supervision orders made in other civil proceedings will continue in force for one year from the date on which the Act comes into force unless they would have ended earlier in any event or the court directs that they should do so (para 26).

19.2.6 Place of safety orders

Any place of safety order or warrant in force at the time the Act is implemented will continue to have effect as if the old law were still in force. Any application for an interim care order, however, will have to be made under the Act and not the previous legislation (para 27).

19.2.7 Recovery of children

The implementation of the Act will not affect the operation of any summons or warrant issued before that date for the recovery of any child missing from care (para 28).

19.2.8 Voluntary organisations: parental rights resolutions

Any resolution transferring parental rights and duties to a voluntary organisation which is in force on implementation of the Act, will continue to have effect for a further six months unless discharged earlier (para 31). A voluntary organisation wishing to retain a child in its care beyond that period will have to apply for an order under s 8, with leave if necessary.

A voluntary organisation may not arrange for the emigration of a child in its care while a parental rights resolution is continued under the transitional provisions. Neither may a local authority take over the parental rights of the organisation, by resolution, during this period. In all other respects the relevant provisions of the Child Care Act 1980 will apply while the resolution is preserved under the transitional provisions.

19.2.9 Foster children

Certain accommodation classified as a private foster home under the previous legislation is re-classified as a children's home under the Act. Different provisions will therefore apply to children thus accommodated once the Act comes into force. Such children will continue to be treated as private foster children provided that an application for registration of the home in question is made within three months of implementation. They will retain this status until the application is granted or, if it has been refused, the time limit for appeal has expired or any appeal has been determined (para 32).

19.2.10 Nurseries and child minding

There is a transitional period of twelve months for nurseries and child minders registered under the previous legislation to be re-registered under the Act. During this period, or until they are re-registered if sooner, The Nurseries and Child Minders Regulation Act 1948 will continue to apply (para 34).

19.2.11 Children living away from home

Sections 85 and 86 impose a duty on certain authorities, organisations or individuals to notify a local authority when a child is accommodated away from home for a consecutive period of more than three months. In calculating whether this duty arises, any period of time a child was accommodated before the Act came into force shall be disregarded (para 35).

19.2.12 Criminal care order

The Act abolishes the power to make care orders in criminal proceedings. The transitional provisions provide for existing criminal care orders to be replaced by orders under the Act, where appropriate, within a period of six months.

Criminal care orders made under the old law will accordingly cease to have effect six months after the Act comes into force, unless discharged earlier (para 36). During this period the local authority may apply for a care or supervision order under s 31, if the grounds apply, or a supervision order with a residence requirement under s 12AA of CYPA 1969. The power to include a residence requirement in a supervision order made in criminal proceedings was introduced by the Act to replace the criminal care order. Under a residence requirement a child may be required to live in local authority accommodation for up to six months. In transitional cases, where a criminal care order is already in force, it will not be necessary to satisfy the usual conditions for a residence requirement contained in s 12AA of CYPA 1969.

During the transitional period any person may apply for a residence order with the leave of the court. A local education authority may also apply for an education supervision order, if appropriate. On making any of these orders, the court must discharge the criminal care order. While a criminal care order is preserved under the transitional arrangements, the relevant provisions of the CYPA 1969 and the CCA 1980 will continue to apply.

19.3 Savings

19.3.1 Consent to marriage

The Act amends the Marriage Act 1949 by simplifying the rules relating to consent to the marriage of a minor. The old rules will continue to apply, however, where a child is the subject of an existing order determining custody, care and control, access or any matter relating to his upbringing or a care order or parental rights resolution made under the previous legislation (para 37).

19.3.2 The Children Act 1975

Certain provisions of the Children Act 1975 amending other legislation will continue to have effect notwithstanding the repeal of the 1975 Act itself. They are:

(a) s 68(4), (5) and (7) (amendments of s 32 CYPA 1969); and

(b) in Sched 3—
  (i) para 13 (amendment of Births and Deaths Registration Act 1953);
  (ii) para 43 (amendment of Perpetuities and Accumulations Act 1964);
  (iii) paras 46 and 47 (amendment of Health Services and Public Health Act 1968); and
  (iv) para 77 (amendment of Parliamentary and Other Pensions Act 1972).

19.3.3 Child Care Act 1980

The amendment of s 106(2)(*a*) CYPA 1933 (certified copies of court orders) by the CCA 1980 shall continue to have effect notwithstanding the repeal of the 1980 Act itself.

Appendix 1

Standard Scale of Fines*

Level 1	£50
Level 2	£100
Level 3	£400
Level 4	£1,000
Level 5	£2,000

* Applicable at the time of going to press

Appendix 2

Effect and Duration of Orders

ORDERS	Age 18	Age 16	Care Order	Adoption Order	Residence Order	Supervision Order	Parents living together for six months
				DISCHARGED BY			
Care	Yes			Yes	Yes	Yes	
Supervision	Yes		Yes	Yes		Yes	
Order under s 4(1) for Parental Responsibility	Yes			Yes			
Order under s 5(1) Appointment of Guardian	Yes			Yes			
Appointment of Guardian under s 5(2) or 5(3)	Yes			Yes			
Parental Responsibility Agreement	Yes			Yes			
SECTION 8 ORDERS Residence	Only in Exceptional Circumstances	Yes	Yes	Yes	Yes		Yes
Contact	Only in Exceptional Circumstances	Yes	Yes	Yes			
Specific Issue	Only in Exceptional Circumstances	Yes	Yes	Yes			
Prohibited Steps	Only in Exceptional Circumstances	Yes	Yes	Yes			Yes

244

Appendix 3

Table of Secondary Legislation

The Act contains 60 enabling provisions for secondary legislation to be made in the form of regulations and ministerial orders and 18 sections make provision for new rules of court. These were not available at the time of going to press but practitioners may find it useful to refer to the following table for a quick guide to matters on which there is likely to be secondary legislation.

Enabling provision	Form	Content
s 4(2)	Regs	Form and method of recording parental responsibility agreements between unmarried parents
s 5(11)	Rules	Circumstances when High Court may exercise its inherent jurisdiction to appoint a guardian of the estate of any child
s 6(6)	Regs	Method of recording disclaimer by guardian
s 7(2)	Regs	Matters which must be dealt with in welfare reports
s 10(7)	Rules	Additional persons who may apply for s 8 orders
s 11(2)	Rules	Time limits for specified steps in proceedings under Part II and provisions to avoid delay
s 17(4)	Order	Amendment of Part 1, Sched 2
s 23(2)(a)	Regs	Placement of children looked after by local authorities with foster parents

Enabling provision	Form	Content
s 23(2)(f)	Regs	Other arrangements by local authorities for accommodation and maintenance of children being looked after
s 23(5)	Regs	Placement of children in care with parents or those with parental responsibility
s 23(9) & Sched 2, para 17(7)	Regs	Circumstances in which a visitor is to be regarded as independent
s 29(6) & Sched 2, para 23(11)	Rules	Appeals against contribution orders
s 29(6) & Sched 2, para 25	Regs	Recovery of contributions in respect of children being looked after by local authorities
s 25(2)	Regs	Use of secure accommodation
s 25(7)	Regs	Exemption from secure accommodation provisions of specified categories of children
s 26(1)	Regs	Review of cases of children being looked after by local authorities
s 26(5)	Regs	Procedure for considering representations
s 26(6)	Regs	Monitoring of arrangements for complaints procedures
s 30(3)	Regs	Procedure where local authority and education authority functions are concurrent
s 30(4)	Regs	Availability of educational grants for children looked after by local authorities
s 31(9)	Order	Specifying person authorised to apply for care or supervision order under s 26(1)
S 32(2)	Rules	Time limits for specified steps in proceedings under Part IV and provisions to avoid delay
s 34(8)	Regs	Parental contact with children in care

246

Table of Secondary Legislation

Enabling provision	Form	Content
s 35(1), Sched 3, para 11	Regs	Local authority functions under a supervision order
s 36(10), Sched 3, para 20	Regs	Modification of existing education enactments where education supervision order in force
s 38(8)(b)	Rules	Persons who may apply for variation of medical etc direction made in respect of an interim order
s 41(2)	Rules	Appointment of guardians ad litem
s 41(5)	Rules	Representation of child by solicitor appointed under or by virtue of s 35
s 41(6)(i)	Rules	Additional proceedings to which guardian ad litem provisions may apply
s 41(9)	Regs	Establishment of guardian ad litem panels
s 41(10)	Rules	Role of guardian ad litem in court
s 43(12)	Rules	Persons who may apply for variation or discharge of a child assessment order
s 44(5)(c)	Regs	Requirements imposed on person with parental responsibility under an emergency protection order
s 44(9)(b)	Rules	Persons who may apply to vary a medical direction in emergency proceedings
s 48(12)	Rules	Manner and form of warrant to assist applicant for an emergency protection order
s 51(4)	Regs	Certification procedure applying to refuges for children at risk
s 52(1)	Rules	Procedure on application for orders under Part V

Enabling provision	Form	Content
s 52(3)	Regs	Provision for transfer of emergency protection order to another local authority
s 53(1) & Sched 4, para 4	Regs	Conduct of community homes
s 59(2)	Regs	Placement of children with foster parents by voluntary organisations
s 59(3)	Regs	Other arrangements by voluntary organisations for accommodating children
s 59(4)	Regs	Procedure for review of cases and consideration of representations by voluntary organisations
s 60(3)(f)	Regs	Exemption of homes otherwise falling within definition of a voluntary home
s 60(4) & Sched 5, para 7	Regs	Conduct of voluntary homes
s 62(3)	Regs	Circumstances in which local authority must visit child accommodated by a voluntary organisation
s 63(3)(b)	Regs	Exemption of certain children's homes from Part VIII
s 63(11) & Sched 6, Para 1(3)	Regs	Manner of application for registration of a children's home
s 63(12) Sched 7, para 4(5)	Regs	Circumstances in which usual fostering limit may be exceeded in an emergency
s 63(12) Sched 7, para 6(2)	Regs	Complaints procedure relating to exemption from usual fostering limit
Sched 6, para 1(5)	Regs	Requirements to be complied with before registration
Sched 6, para 10	Regs	Conduct of registered children's homes
s 66(5) Sched 8, para 7	Regs	Notification of private fostering arrangements

248

Table of Secondary Legislation

Enabling provision	Form	Content
s 67(2)	Regs	Circumstances in which local authority must visit privately fostered child
s 68(1)	Regs	Disqualifications relating to private foster parents
s 71 Sched 9, para 1(1)(*a*)	Regs	Contents of statement to accompany application for registration of child minder or person providing day care facility
Sched 9, para 2(1)	Regs	Persons disqualified from registration as child minder or provider of day care facilities
s 72(3)	Regs	Requirements to be imposed on child minders
s 72(4)	Regs	Requirements to be imposed on person providing day care facilities
s 80(11)	Order	Exemption of certain children's homes and other premises from state inspection
s 87(6)	Regs	Inspection of independent schools
s 92(6) Sched 11, para 1	Order	Jurisdiction of courts: venue for proceedings
Sched 11, para 2	Order	Jurisdiction of courts: transfer of proceedings
Sched 11, para 3	Order	Jurisdiction of courts: hearings by single justice
Sched 11, para 4	Order	Jurisdiction: consequential, incidental or transitional provisions
s 92(9)	Order	Provision for Principal Registry of Family Division to be treated as a county court for purposes of Act
s 93(1)	Rules	Rules of court governing proceedings under the Act
s 94(10)	Order	Appeals relating to transfer of proceedings

Enabling provision	Form	Content
s 95(2)	Rules	Attendance of child at hearing under Part IV or V
s 96(3)	Order	Admissibility of hearsay evidence in civil proceedings relating to children
s 97(1)	Rules	Provision for magistrates' courts to sit in private in proceedings relating to children
s 99(5)	Order	Necessary and consequential amendments to Legal Aid Act 1988
s 101(1)	Regs	Reciprocal arrangements with Northern Ireland for enforcement of certain orders
s 101(3)	Regs	Reciprocal arrangements with Isle of Man and Channel Islands for enforcement of certain orders
s 101(4)	Regs	Discharge of care orders when child taken to live in Northern Ireland, Isle of Man or Channel Islands
s 101(5)	Regs	Consequential amendments to CYPA 1969, ss 25 and 26
s 102(3)	Rules	Manner and form of search warrant issued under s 102
s 108(8)	Order	Necessary and expedient transitional provisions and savings
s 108(9)	Order	Necessary and expedient amendments and repeals

Appendix 4

Children Act 1989, Schedule 12

SCHEDULE 12 Minor Amendments

The Custody of Children Act 1891 (c. 3)
1. The Custody of Children Act 1891 (which contains miscellaneous obsolete provisions with respect to the custody of children) shall cease to have effect.

The Children and Young Persons Act 1933 (c. 12)
2. In section 1(2)(*a*) of the Children and Young Persons Act 1933 (cruelty to persons under sixteen), after the words 'young person' there shall be inserted ', or the legal guardian of a child or young person,'.
3. Section 40 of that Act shall cease to have effect.

The Education Act 1944 (c. 31)
4. In section 40(1) of the Education Act 1944 (enforcement of school attendance), the words from 'or to imprisonment' to the end shall cease to have effect.

The Marriage Act 1949 (c. 76)
5.—(1) In section 3 of the Marriage Act 1949 (consent required to the marriage of a child by common licence or superintendent registrar's certificate), in subsection (1) for the words 'the Second Schedule to this Act' there shall be substituted 'subsection (1A) of this section'.
(2) After that subsection there shall be inserted—
   '(1A) The consents are—
   (a) subject to paragraphs (*b*) to (*d*) of this subsection, the consent of—
      (i) each parent (if any) of the child who has parental responsibility for him; and
      (ii) each guardian (if any) of the child;
   (b) where a residence order is in force with respect to the child, the consent of the person or persons with whom he lives, or is to live, as a result of the order (in substitution for the consents mentioned in paragraph (*a*) of this subsection);
   (c) where a care order is in force with respect to the child, the consent of the local authority designated in the order (in

251

addition to the consents mentioned in paragraph (*a*) of this subsection);

(d) where neither paragraph (*b*) nor (*c*) of this subsection applies but a residence order was in force with respect to the child immediately before he reached the age of sixteen, the consent of the person or persons with whom he lived, or was to live, as a result of the order (in substitution for the consents mentioned in paragraph (*a*) of this subsection).

(1B) In this section "guardian of a child", "parental responsibility", "residence order" and "care order" have the same meaning as in the Children Act 1989.'

The Births and Deaths Registration Act 1953 (c. 20)

6.—(1) Sections 10 and 10A of the Births and Deaths Registration Act 1953 (registration of father, and re-registration, where parents not married) shall be amended as follows.

(2) In sections 10(1) and 10A(1) for paragraph (*d*) there shall be substituted—

'(d) at the request of the mother or that person on production of—

(i) a copy of a parental responsibility agreement made between them in relation to the child; and

(ii) a declaration in the prescribed form by the person making the request stating that the agreement was made in compliance with section 4 of the Children Act 1989 and has not been brought to an end by an order of a court; or

(e) at the request of the mother or that person on production of—

(i) a certified copy of an order under section 4 of the Children Act 1989 giving that person parental responsibility for the child; and

(ii) a declaration in the prescribed form by the person making the request stating that the order has not been brought to an end by an order of a court; or

(f) at the request of the mother or that person on production of—

(i) a certified copy of an order under paragraph 1 of Schedule 1 to the Children Act 1989 which requires that person to make any financial provision for the child and which is not an order falling within paragraph 4(3) of that Schedule; and

(ii) a declaration in the prescribed form by the person making the request stating that the order has not been discharged by an order of a court; or

(g) at the request of the mother or that person on production of—

(i) a certified copy of any of the orders which are mentioned

252

in subsection (1A) of this section which has been made in relation to the child; and

(ii) a declaration in the prescribed form by the person making the request stating that the order has not been brought to an end or discharged by an order of a court.'

(3) After sections 10(1) and 10A(1) there shall be inserted—

'(1A) The orders are—

(a) an order under section 4 of the Family Law Reform Act 1987 that that person shall have all the parental rights and duties with respect to the child;

(b) an order that that person shall have custody or care and control or legal custody of the child made under section 9 of the Guardianship of Minors Act 1971 at a time when such an order could only be made in favour of a parent;

(c) an order under section 9 or 11B of that Act which requires that person to make any financial provision in relation to the child;

(d) an order under section 4 of the Affiliation Proceedings Act 1957 naming that person as putative father of the child.'

(4) In section 10(2) for the words 'or (d)' there shall be substituted 'to (g)'.

(5) In section 10(3) for the words from '"relevant order"' to the end there shall be substituted '"parental responsibility agreement" has the same meaning as in the Children Act 1989'.

(6) In section 10A(2), in paragraphs (b) and (c) for the words 'paragraph (d)' in both places where they occur there shall be substituted 'any of paragraphs (d) to (g)'.

The Army Act 1955 (c. 18)

7. In section 151 of the Army Act 1955 (deductions from pay for maintenance of wife or child), in subsection (1A)(a) for the words 'in the care of a local authority in England or Wales' there shall be substituted 'being looked after by a local authority in England or Wales (within the meaning of the Children Act 1989)'.

8.—(1) Schedule 5A to that Act (powers of court on trial of civilian) shall be amended as follows.

(2) For paragraphs 7(3) and (4) there shall be substituted—

'(3) While an authorisation under a reception order is in force the order shall (subject to sub-paragraph (4) below) be deemed to be a care order for the purposes of the Children Act 1989, and the authorised authority shall be deemed to be the authority designated in that deemed care order.

(3A) In sub-paragraph (3) above "care order" means a care order which is not an interim care order under section 38 of the Children Act 1989.

(4) The Children Act 1989 shall apply to a reception order which is deemed to be a care order by virtue of sub-paragraph (3) above as if sections 31(8) (designated local authority), 91 (duration of care

order etc.) and 101 (effect of orders as between different jurisdictions) were omitted.'

(3) In sub-paragraph (5)(c) for the words from 'attains' to the end there shall be substituted 'attains 18 years of age'.

(4) In paragraph 8(1) for the words 'Children and Young Persons Act 1969' there shall be substituted 'Children Act 1989'.

The Air Force Act 1955 (c. 19)

9. Section 151 (1A) of the Air Force Act 1955 (deductions from pay for maintenance of wife or child) shall have effect subject to the amendment that is set out in paragraph 7 in relation to section 151(1A) of the Army Act 1955.

10. Schedule 5A to that Act (powers of court on trial of civilian) shall have effect subject to the amendments that are set out in paragraph 8(2) to (4) in relation to Schedule 5A to the Army Act 1955.

The Sexual Offences Act 1956 (c. 69)

11. In section 19(3) of the Sexual Offences Act 1956 (abduction of unmarried girl under eighteen from parent or guardian) for the words 'the lawful care or charge of' there shall be substituted 'parental responsibility for or care of'.

12. In section 20(2) of that Act (abduction of unmarried girl under sixteen from parent or guardian) for the words 'the lawful care or charge of' there shall be substituted 'parental responsibility for or care of'.

13. In section 21(3) of that Act (abduction of defective from parent or guardian) for the words 'the lawful care or charge of' there shall be substituted 'parental responsibility for or care of'.

14. In section 28 of that Act (causing or encouraging prostitution of, intercourse with, or indecent assault on, girl under sixteen) for subsections (3) and (4) there shall be substituted—

'(3) The persons who are to be treated for the purposes of this section as responsible for a girl are (subject to subsection (4) of this section)—

(a) her parents;

(b) any person who is not a parent of hers but who has parental responsibility for her; and

(c) any person who has care of her.

(4) An individual falling within subsection (3)(a) or (b) of this section is not to be treated as responsible for a girl if—

(a) a residence order under the Children Act 1989 is in force with respect to her and he is not named in the order as the person with whom she is to live; or

(b) a care order under that Act is in force with respect to her.'

15. Section 38 of that Act (power of court to divest person of authority over girl or boy in case of incest) shall cease to have effect.

16.—(1) In section 43 of that Act (power to search for and recover woman detained for immoral purposes), in subsection (5) for the words 'the lawful care or charge of' there shall be substituted 'parental responsibility for or care of'.

(2) In subsection (6) of that section, for the words 'section forty of the Children and Young Persons Act 1933' there shall be substituted 'Part V of the Children Act 1989'.

17. After section 46 of that Act there shall be inserted—

'**46A Meaning of "parental responsibility"** In this Act "parental responsibility" has the same meaning as in the Children Act 1989.'

The Naval Discipline Act 1957 (c. 53)

18. Schedule 4A to the Naval Discipline Act 1957 (powers of court on trial of civilian) shall have effect subject to the amendments that are set out in paragraph 8(2) to (4) in relation to Schedule 5A to the Army Act 1955.

The Children and Young Persons Act 1963 (c. 37)

19. Section 3 of the Children and Young Persons Act 1963 (children and young persons beyond control) shall cease to have effect.

The Children and Young Persons Act 1969 (c. 54)

20. In section 5 of the Children and Young Persons Act 1969 (restrictions on criminal proceedings for offences by young persons), in subsection (2), for the words 'section 1 of this Act' there shall be substituted 'Part IV of the Children Act 1989'.

21. After section 7(7) of that Act (alteration in treatment of young offenders, etc) there shall be inserted—

'(7B) An order under subsection (7)(c) of this section shall not require a person to enter into a recognisance—

    (a) for an amount exceeding £1,000; or

    (b) for a period exceeding—

        (i) three years; or

        (ii) where the young person concerned will attain the age of eighteen in a period shorter than three years, that shorter period.

(7C) Section 120 of the Magistrates' Courts Act 1980 shall apply to a recognisance entered into in pursuance of an order under subsection (7)(c) of this section as it applies to a recognisance to keep the peace.'

22. In section 12A of that Act (young offenders) for subsections (1) and (2) there shall be substituted—

'(1) This subsection applies to any supervision order made under section 7(7) of this Act unless it requires the supervised person to comply with directions given by the supervisor under section 12(2) of this Act.'

23. After that section there shall be inserted—

'**12AA Requirement for young offender to live in local authority accommodation**—(1) Where the conditions mentioned in subsection (6) of this section are satisfied, a supervision order may impose a

255

requirement ("a residence requirement") that a child or young person shall live for a specified period in local authority accommodation.

(2) A residence requirement shall designate the local authority who are to receive the child or young person and that authority shall be the authority in whose area the child or young person resides.

(3) The court shall not impose a residence requirement without first consulting the designated authority.

(4) A residence requirement may stipulate that the child or young person shall not live with a named person.

(5) The maximum period which may be specified in a residence requirement is six months.

(6) The conditions are that—

(a) a supervision order has previously been made in respect of the child or young person;

(b) that order imposed—

    (i) a requirement under section 12A(3) of this Act; or

    (ii) a residence requirement;

(c) he is found guilty of an offence which—

    (i) was committed while that order was in force;

    (ii) if it had been committed by a person over the age of twenty-one, would have been punishable with imprisonment; and

    (iii) in the opinion of the court is serious; and

(d) the court is satisfied that the behaviour which constituted the offence was due, to a significant extent, to the circumstances in which he was living,

except that the condition in paragraph (d) of this subsection does not apply where the condition in paragraph (b)(ii) is satisfied.

(7) For the purposes of satisfying itself as mentioned in subsection (6)(d) of this section, the court shall obtain a social inquiry report which makes particular reference to the circumstances in which the child or young person was living.

(8) Subsection (7) of this section does not apply if the court already has before it a social inquiry report which contains sufficient information about the circumstances in which the child or young person was living.

(9) A court shall not include a residence requirement in respect of a child or young person who is not legally represented at the relevant time in that court unless—

(a) he has applied for legal aid for the purposes of the proceedings and the application was refused on the ground that it did not appear that his resources were such that he required assistance; or

(b) he has been informed of his right to apply for legal aid for the purposes of the proceedings and has had the opportunity to do so, but nevertheless refused or failed to apply.

(10) In subsection (9) of this section—

(a) "the relevant time" means the time when the court is considering whether or not to impose the requirement; and

(b) "the proceedings" means—

(i) the whole proceedings; or

(ii) the part of the proceedings relating to the imposition of the requirement.

(11) A supervision order imposing a residence requirement may also impose any of the requirements mentioned in sections 12, 12A, 12B or 12C of this Act.

(12) In this section "social inquiry report" has the same meaning as in section 2 of the Criminal Justice Act 1982.'

24.—(1) In section 15 of that Act (variation and discharge of supervision orders), in subsections (1)(a), (2A), (3)(e) and (4) after the word '12A', in each place where it occurs, there shall be inserted '12AA'.

(2) In subsection (4) of that section for the words '(not being a juvenile court)' there shall be substituted 'other than a juvenile court'.

25.—(1) In section 16 of that Act (provisions supplementary to section 15), in subsection (3) for the words 'either direct' to the end there shall be substituted—

'(i) direct that he be released forthwith; or

(ii) remand him.'

(2) In subsection (4) of that section—

(a) in paragraph (a) for the words 'an interim order made by virtue of' there shall be substituted 'a remand under';

(b) in paragraph (b) for the words 'makes an interim order in respect of' there shall be substituted 'remands', and

(c) for the words 'make an interim order in respect of' there shall be substituted 'remand'.

(3) In subsections (5)(b) and (c) and (6)(a) after the word '12A', in each place where it occurs, there shall be inserted '12AA'.

26. For section 23 of that Act (remand to care of local authorities etc) there shall be substituted—

'23 Remand to local authority accommodation, committal of young persons of unruly character, etc—(1) Where a court—

(a) remands or commits for trial a child charged with homicide or remands a child convicted of homicide; or

(b) remands a young person charged with or convicted of one or more offences or commits him for trial or sentence,

and he is not released on bail, then, unless he is a young person who is certified by the court to be of unruly character, the court shall remand him to local authority accommodation.

(2) A court remanding a person to local authority accommodation shall designate the authority who are to receive him and that authority shall be the authority in whose area it appears to the court that—

(a) he resides; or

(b) the offence or one of the offences was committed.

(3) Where a person is remanded to local authority accommodation,

257

it shall be lawful for any person acting on behalf of the designated authority to detain him.

(4) The court shall not certify a young person as being of unruly character unless—

(a) he cannot safely be remanded to local authority accommodation; and

(b) the conditions prescribed by order made by the Secretary of State under this subsection are satisfied in relation to him.

(5) Where the court certifies that a young person is of unruly character, it shall commit him—

(a) to a remand centre, if it has been notified that such a centre is available for the reception from the court of such persons; and

(b) to a prison, if it has not been so notified.

(6) Where a young person is remanded to local authority accommodation, a court may, on the application of the designated authority, certify him to be of unruly character in accordance with subsection (4) of this section (and on so doing he shall cease to be remanded to local authority accommodation and subsection (5) of this section shall apply).

(7) For the purposes of subsection (6) of this section, "a court" means—

(a) the court which remanded the young person; or

(b) any magistrates' court having jurisdiction in the place where that person is for the time being,

and in this section "court" and "magistrates' court" include a justice.

(8) This section has effect subject to—

(a) section 37 of the Magistrates' Courts Act 1980 (committal to the Crown Court with a view to a sentence of detention in a young offender institution); and

(b) section 128(7) of that Act (remands to the custody of a constable for periods of not more than three days),

but section 128(7) shall have effect in relation to a child or young person as if for the reference to three clear days there were substituted a reference to twenty-four hours.'

27.—(1) In section 32 of that Act (detention of absentees), for subsection (1A) there shall be substituted the following subsections—

'(1A) If a child or young person is absent, without the consent of the responsible person—

(a) from a place of safety to which he has been taken under section 16(3) of this Act; or

(b) from local authority accommodation—

(i) in which he is required to live under section 12AA of this Act; or

(ii) to which he has been remanded under section 23(1) of this Act,

258

he may be arrested by a constable anywhere in the United Kingdom or Channel Islands without a warrant.

(1B) A person so arrested shall be conducted to—

(a) the place of safety;

(b) the local authority accommodation; or

(c) such other place as the responsible person may direct,

at the responsible person's expense.

(1C) In this section "the responsible person" means the person who made the arrangements under section 16(3) of this Act or, as the case may be, the authority designated under section 12AA or 23 of this Act.'

(2) In subsection (2B) of that section for the words 'person referred to in subsection (1A)(a) or (b) (as the case may be) of this section' there shall be substituted 'responsible person'.

28. In section 34(1) of that Act (transitional modifications of Part I for persons of specified ages)—

(a) in paragraph (a), for the words '13(2) or 28(4) or (5)' there shall be substituted 'or 13(2)'; and

(b) in paragraph (e), for the words 'section 23(2) or (3)' there shall be substituted 'section 23(4) to (6)'.

29. In section 70(1) of that Act (interpretation)—

(a) after the definition of 'local authority' there shall be inserted—

'"local authority accommodation" means accommodation provided by or on behalf of a local authority (within the meaning of the Children Act 1989)'; and

(b) in the definition of 'reside' for '12(4) and (5)' there shall be substituted '12B(1) and (2)'.

30. In section 73 of that Act (extent, etc)—

(a) in subsection (4)(a) for '32(1), (3) and (4)' there shall be substituted '32(1) to (1C) and (2A) to (4)'; and

(b) in subsection (6) for '32(1), (1A)' there shall be substituted '32(1) to (1C)'.

The Matrimonial Causes Act 1973 (c. 18)

31. For section 41 of the Matrimonial Causes Act 1973 (restrictions on decrees for dissolution, annulment or separation affecting children) there shall be substituted—

'**41. Restrictions on decrees for dissolution, annulment or separation affecting children**—(1) In any proceedings for a decree of divorce or nullity of marriage, or a decree of judicial separation, the court shall consider—

(a) whether there are any children of the family to whom this section applies; and

(b) where there are any such children, whether (in the light of the arrangements which have been, or are proposed to be, made for their upbringing and welfare) it should exercise any of its powers under the Children Act 1989 with respect to any of them.

259

(2) Where, in any case to which this section applies, it appears to the court that—

(a) the circumstances of the case require it, or are likely to require it, to exercise any of its powers under the Act of 1989 with respect to any such child;

(b) it is not in a position to exercise that power or (as the case may be) those powers without giving further consideration to the case; and

(c) there are exceptional circumstances which make it desirable in the interests of the child that the court should give a direction under this section,

it may direct that the decree of divorce or nullity is not to be made absolute, or that the decree of judicial separation is not to be granted, until the court orders otherwise.

(3) This section applies to—

(a) any child of the family who has not reached the age of sixteen at the date when the court considers the case in accordance with the requirements of this section; and

(b) any child of the family who has reached that age at that date and in relation to whom the court directs that this section shall apply.'

32. In section 42 of that Act, subsection (3) (declaration by court that party to marriage unfit to have custody of children of family) shall cease to have effect.

33. In section 52(1) of that Act (interpretation), in the definition of 'child of the family', for the words 'has been boarded-out with those parties' there shall be substituted 'is placed with those parties as foster parents'.

The National Health Service Act 1977 (c. 49)

34. In Schedule 8 to the National Health Service Act 1977 (functions of local social services authorities), the following sub-paragraph shall be added at the end of paragraph 2—

'(4A) This paragraph does not apply in relation to persons under the age of 18.'

The Child Care Act 1980 (c. 5)

35. Until the repeal of the Child Care Act 1980 by this Act takes effect, the definition of 'parent' in section 87 of that Act shall have effect as if it applied only in relation to Part I and sections 13, 24, 64 and 65 of that Act (provisions excluded by section 2(1)(f) of the Family Law Reform Act 1987 from the application of the general rule in that Act governing the meaning of references to relationships between persons).

The Education Act 1981 (c. 60)

36. The following section shall be inserted in the Education Act 1981, after section 3—

'**3A Provision outside England and Wales for certain children**—(1) A local authority may make such arrangements as they think fit to enable any child in respect of whom they maintain a statement under section 7 to attend an establishment outside England and Wales which specialises in providing for children with special needs.

(2) In subsection (1) above 'children with special needs' means children who have particular needs which would be special educational needs if those children were in England and Wales.

(3) Where an authority make arrangements under this section with respect to a child, those arrangements may, in particular, include contributing to or paying—

(a) fees charged by the establishment;

(b) expenses reasonably incurred in maintaining him while he is at the establishment or travelling to or from it;

(c) those travelling expenses;

(d) expenses reasonably incurred by any person accompanying him while he is travelling or staying at the establishment.

(4) This section is not to be taken as in any way limiting any other powers of a local education authority.'.

The Child Abduction Act 1984 (c. 37)

37.—(1) Section 1 of the Child Abduction Act 1984 (offence of abduction by parent, etc.) shall be amended as follows.

(2) For subsections (2) to (4) there shall be substituted—

'(2) A person is connected with a child for the purposes of this section if—

(a) he is a parent of the child; or

(b) in the case of a child whose parents were not married to each other at the time of his birth, there are reasonable grounds for believing that he is the father of the child; or

(c) he is a guardian of the child; or

(d) he is a person in whose favour a residence order is in force with respect to the child; or

(e) he has custody of the child.

(3) In this section "the appropriate consent", in relation to a child, means—

(a) the consent of each of the following—

(i) the child's mother;

(ii) the child's father, if he has parental responsibility for him;

(iii) any guardian of the child;

(iv) any person in whose favour a residence order is in force with respect to the child;

(v) any person who has custody of the child; or

(b) the leave of the court granted under or by virtue of any provision of Part II of the Children Act 1989; or

(c) if any person has custody of the child, the leave of the court which awarded custody to him.

(4) A person does not commit an offence under this section by

taking or sending a child out of the United Kingdom without obtaining the appropriate consent if—

(a) he is a person in whose favour there is a residence order in force with respect to the child, and

(b) he takes or sends him out of the United Kingdom for a period of less than one month.

(4A) Subsection (4) above does not apply if the person taking or sending the child out of the United Kingdom does so in breach of an order under Part II of the Children Act 1989.'

(3) In subsection (5) for the words from 'but' to the end there shall be substituted—

'(5A) Subsection (5)(c) above does not apply if—

(a) the person who refused to consent is a person—

(i) in whose favour there is a residence order in force with respect to the child; or

(ii) who has custody of the child; or

(b) the person taking or sending the child out of the United Kingdom is, by so acting, in breach of an order made by a court in the United Kingdom.'

(4) For subsection (7) there shall be substituted—

'(7) For the purposes of this section—

(a) "guardian of a child", "residence order" and "parental responsibility" have the same meaning as in the Children Act 1989; and

(b) a person shall be treated as having custody of a child if there is in force an order of a court in the United Kingdom awarding him (whether solely or jointly with another person) custody, legal custody or care and control of the child.'

(5) In subsection (8) for the words from 'or voluntary organisation' to 'custodianship proceedings or' there shall be substituted 'detained in a place of safety, remanded to a local authority accommodation or the subject of'.

38.—(1) In section 2 of that Act (offence of abduction of child by other persons), in subsection (1) for the words from 'Subject' to 'above' there shall be substituted 'Subject to subsection (3) below, a person, other than one mentioned in subsection (2) below'.

(2) For subsection (2) of that section there shall be substituted—

'(2) The persons are—

(a) where the father and mother of the child in question were married to each other at the time of his birth, the child's father and mother;

(b) where the father and mother of the child in question were not married to each other at the time of his birth, the child's mother; and

(c) any other person mentioned in section 1(2)(c) to (e) above.

(3) In proceedings against any person for an offence under this section, it shall be a defence for that person to prove—

262

(a) where the father and mother of the child in question were not married to each other at the time of his birth—
    (i) that he is the child's father; or
    (ii) that, at the time of the alleged offence, he believed, on reasonable grounds, that he was the child's father; or

(b) that, at the time of the alleged offence, he believed that the child had attained the age of sixteen.'

39. At the end of section 3 of that Act (construction of references to taking, sending and detaining) there shall be added 'and

(d) references to a child's parents and to a child whose parents were (or were not) married to each other at the time of his birth shall be construed in accordance with section 1 of the Family Law Reform Act 1987 (which extends their meaning).'

40.—(1) The Schedule to that Act (modifications of section 1 for children in certain cases) shall be amended as follows.

(2) In paragraph 1(1) for the words 'or voluntary organisation' there shall be substituted 'within the meaning of the Children Act 1989'.

(3) for paragraph 2(1) there shall be substituted—

'(1) This paragraph applies in the case of a child who is—

(a) detained in a place of safety under section 16(3) of the Children and Young Persons Act 1969; or

(b) remanded to local authority accommodation under section 23 of that Act.'

(4) In paragraph 3(1)—

(a) in paragraph (a) for the words 'section 14 of the Children Act 1975' there shall be substituted 'section 18 of the Adoption Act 1976'; and

(b) in paragraph (d) for the words 'section 25 of the Children Act 1975 or section 53 of the Adoption Act 1958' there shall be substituted 'section 55 of the Adoption Act 1976'.

(5) In paragraph 3(2)(a)—

(a) in sub-paragraph (i), for the words from 'order or', to 'Children Act 1975' there shall be substituted 'section 18 order or, if the section 18 order has been varied under section 21 of that Act so as to give parental responsibility to another agency', and

(b) in sub-paragraph (ii), for the words '(c) or (e)' there shall be substituted 'or (c)'.

(6) At the end of paragraph 3 there shall be added—

'(3) Sub-paragraph (2) above shall be construed as if the references to the court included, in any case where the court is a magistrates' court, a reference to any magistrates' court acting for the same area as that court'.

(7) For paragraph 5 there shall be substituted—

'5. In this Schedule—

(a) "adoption agency" and "adoption order" have the same meaning as in the Adoption Act 1976; and

(b) "area", in relation to a magistrates' court, means the petty

263

sessions area (within the meaning of the Justices of the Peace Act 1979) for which the court is appointed.'

The Foster Children (Scotland) Act 1984 (c. 56)

41. In section 1 of the Foster Children (Scotland) Act 1984 (definition of foster child)—

(a) for the words 'he is— (a)' there shall be substituted '(a) he is'; and

(b) the words 'for a period of more than 6 days' and the words from 'The period' to the end shall cease to have effect.

42. In section 2(2) of that Act (exceptions to section 1), for paragraph (f) there shall be substituted—

'(f) if he has been in that person's care for a period of less than 28 days and that person does not intend to undertake his care for any longer period.'

43. In section 7(1) of that Act (persons disqualified from keeping foster children)—

(a) the word 'or' at the end of paragraph (e) shall be omitted; and

(b) after paragraph (f) there shall be inserted 'or

(g) he is disqualified from fostering a child privately (within the meaning of the Children Act 1989) by regulations made under section 68 of that Act,'.

The Disabled Persons (Services, Consultation and Representation) Act 1986 (c. 33)

44. In section 2(5) of the Disabled Persons (Services, Consultation and Representation) Act 1986 (circumstances in which authorised representative has right to visit etc. disabled person), after paragraph (d) there shall be inserted—

'(dd) in accommodation provided by any educational establishment'.

The Legal Aid Act 1988 (c. 34)

45. In paragraph 2 of Part I of Schedule 2 to the Legal Aid Act 1988 (proceedings in magistrates' courts to which the civil legal aid provisions of Part IV of the Act apply), the following sub-paragraph shall be added at the end—

'(g) proceedings under the Children Act 1989'.

Appendix 5

Children Act 1989, Schedule 13

SCHEDULE 13 CONSEQUENTIAL AMENDMENTS

The Wills Act 1837 (c. 26)

1. In section 1 of the Wills Act 1837 (interpretation), in the definition of 'will', for the words 'and also to a disposition by will and testament or devise of the custody and tuition of any child' there shall be substituted 'and also to an appointment by will of a guardian of a child'.

The Children and Young Persons Act 1933 (c. 12)

2. In section 1(1) of the Children and Young Persons Act 1933 (cruelty to persons under sixteen) for the words 'has the custody, charge or care of' there shall be substituted 'has responsibility for'.

3. In the following sections of that Act—

(a) 3(1) (allowing persons under sixteen to be in brothels);

(b) 4(1) and (2) (causing or allowing persons under sixteen to be used for begging);

(c) 11 (exposing children under twelve to risk of burning); and

(d) 25(1) (restrictions on persons under eighteen going abroad for the purpose of performing for profit),

for the words 'the custody, charge or care of' there shall, in each case, be substituted 'responsibility for'.

4. In section 10(1A) of that Act (vagrants preventing children from receiving education), for the words from 'to bring the child' to the end there shall be substituted 'to make an application in respect of the child or young person for an education supervision order under section 36 of the Children Act 1989'.

5. For section 17 of that Act (interpretation of Part I) there shall be substituted the following section—

'**17. Interpretation of Part I**—(1) For the purposes of this Part of this Act, the following shall be presumed to have responsibility for a child or young person—

(a) any person who—

(i) has parental responsibility for him (within the meaning of the Children Act 1989); or

(ii) is otherwise legally liable to maintain him; and

265

(b) any person who has care of him.

(2) A person who is presumed to be responsible for a child or young person by virtue of subsection (1)(a) shall not be taken to have ceased to be responsible for him by reason only that he does not have care of him.'

6.—(1) In section 34 of that Act (attendance at court of parent of child or young person charged with an offence etc.), in subsection (1) after the word 'offence' there shall be inserted 'is the subject of an application for a care or supervision order under Part IV of the Children Act 1989'.

(2) In subsection (7) of that section after the words 'Children and Young Persons Act 1969' there shall be inserted 'or Part IV of the Children Act 1989'.

(3) After subsection (7) of that section there shall be inserted—

'(7A) If it appears that at the time of his arrest the child or young person is being provided with accommodation by or on behalf of a local authority under section 20 of the Children Act 1989, the local authority shall also be informed as described in subsection (3) above as soon as it is reasonably practicable to do so.'

7. In section 107(1) of that Act (interpretation)—

(a) in the definition of 'guardian', for the words 'charge of or control over' there shall be substituted 'care of';

(b) for the definition of legal guardian there shall be substituted—

'"legal guardian", in relation to a child or young person, means a guardian of a child as defined in the Children Act 1989'.

The Education Act 1944 (c. 31)

8.—(1) Section 40 of the Education Act 1944 (enforcement of school attendance) shall be amended as follows.

(2) For subsection (2) there shall be substituted—

'(2) Proceedings for such offences shall not be instituted except by a local education authority.

(2A) Before instituting such proceedings the local education authority shall consider whether it would be appropriate, instead of or as well as instituting the proceedings, to apply for an education supervision order with respect to the child.'

(3) For subsections (3) and (4) there shall be substituted—

'(3) The court—

(a) by which a person is convicted of an offence against section 37 of this Act; or

(b) before which a person is charged with an offence under section 39 of this Act,'

may direct the local education authority instituting the proceedings to apply for an education supervision order with respect to the child unless the authority, having consulted the appropriate local authority, decide that the child's welfare will be satisfactorily safeguarded even though no education supervision order is made.

(3A) Where, following such a direction, a local education authority decide not to apply for an education supervision order they shall inform the court of the reasons for their decision.

(3B) Unless the court has directed otherwise, the information required under subsection (3A) shall be given to the court before the end of the period of eight weeks beginning with the date on which the direction was given.

(4) Where—

(a) a local education authority apply for an education supervision order with respect to a child who is the subject of a school attendance order; and

(b) the court decides that section 36(3) of the Children Act 1989 prevents it from making the order;

the court may direct that the school attendance order shall cease to be in force.'

(4) After subsection (4) there shall be inserted—

'(5) In this section—

"appropriate local authority" has the same meaning as in section 36(9) of the Children Act 1989; and

"education supervision order" means an education supervision order under that Act.'

9. In section 71 of that Act (complaints with respect to independent schools), the following paragraph shall be added after paragraph (d), in subsection (1)—

'(e) there has been a failure, in relation to a child provided with accommodation by the school, to comply with the duty imposed by section 87 of the Children Act 1989 (welfare of children accommodated in independent schools);'.

10. After section 114(1C) of that Act (interpretation) there shall be inserted the following subsections—

'(1D) In this Act, unless the context otherwise requires, "parent", in relation to a child or young person, includes any person—

(a) who is not a parent of his but who has parental responsibility for him, or

(b) who has care of him,

except for the purposes of the enactments mentioned in subsection (1E) of this section, where it only includes such a person if he is an individual.

(1E) The enactments are—

(a) sections 5(4), 15(2) and (6), 31 and 65(1) of, and paragraph 7(6) of Schedule 2 to, the Education (No 2) Act 1986; and

(b) sections 53(8), 54(2), 58(5)(k), 60 and 61 of the Education Reform Act 1988.

(1F) For the purposes of subsection (1D) of this section—

(a) "parental responsibility" has the same meaning as in the Children Act 1989; and

(b) in determining whether an individual has care of a child or young person any absence of the child or young person at a hospital or boarding school and any other temporary absence shall be disregarded.'

The National Assistance Act 1948 (c. 29)

11.—(1) In section 21(1)(a) of the National Assistance Act 1948 (persons for whom local authority is to provide residential accommodation) after the word 'persons' there shall be inserted 'aged eighteen or over'.

(2) In section 29(1) of that Act (welfare arrangements for blind, deaf, dumb and crippled persons) after the words 'that is to say persons' and after the words 'and other persons' there shall, in each case, be inserted 'aged eighteen or over'.

The Reserve and Auxiliary Forces (Protection of Civil Interests) Act 1951 (c. 65)

12. For section 2(1)(d) of the Reserve and Auxiliary Forces (Protection of Civil Interests) Act 1951 (cases in which leave of an appropriate court is required before enforcing certain orders for the payment of money), there shall be substituted—

'(d) an order for alimony, maintenance or other payment made under sections 21 to 33 of the Matrimonial Causes Act 1973 or made, or having effect as if made, under Schedule 1 to the Children Act 1989'.

The Mines and Quarries Act 1954 (c. 70)

13. In section 182(1) of the Mines and Quarries Act 1954 (interpretation), in the definition of 'parent', for the words from 'or guardian' to first 'young person' there shall be substituted 'of a young person or any person who is not a parent of his but who has parental responsibility for him (within the meaning of the Children Act 1989)'.

The Administration of Justice Act 1960 (c. 65)

14. In section 12 of the Administration of Justice Act 1960 (publication of information relating to proceedings in private), in subsection (1) for paragraph (a) there shall be substituted—

'(a) where the proceedings—

(i) relate to the exercise of the inherent jurisdiction of the High Court with respect to minors;
(ii) are brought under the Children Act 1989; or
(iii) otherwise relate wholly or mainly to the maintenance or upbringing of a minor;'.

The Factories Act 1961 (c. 34)

15. In section 176(1) of the Factories Act 1961 (interpretation), in the definition of 'parent', for the words from 'or guardian' to first 'young person' there shall be substituted 'of a child or young person or any person who is not a parent of his but who has parental responsibility for him (within the meaning of the Children Act 1989)'.

The Criminal Justice Act 1967 (c. 80)
16. In section 67(1A)(c) of the Criminal Justice Act 1967 (computation of sentences of imprisonment passed in England and Wales) for the words 'in the care of a local authority' there shall be substituted 'remanded to local authority accommodation'.

The Health Services and Public Health Act 1968 (c. 46)
17.—(1) In section 64(3)(a) of the Health Services and Public Health Act 1968 (meaning of 'relevant enactments' in relation to power of Minister of Health or Secretary of State to provide financial assistance), for sub-paragraph (xix) inserted by paragraph 19 of Schedule 5 to the Child Care Act 1980 there shall be substituted—
    '(xx) the Children Act 1989.'
(2) In section 65(3)(b) of that Act (meaning of 'relevant enactments' in relation to power of local authority to provide financial and other assistance), for sub-paragraph (xx) inserted by paragraph 20 of Schedule 5 to the Child Care Act 1980 there shall be substituted—
    '(xxi) the Children Act 1989.'

The Social Work (Scotland) Act 1968 (c. 49)
18. In section 2(2) of the Social Work (Scotland) Act 1968 (matters referred to social work committee) after paragraph (j) there shall be inserted—
    '(k) section 19 and Part X of that Children Act 1989,'.
19. In section 5(2)(c) of that Act (power of Secretary of State to make regulations) for the words 'and (j)' there shall be substituted 'to (k)'.
20. In section 21(3) of that Act (mode of provision of accommodation and maintenance) for the words 'section 21 of the Child Care Act 1980' there shall be substituted 'section 23 of the Children Act 1989'.
21. In section 74(6) of that Act (parent of child in residential establishment moving to England or Wales) for the words from 'Children and Young Persons Act 1969' to the end there shall be substituted 'Children Act 1989, but as if section 31(8) were omitted'.
22. In section 75(2) of that Act (parent of child subject to care order etc moving to Scotland), for the words 'Children and Young Persons Act 1969' there shall be substituted 'Children Act 1989'.
23. In section 86(3) of that Act (meaning of ordinary residence for purpose of adjustments between authority providing accommodation and authority of area of residence), the words 'the Child Care Act 1980 or' shall be omitted and after the words 'education authority' there shall be inserted 'or placed with local authority foster parents under the Children Act 1989'.

The Civil Evidence Act 1968 (c. 64)
24. In section 12(5)(b) of the Civil Evidence Act 1968 (findings of paternity etc as evidence in civil proceedings—meaning of 'relevant proceedings') for sub-paragraph (iv) there shall be substituted—
    '(iv) paragraph 23 of Schedule 2 to the Children Act 1989.'

The Administration of Justice Act 1970 (c. 31)
25. In Schedule 8 to the Administration of Justice Act 1970 (maintenance orders for purposes of Maintenance Orders Act 1958 and the 1970 Act), in paragraph 6 for the words 'section 47 or 51 of the Child Care Act 1980' there shall be substituted 'paragraph 23 of Schedule 2 to the Children Act 1989'.

The Local Authority Social Services Act 1970 (c. 42)
26.—(1) In Schedule 1 to the Local Authority Social Services Act 1970 (enactments conferring functions assigned to social service committee)—
   (a) in the entry relating to the Mental Health Act 1959, for the words 'sections 8 and 9' there shall be substituted 'section 8'; and
   (b) in the entry relating to the Children and Young Persons Act 1969, for the words 'sections 1, 2 and 9' there shall be substituted 'section 9'.
(2) At the end of that Schedule there shall be added—

'Children Act 1989.	Welfare reports.
The whole Act, in so far as it confers functions on a local authority within the meaning of that Act.	Consent to application for residence order in respect of child in care.
	Family assistance orders.
	Functions under Part III of the Act (local authority support for children and families).
	Care and supervision.
	Protection of children.
	Functions in relation to community homes, voluntary homes and voluntary organisations, registered children's homes, private arrangements for fostering children, child minding and day care for young children.
	Inspection of children's homes on behalf of Secretary of State.
	Research and returns of information.
	Functions in relation to children accommodated by health authorities and local education authorities or in residential care, nursing or mental nursing homes or in independent schools.'

The Chronically Sick and Disabled Persons Act 1970 (c. 44)
27. After section 28 of the Chronically Sick and Disabled Persons Act 1970 there shall be inserted—
   '28A Application of Act to authorities having functions under the Children Act 1989 This Act applies with respect to disabled children

in relation to whom a local authority have functions under Part III of the Children Act 1989 as it applies in relation to persons to whom section 29 of the National Assistance Act 1948 applies.'

The Courts Act 1971 (c. 23)

28. In Part I of Schedule 9 to the Courts Act 1971 (substitution of references to Crown Court), in the entry relating to the Children and Young Persons Act 1969, for the words 'Sections 2(12), 3(8), 16(8), 21(4)(5)' there shall be substituted 'Section 16(8).'.

The Attachment of Earnings Act 1971 (c. 32)

29. In Schedule 1 to the Attachment of Earnings Act 1971 (maintenance orders to which that Act applies), in paragraph 7, for the words 'section 47 or 51 of the Child Care Act 1980' there shall be substituted 'paragraph 23 of Schedule 2 to the Children Act 1989'.

The Tribunals and Inquiries Act 1971 (c. 62)

30. In Schedule 1 to the Tribunals and Inquiries Act 1971 (tribunals under direct supervision of the Council on Tribunals) for paragraph 4 there shall be substituted—

'Registration of voluntary homes and children's homes under the Children Act 1989.   4. Registered Homes Tribunals constituted under Part III of the Registered Homes Act 1984.'

The Local Government Act 1972 (c. 70)

31.—(1) In section 102(1) of the Local Government Act 1972 (appointment of committees) for the words 'section 31 of the Child Care Act 1980' there shall be substituted 'section 53 of the Children Act 1989'.

(2) In Schedule 12A to that Act (access to information: exempt information), in Part III (interpretation), in paragraph 1(1)(b) for the words 'section 20 of the Children and Young Persons Act 1969' there shall be substituted 'section 31 of the Children Act 1989'.

The Employment of Children Act 1973 (c. 24)

32.—(1) In section 2 of the Employment of Children Act 1973 (supervision by education authorities), in subsection (2)(a) for the words 'guardian or a person who has actual custody of' there shall be substituted 'any person responsible for'.

(2) After that subsection there shall be inserted—

'(2A) For the purposes of subsection (2)(a) above a person is responsible for a child—

(a) in England and Wales, if he has parental responsibility for the child or care of him; and

(b) in Scotland, if he is his guardian or has actual custody of him.'.

The Domicile and Matrimonial Proceedings Act 1973 (c. 45)

33.—(1) In Schedule 1 to the Domicile and Matrimonial Proceedings Act 1973 (proceedings in divorce etc stayed by reference to proceedings in other jurisdiction), paragraph 11(1) shall be amended as follows—

271

(a) at the end of the definition of 'lump sum' there shall be added 'or an order made in equivalent circumstances under Schedule 1 to the Children Act 1989 and of a kind mentioned in paragraph 1(2)(c) of that Schedule';

(b) in the definition of 'relevant order', at the end of paragraph (b), there shall be added 'or an order made in equivalent circumstances under Schedule 1 to the Children Act 1989 and of a kind mentioned in paragraph 1(2)(a) or (b) of that Schedule';

(c) in paragraph (c) of that definition, after the word 'children)' there shall be inserted 'or a section 8 order under the Children Act 1989'; and

(d) in paragraph (d) of that definition for the words 'the custody, care or control' there shall be substituted 'care'.

(2) In paragraph 11(3) of that Schedule—

(a) the word 'four' shall be omitted; and

(b) for the words 'the custody of a child and the education of a child' there shall be substituted 'or any provision which could be made by a section 8 order under the Children Act 1989'.

The Powers of Criminal Courts Act 1973 (c. 62)

34. In Schedule 3 to the Powers of Criminal Courts Act 1973 (the probation and after-care service and its functions), in paragraph 3(2A) after paragraph (b) there shall be inserted—

'and

(c) directions given under paragraph 2 or 3 of Schedule 3 to the Children Act 1989'.

The Rehabilitation of Offenders Act 1974 (c. 53)

35.—(1) Section 7(2) of the Rehabilitation of Offenders Act 1974 (limitations on rehabilitation under the Act) shall be amended as follows.

(2) For paragraph (c) there shall be substituted—

'(c) in any proceedings relating to adoption, the marriage of any minor, the exercise of the inherent jurisdiction of the High Court with respect to minors or the provision by any person of accommodation, care or schooling for minors;

(cc) in any proceedings brought under the Children Act 1989;'

(3) For paragraph (d) there shall be substituted—

'(d) in any proceedings relating to the variation or discharge of a supervision order under the Children and Young Persons Act 1969, or on appeal from any such proceedings'.

The Domestic Proceedings and Magistrates' Courts Act 1978 (c. 22)

36. For section 8 of the Domestic Proceedings and Magistrates' Courts Act 1978 (orders for the custody of children) there shall be substituted—

'8 Restrictions on making of orders under this Act: welfare of children Where an application is made by a party to a marriage for an order under section 2, 6 or 7 of this Act, then, if there is a child of the family who is under the age of eighteen, the court shall not dismiss or make a final order on the application until it has decided whether to exercise any of its powers under the Children Act 1989 with respect to the child.'

37. In section 19(3A)(b) (interim orders) for the words 'subsections (2) and' there shall be substituted 'subsection'.

38. For section 20(12) of that Act (variation and revocation of orders for periodical payments) there shall be substituted—

'(12) An application under this section may be made—

(a) where it is for the variation or revocation of an order under section 2, 6, 7 or 19 of this Act for periodical payments, by either party to the marriage in question; and

(b) where it is for the variation of an order under section 2(1)(c), 6, or 7 of this Act for periodical payments to or in respect of a child, also by the child himself, if he has attained the age of sixteen.'

39.—(1) For section 20A of that Act (revival of orders for periodical payments) there shall be substituted—

'**20A Revival of orders for periodical payments**—(1) Where an order made by a magistrates' court under this Part of this Act for the making of periodical payments to or in respect of a child (other than an interim maintenance order) ceases to have effect—

(a) on the date on which the child attains the age of sixteen, or

(b) at any time after that date but before or on the date on which he attains the age of eighteen,

the child may apply to the court which made the order for an order for its revival.

(2) If on such an application it appears to the court that—

(a) the child is, will be or (if an order were made under this subsection) would be receiving instruction at an educational establishment or undergoing training for a trade, profession or vocation, whether or not while in gainful employment, or

(b) there are special circumstances which justify the making of an order under this subsection,

the court shall have power by order to revive the order from such date as the court may specify, not being earlier than the date of the making of the application.

(3) Any order revived under this section may be varied or revoked under section 20 in the same way as it could have been varied or revoked had it continued in being.'

40. In section 23(1) of that Act (supplementary provisions with respect to the variation and revocation of orders) for the words '14(3), 20 or 21' there shall be substituted '20' and for the words 'section 20 of this Act' there shall be substituted 'that section'.

41.—(1) in section 25 of that Act (effect on certain orders of parties living together), in subsection (1)(a) for the words '6 or 11(2)' there shall be substituted 'or 6'.

(2) In subsection (2) of that section—

(a) in paragraph (a) for the words '6 or 11(2)' there shall be substituted 'or 6'; and

(b) after paragraph (a) there shall be inserted 'or'.

42. In section 29(5) of that Act (appeals) for the words 'sections 14(3), 20 and 21' there shall be substituted 'section 20'.

43. In section 88(1) of that Act (interpretation)—

(a) in the definition of 'child', for the words from 'an illegitimate' to the end there shall be substituted 'a child whose father and mother were not married to each other at the time of his birth'; and

(b) in the definition of 'child of the family', for the words 'being boarded-out with those parties' there shall be substituted 'placed with those parties as foster parents'.

The Magistrates' Courts Act 1980 (c. 43)

44.—(1) In section 59(2) of the Magistrates' Courts Act 1980 (periodical payments through justices' clerk) for the words 'the Guardianship of Minors Acts 1971 and 1973' there shall be substituted '(or having effect as if made under) Schedule 1 to the Children Act 1989'.

(2) For section 62(5) of that Act (payments to children) there shall be substituted—

'(5) In this section references to the person with whom a child has his home—

(a) in the case of any child who is being looked after by a local authority (within the meaning of section 22 of the Children Act 1989), are references to that local authority; and

(b) in any other case, are references to the person who, disregarding any absence of the child at a hospital or boarding school and any other temporary absence, has care of the child.'.

The Supreme Court Act 1981 (c. 54)

45.—(1) In section 18 of the Supreme Court Act 1981 (restrictions on appeals to Court of Appeal)—

(a) in subsection (1)(h)(i), for the word 'custody' there shall be substituted 'residence'; and

(b) in subsection (1)(h)(ii) for the words 'access to', in both places, there shall be substituted 'contact with'.

(2) In section 41 of that Act (wards of court), the following subsection shall be inserted after subsection (2)—

'(2A) subsection (2) does not apply with respect to a child who is the subject of a care order (as defined by section 105 of the Children Act 1989).'

(3) In Schedule 1 to that Act (distribution of business in High Court), for paragraph 3(b)(ii) there shall be substituted—

'(ii) the exercise of the inherent jurisdiction of the High Court with respect to minors, the maintenance of minors and any proceedings under the Children Act 1989, except proceedings solely for the appointment of a guardian of a minor's estate;'.

The Armed Forces Act 1981 (c. 55)

46. In section 14 of the Armed Forces Act 1981 (temporary removal to, and detention in, place of safety abroad or in the United Kingdom of service children in need of care and control), in subsection (9A) for the words 'the Children and Young Persons Act 1933, the Children and Young Persons Act 1969' there shall be substituted 'the Children Act 1989'.

The Civil Jurisdiction and Judgments Act 1982 (c. 27)

47. In paragraph 5(a) of Schedule 5 to the Civil Jurisdiction and Judgments Act 1982 (maintenance and similar payments excluded from Schedule 4 to that Act) for the words 'section 47 or 51 of the Child Care Act 1980' there shall be substituted 'paragraph 23 of Schedule 2 to the Children Act 1989'.

The Mental Health Act 1983 (c. 20)

48.—(1) For section 27 of the Mental Health Act 1983 (children and young persons in care of local authority) there shall be substituted the following section—

'**27 Children and young persons in care** Where—

(a) a patient who is a child or young person is in the care of a local authority by virtue of a care order within the meaning of the Children Act 1989; or

(b) the rights and powers of a parent of a patient who is a child or young person are vested in a local authority by virtue of section 16 of the Social Work (Scotland) Act 1968,

the authority shall be deemed to be the nearest relative of the patient in preference to any person except the patient's husband or wife (if any).'

(2) Section 28 of that Act (nearest relative of minor under guardianship, etc) is amended as mentioned in sub-paragraphs (3) and (4).

(3) For subsection (1) there shall be substituted—

'(1) Where—

(a) a guardian has been appointed for a person who has not attained the age of eighteen years; or

(b) a residence order (as defined by section 8 of the Children Act 1989) is in force with respect to such a person,

the guardian (or guardians, where there is more than one) or the person named in the residence order shall, to the exclusion of any other person, be deemed to be his nearest relative.'

(4) For subsection (3) there shall be substituted—

'(3) In this section "guardian" does not include a guardian under this Part of this Act.'

(5) In section 131(2) of that Act (informal admission of patients aged sixteen or over) for the words from 'notwithstanding' to the end there shall be substituted 'even though there are one or more persons who have parental responsibility for him (within the meaning of the Children Act 1989)'.

275

The Registered Homes Act 1984 (c. 23)

49.—(1) In section 1(5) of the Registered Homes Act 1984 (requirement of registration) for paragraphs (d) and (e) there shall be substituted—

'(d) any community home, voluntary home or children's home within the meaning of the Children Act 1989.'

(2) In section 39 of that Act (preliminary) for paragraphs (a) and (b) there shall be substituted—

'(a) the Children Act 1989.'

The Mental Health (Scotland) Act 1984 (c. 36)

50. For section 54 of the Mental Health (Scotland) Act 1984 (children and young persons in care of local authority) there shall be substituted the following section—

'**54 Children and young persons in care of local authority** Where—

(a) the rights and powers of a parent of a patient who is a child or young person are vested in a local authority by virtue of section 16 of the Social Work (Scotland) Act 1968; or

(b) a patient who is a child or young person is in the care of a local authority by virtue of a care order made under the Children Act 1989,

the authority shall be deemed to be the nearest relative of the patient in preference to any person except the patient's husband or wife (if any).'

The Matrimonial and Family Proceedings Act 1984 (c. 42)

51. In section 38(2)(b) of the Matrimonial and Family Proceedings Act 1984 (transfer of family proceedings from High Court to county court) after the words 'a ward of court' there shall be inserted 'or any other proceedings which relate to the exercise of the inherent jurisdiction of the High Court with respect to minors'.

The Police and Criminal Evidence Act 1984 (c. 60)

52. In section 37(14) of the Police and Criminal Evidence Act 1984 (duties of custody officer before charge) after the words 'Children and Young Persons Act 1969' there shall be inserted 'or in Part IV of the Children Act 1989'.

53.—(1) In section 38 of that Act (duties of custody officer after charge), in subsection (6) for the words from 'make arrangements' to the end there shall be substituted 'secure that the arrested juvenile is moved to local authority accommodation'.

(2) After that subsection there shall be inserted—

'(6A) In this section "local authority accommodation" means accommodation provided by or on behalf of a local authority (within the meaning of the Children Act 1989).

(6B) Where an arrested juvenile is moved to local authority accommodation under subsection (6) above, it shall be lawful for any person acting on behalf of the authority to detain him.'.

(3) In subsection (8) of that section for the words 'Children and Young Persons Act 1969' there shall be substituted 'Children Act 1989'.

54. In section 39(4) of that Act (responsibilities in relation to persons detained) for the words 'transferred to the care of a local authority in pursuance of arrangements made' there shall be substituted 'moved to local authority accommodation'.

55. In Schedule 2 to that Act (preserved powers of arrest) in the entry relating to the Children and Young Persons Act 1969 for the words 'Sections 28(2) and' there shall be substituted 'Section'.

The Surrogacy Arrangements Act 1985 (c. 49)

56. In section 1(2)(b) of the Surrogacy Arrangements Act 1985 (meaning of 'surrogate mother', etc) for the words 'the parental rights being exercised' there shall be substituted 'parental responsibility being met'.

The Child Abduction and Custody Act 1985 (c. 60)

57.—(1) In sections 9(a) and 20(2)(a) of the Child Abduction and Custody Act 1985 (orders with respect to which court's powers suspended), for the words 'any other order under section 1(2) of the Children and Young Persons Act 1969' there shall be substituted 'a supervision order under section 31 of the Children Act 1989'.

(2) At the end of section 27 of that Act (interpretation), there shall be added—

'(4) In this Act a decision relating to rights of access in England and Wales means a decision as to the contact which a child may, or may not, have with any person.'

(3) In Part I of Schedule 3 to that Act (orders in England and Wales which are custody orders for the purposes of the Act), for paragraph 1 there shall be substituted—

'1. The following are the orders referred to in section 27(1) of this Act—

(a) a care order under the Children Act 1989 (as defined by section 31(11) of that Act, read with section 105(1) and Schedule 14);

(b) a residence order (as defined by section 8 of the Act of 1989); and

(c) any order made by a court in England and Wales under any of the following enactments—

(i) section 9(1), 10(1)(a) or 11(a) of the Guardianship of Minors Act 1971;

(ii) section 42(1) or (2) or 43(1) of the Matrimonial Causes Act 1973;

(iii) section 2(2)(b), (4)(b) or (5) of the Guardianship Act 1973 as applied by section 34(5) of the Children Act 1975;

(iv) section 8(2)(a), 10(1) or 19(1)(ii) of the Domestic Proceedings and Magistrates Courts Act 1978;

(v) section 26(1)(b) of the Adoption Act 1976.'

277

The Disabled Persons (Services, Consultation and Representation) Act 1986
(c. 33)

58. In section 1(3) of the Disabled Persons (Services, Consultation and Representation) Act 1986 (circumstances in which regulations may provide for the appointment of authorised representatives of disabled persons)—

(a) in paragraph (a), for the words 'parent or guardian of a disabled person under the age of sixteen' there shall be substituted—

'(i) the parent of a disabled person under the age of sixteen, or

(ii) any other person who is not a parent of his but who has parental responsibility for him'; and

(b) in paragraph (b), for the words 'in the care of' there shall be substituted 'looked after by'.

59.—(1) Section 2 of that Act (circumstances in which authorised representative has right to visit etc disabled person) shall be amended as follows.

(2) In subsection 3(a) for the words from second 'the' to 'by' there shall be substituted 'for the words "if so requested by the disabled person" there shall be substituted "if so requested by any person mentioned in section 1(3)(a)(i) or (ii)".'

(3) In subsection (5) after paragraph (b) there shall be inserted—

'(bb) in accommodation provided by or on behalf of a local authority under Part III of the Children Act 1989, or'.

(4) After paragraph (c) of subsection (5) there shall be inserted—

'(cc) in accommodation provided by a voluntary organisation in accordance with arrangements made by a local authority under section 17 of the Children Act 1989, or'.

60. In section 5(7)(b) of that Act (disabled persons leaving special education) for the word 'guardian' there shall be substituted 'other person who is not a parent of his but who has parental responsibility for him'.

61.—(1) In section 16 of that Act (interpretation) in the definition of 'disabled person', in paragraph (a) for the words from 'means' to 'applies' there shall be substituted 'means—

"(i) in the case of a person aged eighteen or over, a person to whom section 29 of the 1948 Act applies, and

(ii) in the case of a person under the age of eighteen, a person who is disabled within the meaning of Part III of the Children Act 1989"'.

(2) After the definition of 'parent' in that section there shall be inserted—

'"parental responsibility" has the same meaning as in the Children Act 1989.'

(3) In the definition of 'the welfare enactments' in that section, in paragraph (a) after the words 'the 1977 Act' there shall be inserted 'and Part III of the Children Act 1989'.

(4) At the end of that section there shall be added—

'(2) In this Act any reference to a child who is looked after by a local authority has the same meaning as in the Children Act 1989.'

278

The Family Law Act 1986 (c. 55)

62.—(1) The Family Law Act 1986 shall be amended as follows.

(2) Subject to paragraphs 63 to 71, in Part I—

(a) for the words 'custody order', in each place where they occur, there shall be substituted 'Part I order';

(b) for the words 'proceedings with respect to the custody of', in each place where they occur, there shall be substituted 'Part I proceedings with respect to'; and

(c) for the words 'matters relating to the custody of', in each place where they occur, there shall be substituted 'Part I matters relating to'.

(3) For section 42(7) (general interpretation of Part I) there shall be substituted—

'(7) In this Part—

(a) references to Part I proceedings in respect of a child are references to any proceedings for a Part I order or an order corresponding to a Part I order and include, in relation to proceedings outside the United Kingdom, references to proceedings before a tribunal or other authority having power under the law having effect there to determine Part I matters; and

(b) references to Part I matters are references to matters that might be determined by a Part I order or an order corresponding to a Part I order.'

63.—(1) In section 1 (orders to which Part I of the Act of 1986 applies), in subsection (1)—

(a) for paragraph (a) there shall be substituted—

'(a) a section 8 order made by a court in England and Wales under the Children Act 1989, other than an order varying or discharging such an order'; and

(b) for paragraph (d) there shall be substituted the following paragraphs—

'(d) an order made by a court in England and Wales in the exercise of the inherent jurisdiction of the High Court with respect to children—

(i) so far as it gives care of a child to any person or provides for contact with, or the education of, a child; but

(ii) excluding an order varying or revoking such an order;

(e) an order made by the High Court in Northern Ireland in the exercise of its jurisdiction relating to wardship—

(i) so far as it gives care and control of a child to any person or provides for the education of or access to a child; but

(ii) excluding an order relating to a child of whom care or care and control is (immediately after the making of the order) vested in the Department of Health and Social Services or a Health and Social Services Board.'

279

(2) In subsection (2) of that section, in paragraph (c) for '(d)' there shall be substituted '(e)'.

(3) For subsections (3) to (5) of that section there shall be substituted—

'(3) In this Part, "Part I order"—

(a) includes any order which would have been a custody order by virtue of this section in any form in which it was in force at any time before its amendment by the Children Act 1989; and

(b) (subject to sections 32 and 40 of this Act) excludes any order which would have been excluded from being a custody order by virtue of this section in any such form.'

64. For section 2 there shall be substituted the following sections—

'2 **Jurisdiction: general**—(1) A court in England and Wales shall not have jurisdiction to make a section $1(1)(a)$ order with respect to a child in or in connection with matrimonial proceedings in England and Wales unless the condition in section 2A of this Act is satisfied.

(2) A court in England and Wales shall not have jurisdiction to make a section $1(1)(a)$ order in a non-matrimonial case (that is to say, where the condition in section 2A of this Act is not satisfied) unless the condition in section 3 of this Act is satisfied.

(3) A court in England and Wales shall not have jurisdiction to make a section $1(1)(d)$ order unless—

(a) the condition in section 3 of this Act is satisfied, or

(b) the child concerned is present in England and Wales on the relevant date and the court considers that the immediate exercise of its powers is necessary for his protection.

2A Jurisdiction in or in connection with matrimonial proceedings—(1) The condition referred to in section 2(1) of this Act is that the matrimonial proceedings are proceedings in respect of the marriage of the parents of the child concerned and—

(a) the proceedings—

(i) are proceedings for divorce or nullity of marriage, and

(ii) are continuing;

(b) the proceedings—

(i) are proceedings for judicial separation,

(ii) are continuing,

and the jurisdiction of the court is not excluded by subsection (2) below; or

(c) the proceedings have been dismissed after the beginning of the trial but—

(i) the section $1(1)(a)$ order is being made forthwith, or

(ii) the application for the order was made on or before the dismissal.

(2) For the purposes of subsection (1)(b) above, the jurisdiction of the court is excluded if, after the grant of a decree of judicial separation, on the relevant date, proceedings for divorce or nullity

in respect of the marriage are continuing in Scotland or Northern Ireland.

(3) Subsection (2) above shall not apply if the court in which the other proceedings there referred to are continuing has made—

(a) an order under section 13(6) or 21(5) of this Act (not being an order made by virtue of section 13(6)(a)(i)), or

(b) an order under section 14(2) or 22(2) of this Act which is recorded as being made for the purpose of enabling Part I proceedings to be taken in England and Wales with respect to the child concerned.

(4) Where a court—

(a) has jurisdiction to make a section 1(1)(a) order in or in connection with matrimonial proceedings, but

(b) considers that it would be more appropriate for Part I matters relating to the child to be determined outside England and Wales,

the court may by order direct that, while the order under this subsection is in force, no section 1(1)(a) order shall be made by any court in or in connection with those proceedings.'

65.—(1) In section 3 (habitual residence or presence of child concerned) in subsection (1) for 'section 2' there shall be substituted 'section 2(2)'.

(2) In subsection (2) of that section for the words 'proceedings for divorce, nullity or judicial separation' there shall be substituted 'matrimonial proceedings'.

66.—(1) In section 6 (duration and variation of Part I orders), for subsection (3) there shall be substituted the following subsections—

'(3) A court in England and Wales shall not have jurisdiction to vary a Part I order if, on the relevant date, matrimonial proceedings are continuing in Scotland or Northern Ireland in respect of the marriage of the parents of the child concerned.

(3A) Subsection (3) above shall not apply if—

(a) the Part I order was made in or in connection with proceedings for divorce or nullity in England and Wales in respect of the marriage of the parents of the child concerned; and

(b) those proceedings are continuing.

(3B) Subsection (3) above shall not apply if—

(a) the Part I order was made in or in connection with proceedings for judicial separation in England and Wales;

(b) those proceedings are continuing; and

(c) the decree of judicial separation has not yet been granted.'

(2) In subsection (5) of that section for the words from 'variation of' to 'if the ward' there shall be substituted 'variation of a section 1(1)(d) order if the child concerned'.

(3) For subsections (6) and (7) of that section there shall be substituted the following subsections—

'(6) Subsection (7) below applies where a Part I order which is—

(a) a residence order (within the meaning of the Children Act 1989) in favour of a person with respect to a child,

(b) an order made in the exercise of the High Court's inherent jurisdiction with respect to children by virtue of which a person has care of a child, or

(c) an order—

    (i) of a kind mentioned in section 1(3)(a) of this Act,

    (ii) under which a person is entitled to the actual possession of a child,

ceases to have effect in relation to that person by virtue of subsection (1) above.

(7) Where this subsection applies, any family assistance order made under section 16 of the Children Act 1989 with respect to the child shall also cease to have effect.

(8) For the purposes of subsection (7) above the reference to a family assistance order under section 16 of the Children Act 1989 shall be deemed to include a reference to an order for the supervision of a child made under—

(a) section 7(4) of the Family Law Reform Act 1969,

(b) section 44 of the Matrimonial Causes Act 1973,

(c) section 2(2)(a) of the Guardianship Act 1973,

(d) section 34(5) or 36(3)(b) of the Children Act 1975, or

(e) section 9 of the Domestic Proceedings and Magistrates' Courts Act 1978;

but this subsection shall cease to have effect once all such orders for the supervision of children have ceased to have effect in accordance with Schedule 14 to the Children Act 1989.'

67. For section 7 (interpretation of Chapter II) there shall be substituted—

'7 **Interpretation of Chapter II**—In this Chapter—

(a) "child" means a person who has not attained the age of eighteen;

(b) "matrimonial proceedings" means proceedings for divorce, nullity of marriage or judicial separation;

(c) "the relevant date" means, in relation to the making or variation of an order—

    (i) where an application is made for an order to be made or varied, the date of the application (or first application, if two or more are determined together), and

    (ii) where no such application is made, the date on which the court is considering whether to make or, as the case may be, vary the order; and

(d) "section 1(1)(a) order" and "section 1(1)(d) order" mean orders falling within section 1(1)(a) and (d) of this Act respectively.'

68. In each of the following sections—

(a) section 11(2)(a) (provisions supplementary to sections 9 and 10),

(b) section 13(5)(a) (jurisdiction ancillary to matrimonial proceedings),

(c) section 20(3)(a) (habitual residence or presence of child),

(d) section 21(4)(a) (jurisdiction in divorce proceedings, etc.), and

(e) section 23(4)(a) (duration and variation of custody orders),

for '4(5)' there shall be substituted '2A(4)'.

69. In each of the following sections—

(a) section 19(2) (jurisdiction in cases other than divorce, etc.),

(b) section 20(6) (habitual residence or presence of child), and

(c) section 23(5) (duration and variation of custody orders),

for 'section 1(1)(d)' there shall be substituted 'section 1(1)(e)'.

70. In section 34(3) (power to order recovery of child) for paragraph (a) there shall be substituted—

'(a) section 14 of the Children Act 1989'.

71.—(1) In section 42 (general interpretation of Part I), in subsection (4)(a) for the words 'has been boarded out with those parties' there shall be substituted 'is placed with those parties as foster parents'.

(2) In subsection (6) of that section, in paragraph (a) after the word 'person' there shall be inserted 'to be allowed contact with or'.

The Local Government Act 1988 (c. 9)

72. In Schedule 1 to the Local Government Act 1988 (competition) at the end of paragraph 2(4) (cleaning of buildings: buildings to which competition provisions do not apply) for paragraph (c) there shall be substituted—

'(c) section 53 of the Children Act 1989.'

Amendments of local Acts

73.—(1) Section 16 of the Greater London Council (General Powers) Act 1981 (exemption from provisions of Part IV of the Act of certain premises) shall be amended as follows.

(2) After paragraph (g) there shall be inserted—

'(gg) used as a children's home as defined in section 63 of the Children Act 1989'.

(3) In paragraph (h)—

(a) for the words 'section 56 of the Child Care Act 1980' there shall be substituted 'section 60 of the Children Act 1989';

(b) for the words 'section 57' there shall be substituted 'section 60'; and

(c) for the words 'section 32' there shall be substituted 'section 53'.

(4) In paragraph (i), for the words 'section 8 of the Foster Children Act 1980' there shall be substituted 'section 67 of the Children Act 1989'.

74.—(1) Section 10(2) of the Greater London Council (General Powers) Act 1984 (exemption from provisions of Part IV of the Act of certain premises) shall be amended as follows.

(2) In paragraph (d)—

(a) for the words 'section 56 of the Child Care Act 1980' there shall be substituted 'section 60 of the Children Act 1989';

(b) for the words 'section 57' there shall be substituted 'section 60'; and

(c) for the words 'section 31' there shall be substituted 'section 53'.

(3) In paragraph (e), for the words 'section 8 of the Foster Children Act 1980' there shall be substituted 'section 67 of the Children Act 1989'.

(4) In paragraph (l) for the words 'section 1 of the Children's Homes Act 1982' there shall be substituted 'section 63 of the Children Act 1989'.

Appendix 6

Children Act 1989, Schedule 15

SCHEDULE 15   REPEALS

Chapter	Short title	Extent of repeal
1891 c. 3.	The Custody of Children Act 1891.	The whole Act.
1933 c. 12.	The Children and Young Persons Act 1933.	In section 14(2), the words from 'may also' to 'together, and'. In section 34(8), '(a)' and the words from 'and (b)' to the end. Section 40. In section 107(1), the definitions of 'care order' and 'interim order'.
1944 c. 31.	The Education Act 1944.	In section 40(1), the words from 'or to imprisonment' to the end. In section 114(1), the definition of parent.
1948 c. 53.	The Nurseries and Child-Minders Regulation Act 1948.	The whole Act.
1949 c. 76.	The Marriage Act 1949.	In section 3(1), the words 'unless the child is subject to a custodianship order, when the consent of the custodian and, where the custodian is the husband or wife of a parent of the child of that parent shall be required'. Section 78(1A). Schedule 2.
1956 c. 69.	The Sexual Offences Act 1956.	Section 38.
1959 c. 72.	The Mental Health Act 1959.	Section 9.
1963 c. 37.	The Children and Young Persons Act 1963.	Section 3. Section 23.

285

Chapter	Short title	Extent of repeal
		In section 29(1), the words 'under section 1 of the Children and Young Persons Act 1969 or'.
		Section 53(3).
		In Schedule 3, paragraph 11.
1964 c. 42.	The Administration of Justice Act 1964.	In section 38, the definition of 'domestic court'.
1968 c. 46.	The Health Services and Public Health Act 1968.	Section 60.
		In section 64(3)(a), sub-paragraphs (vi), (vii), (ix) and (xv).
		In section 65(3)(b), paragraphs (vii), (viii) and (x).
1968 c. 49.	The Social Work (Scotland) Act 1968.	Section 1(4)(a).
		Section 5(2)(d).
		In section 86(3), the words 'the Child Care Act 1980 or'.
		In Schedule 8, paragraph 20.
1969 c. 46.	The Family Law Reform Act 1969.	Section 7.
1969 c. 54.	The Children and Young Persons Act 1969.	Sections 1 to 3.
		In section 7, in subsection (7) the words 'to subsection (7A) of this section and', paragraph (a) and the words from 'and subsection (13) of section 2 of this Act' to the end; and subsection (7A).
		Section 7A.
		In section 8(3), the words from 'and as if the reference to acquittal' to the end.
		In section 9(1), the words 'proceedings under section 1 of this Act or'.
		Section 11A.
		Section 14A.
		In section 15, in subsection (1) the words 'and may on discharging the supervision order make a care order (other than an interim order) in respect of the supervised person'; in subsection (2) the words 'and the supervision order was not made by virtue of section 1 of this Act or on the occasion of the discharge of a care order'; in subsection

286

Chapter	Short title	Extent of repeal
		(2A), the words 'or made by a court on discharging a care order made under that subsection'; and in subsection (4), the words 'or made by a court on discharging a care order made under that section'.
		In section 16, in subsection (6)(a), the words 'a care order or'; and in subsection (8) the words 'or, in a case where a parent or guardian of his was a party to the proceedings on an application under the preceding section by virtue of an order under section 32A of this Act, the parent or guardian'.
		In section 17, paragraphs (b) and (c).
		Sections 20 to 22.
		Section 27(4).
		Section 28.
		Sections 32A to 32C.
		In section 34(2) the words 'under section 1 of this Act or', the words '2(3) or' and the words 'and accordingly in the case of such a person the reference in section 1(1) of this Act to the said section 2(3) shall be construed as including a reference to this subsection'.
		In section 70, in subsection (1), the definitions of 'care order' and 'interim order'; and in subsection (2) the words '21(2), 22(4) or (6) or 28(5)' and the words 'care order or warrant'.
		In Schedule 5, paragraphs 12(1), 37, 47 and 48.
1970 c. 34.	The Marriage (Registrar General's Licence) Act 1970.	In section 3(b), the words from 'as amended' to '1969'.
1970 c. 42.	The Local Authority Social Services Act 1970.	In Schedule 1, in the entry relating to the Children and Young Persons Act 1969, the words 'welfare, etc. of foster

Chapter	Short title	Extent of repeal
		children'; the entries relating to the Matrimonial Causes Act 1973, section 44, the Domestic Proceedings and Magistrates' Courts Act 1978, section 9, the Child Care Act 1980 and the Foster Children Act 1980.
1971 c. 3.	The Guardianship of Minors Act 1971.	The whole Act.
1971 c. 23.	The Courts Act 1971.	In Schedule 8, paragraph 59(1).
1972 c. 18.	The Maintenance Orders (Reciprocal Enforcement) Act 1972.	Section 41.
1972 c. 70.	The Local Government Act 1972.	In Schedule 23, paragraphs 4 and 9(3).
1972 c. 71.	The Criminal Justice Act 1972.	Section 51(1).
1973 c. 18.	The Matrimonial Causes Act 1973.	Sections 42 to 44. In section 52(1), the definition of 'custody'. In Schedule 2, paragraph 11.
1973 c. 29.	The Guardianship Act 1973.	The whole Act.
1973 c. 45.	The Domicile and Matrimonial Proceedings Act 1973.	In Schedule 1, in paragraph 11(1) the definitions of 'custody' and 'education' and in paragraph 11(3) the word 'four'.
1973 c. 62.	The Powers of Criminal Courts Act 1973.	In section 13(1), the words 'and the purposes of section 1(2)(bb) of the Children and Young Persons Act 1969'. In Schedule 3, in paragraph 3(2A), the word 'and' immediately preceding paragraph (b).
1974 c. 53.	The Rehabilitation of Offenders Act 1974.	In section 1(4)(b) the words 'or in care proceedings under section 1 of the Children and Young Persons Act 1969'. In section 5, in subsection 5(e), the words 'a care order or'; and in subsection (10) the words 'care order or'.
1975 c. 72.	The Children Act 1975.	The whole Act.
1976 c. 36.	The Adoption Act 1976.	Section 11(5). Section 14(3). In section 15, in subsection (1), the words from 'subject' to 'cases)' and subsection (4). Section 26.

Chapter	Short title	Extent of repeal
		In section 28(5), the words 'or the organisation'.
		Section 34.
		Section 36(1)(c).
		Section 37(1), (3) and (4).
		Section 55(4).
		In section 57, in subsection (2), the words from 'and the court' to the end and subsections (4) to (10).
		In section 72(1), the definition of 'place of safety', in the definition of 'local authority' the words from 'and' to the end and, in the definition of 'specified order', the words 'Northern Ireland or'.
		In Schedule 3, paragraphs 8, 11, 19, 21, and 22.
1977 c. 45.	The Criminal Law Act 1977.	Section 58(3).
1977 c. 49.	The National Health Service Act 1977.	In section 21, in subsection (1)(a) the words 'and young children'.
		In Schedule 8, in paragraph 1(1), the words from 'and of children' to the end; in paragraph 2(2) the words from 'or (b) to persons who' to 'arrangements'; and in paragraph 3(1) '(a)' and the words from 'or (b) a child' to 'school age'.
		In Schedule 15, paragraphs 10 and 25.
1978 c. 22.	The Domestic Proceedings and Magistrates' Courts Act 1978.	Sections 9 to 15.
		In section 19, in subsection (1) the words 'following powers, that is to say' and sub-paragraph (ii), subsections (2) and (4), in subsection (7) the words 'and one interim custody order' and in subsection (9) the words 'or 21'.
		In section 20, subsection (4) and in subsection (9) the words 'subject to the provisions of section 11(8) of this Act'.
		Section 21.

Chapter	Short title	Extent of repeal
		In section 24, the words 'or 21' in both places where they occur.
		In section 25, in subsection (1) paragraph (b) and the word 'or' immediately preceding it and in subsection (2) paragraphs (c) and (d).
		Section 29(4).
		Sections 33 and 34.
		Sections 36 to 53.
		Sections 64 to 72.
		Sections 73(1) and 74(1) and (3).
		In section 88(1), the definition of 'actual custody'.
		In Schedule 2, paragraphs 22, 23, 27, 29, 31, 36, 41 to 43, 46 to 50.
1978 c. 28.	The Adoption (Scotland) Act 1978.	In section 20(3)(c), the words 'section 12(3)(b) of the Adoption Act 1976 or of'.
		In section 45(5), the word 'approved'.
		Section 49(4).
		In section 65(1), in the definition of 'local authority', the words from 'and' to the end and, in the definition of 'specified order', the words 'Northern Ireland or'.
1978 c. 30.	The Interpretation Act 1978.	In Schedule 1, the entry with respect to the construction of certain expressions relating to children.
1980 c. 5.	The Child Care Act 1980.	The whole Act.
1980 c. 6.	The Foster Children Act 1980.	The whole Act.
1980 c. 43.	The Magistrates' Courts Act 1980.	In section 65(1), paragraphs (e) and (g) and the paragraph (m) inserted in section 65 by paragraph 82 of Schedule 2 to the Family Law Reform Act 1987.
		In section 81(8), in the definition of 'guardian' the words 'by deed or will' and in the definition of 'sums adjudged to be paid by a conviction' the words from 'as applied' to the end.
		In section 143(2), paragraph (i).

Chapter	Short title	Extent of repeal
		In Schedule 7, paragraphs 78, 83, 91, 92, 110, 116, 117, 138, 157, 158, 165, 166 and 199 to 201.
1981 c. 60.	The Education Act 1981.	In Schedule 3, paragraph 9.
1982 c. 20.	The Children's Homes Act 1982.	The whole Act.
1982 c. 48.	The Criminal Justice Act 1982.	Sections 22 to 25. Section 27. In Schedule 14, paragraphs 45 and 46.
1983 c. 20.	The Mental Health Act 1983.	In section 26(5), paragraph (d) and the word 'or' immediately preceding it. In section 28(1), the words '(including an order under section 38 of the Sexual Offences Act 1956)'. In Schedule 4, paragraphs 12, 26(a), (b) and (c), 35, 44, 50 and 51.
1983 c. 41.	The Health and Social Services and Social Security Adjudications Act 1983.	Section 4(1). Sections 5 and 6. In section 11, in subsection (2) the words 'the Child Care Act 1980 and the Children's Homes Act 1982'. In section 19, subsections (1) to (5). Schedule 1. In Schedule 2, paragraphs 3, 9 to 14, 20 to 24, 27, 28, 34, 37 and 46 to 62. In Schedule 4, paragraphs 38 to 48. In Schedule 9, paragraphs 5, 16 and 17.
1984 c. 23.	The Registered Homes Act 1984.	In Schedule 1, in paragraph 5, sub-paragraph (a) and paragraphs 6, 7 and 8.
1984 c. 28.	The County Courts Act 1984.	In Schedule 2, paragraph 56.
1984 c. 37.	The Child Abduction Act 1984.	In section 3, the word 'and' immediately preceding paragraph (c). In the Schedule, in paragraph 1(2) the words 'or voluntary organisation' and paragraph 3(1)(e).
1984 c. 42.	The Matrimonial and Family Proceedings Act 1984.	In Schedule 1, paragraphs 19 and 23.

Children Act 1989—A Practical Guide

Chapter	Short title	Extent of repeal
1984 c. 56.	The Foster Children (Scotland) Act 1984.	In section 1, the words 'for a period of more than 6 days' and the words from 'The period' to the end. In section 7(1), the word 'or' at the end of paragraph (e). In Schedule 2, paragraphs 1 to 3 and 8.
1984 c. 60.	The Police and Criminal Evidence Act 1984.	In section 37(15), the words 'and is not excluded from this Part of this Act by section 52 below'. Section 39(5). Section 52. In section 118(1), in the definition of parent or guardian, paragraph (b) and the word 'and' immediately preceding it. In Schedule 2, the entry relating to section 16 of the Child Care Act 1980. In Schedule 6, paragraphs 19(a) and 22.
1985 c. 23.	The Prosecution of Offences Act 1985.	Section 27.
1985 c. 60.	The Child Abduction and Custody Act 1985.	Section 9(c). Section 20(2)(b) and (c). Section 25(3) and (5). In Schedule 3, paragraph 1(2).
1986 c. 28.	The Children and Young Persons (Amendment) Act 1986.	The whole Act.
1986 c. 33.	The Disabled Persons (Services, Consultation and Representation) Act 1986.	In section 16, in the definition of 'guardian', paragraph (a).
1986 c. 45.	The Insolvency Act 1986.	In section 281(5)(b), the words 'in domestic proceedings'.
1986 c. 50.	The Social Security Act 1986.	In Schedule 10, paragraph 51.
1986 c. 55.	The Family Law Act 1986.	In section 1(2), in paragraph (a) the words '(a) or' and paragraph (b). Section 3(4) to (6). Section 4. Section 35(1). In section 42(6), in paragraph (b) the words 'section 42(6) of the Matrimonial Causes Act 1973 or', in paragraph (c) the words 'section 42(7) of

292

Chapter	Short title	Extent of repeal
		that Act or' and in paragraph (d) the words 'section 19(6) of the Domestic Proceedings and Magistrates' Courts Act 1978 or'.
		In Schedule 1, paragraphs 10, 11, 13, 16, 17, 20 and 23.
1987 c. 42.	The Family Law Reform Act 1987.	Section 3.
		Sections 4 to 7.
		Sections 9 to 16.
		In Schedule 2, paragraphs 11, 14, 51, 67, 68, 94 and 95.
		In Schedule 3, paragraphs 11 and 12.
1988 c. 34.	The Legal Aid Act 1988.	Section 3(4)(c).
		Section 27.
		Section 28.
		In section 30, subsections (1) and (2).
		In Part I of Schedule 2, paragraph 2(a) and (e).

Index

Index

Index

298

299

Index

Index